ORDER UPON THE LAND

THE ANDREW H. CLARK SERIES
IN THE HISTORICAL GEOGRAPHY OF NORTH AMERICA

Order
Upon the Land

The U.S. Rectangular Land Survey
and the Upper Mississippi Country

Hildegard Binder Johnson

New York
Oxford University Press
London   1976   Toronto

FOR GISELA AND KARIN
AND TO THE MEMORY OF MY FATHER AND MOTHER

The charming landscape which I saw this morning is indubitably made up of some twenty or thirty farms. Miller owns this field, Locke that, and Manning the woodland beyond. But none of them owns the landscape. There is a property in the horizon which no man has but he whose eye can integrate all the parts, that is, the poet. This is the best part of these men's farms, yet this their warranty deeds give no title.

Ralph Waldo Emerson

PREFACE

The U.S. rectangular survey, which organizes land into six-by-six-mile townships divided into thirty-six sections of one square mile each, is the cadastral system under which much of the land of the United States was surveyed. Originating with the Ordinance of 1785, the federal survey may have been inspired by European precedents as old as centuriation, the Roman system of land division. Many books describe the U.S. system; the raison d'être of this book, however, is not only to discuss the survey's possible antecedents or genesis but to take a look at how it affected the settlement landscape of a part of rural America I have come to know well—the Upper Mississippi Hill Country. Moreover, in an area with the roughness of surface that one finds in the Hill Country, many of the problems of the establishment and use of the survey system can be discussed discerningly.

Most Americans and Canadians accept the survey system that so strongly affects their lives and perception of the landscape in the same way that they accept a week of seven days, a decimal numerical system, or an alphabet of twenty-six letters—as natural, inevitable, or perhaps in some inscrutable way, divinely ordained. Clarence Glacken pointed out in his preface to Norman Thrower's *Original Survey and Land Subdivisions* that in contrast foreigners find the system most striking, particularly in its landscape impact. The visual effect from the air has been pointed out by Europeans; to them the section landscape is the typical American landscape. It was Norman Thrower, English born, who recently expressed regret that on a flight from Los Angeles to Kansas the pilot had pointed out the Grand Canyon but had said not one word about the survey.

This reaction of the outsider, who sees the rectangular survey as exotic, was very much mine when I first came to the Middle West. The small towns were ugly and uninteresting, and the rural landscape was appallingly monotonous. A good deal of my attitude simply reflected a narrow perspective; untrained eyes do not really see the unfamiliar. I hope it will not seem presumptuous if I tell a little about the mindscape of a young German immigrant, many years ago.

Growing up in the metropolitan environment of Berlin meant that I experienced "nature" in beautifully maintained parks, along the banks of canals, in plantings of shrubbery in front of buildings. During vacations in the Harz or Thuringian mountains, adventurous walks led along well-trodden footpaths to lookouts displaying picturesque scenes of intensively cultivated landscapes. On the beaches of the Baltic and North seas the silhouettes of a hotel or the roofs of a fishing village were never far away. Nature in my experience was always imbedded in a cultural historical landscape; I was able to find pleasure in a weathered stone cross overgrown by weeds at the bend of an ancient imperial road or in ivy-covered monuments in old churchyards. The forests never seemed wild and in retrospect, when compared with American national parks, they hardly were.

Environments were explained to me as a historical past in the lively present, a most visible past indeed. The context was humanistic rather than scientific, perhaps an unfortunate viewpoint, but unquestionably one that affected my way of looking at landscapes. Informal education is a very potent education. When I was a child, I recall my father telling me on one of our frequent walks that the one-story farmhouse we were passing on the main street of Berlin-Schöneberg was built in 1810, the three-story villa on its left side in 1860, and the five-story apartment house to the right, in 1910. We crossed the street to look at all three together, a view that came back like a flash many years later when I first read Derwent Whittlesey's article on sequent occupance. I still like to think of those houses as an example of the desirability to preserve landmarks in situ—even if the old farmhouse, after the three buildings had survived the bombings, was razed after World War II. It was a good example of urban development—from an agricultural village to a city's suburb.

As students we learned on excursions to recognize the influence of legal codes, religion, or building ordinances on the formal appearance of the landscape. The skylines of small towns still partially walled and compact had high-rising centers formed by cathedral, town hall, and patricians' houses, surrounded by modest cottages with few windows close to the protective walls. In contrast, residential towns planned by a former duke or king, with parks and grand avenues, taught us a feeling for a different urban order. A single, often rather large church dominated a village which was either all Catholic or all Protestant because of the ruler's religious faith. Field layouts could change from one side of a river to the other (along the Rhine near Remagen, for example) because different laws of inheritance prevailed on either side.

For many years after my arrival in Minnesota, the landscape remained a visual blight of my own making because of the nature of my training in chronological scale and visual observation. I did not ask the right questions. But one day I did, when my common sense was challenged by the sight of a narrow path leading on a diagonal along the steep-sided valley of Minnesota's Whitewater River. Why was it there? The advice of Robert Platt, one of the great field geographers of this century, that a hired hand could probably give me the best explanation, proved to be right. I learned from an old man (a former hired hand) that along the path, loads of hay had been hauled down from the upland field for a valley farmer who ran a "two-story" farm. The farm included—impractically, it seemed—both upland and valley bottom with a steep slope in between and straight fence lines crossing at right angles on the face of a steep hill. It was my curiosity about this layout that led to my study of the geometry of the midwestern landscape. To this study I owe a growing affection for the Upper Mississippi Hill Country.

Sixty-nine per cent of the land in forty-eight states is contiguously covered by the rectangular survey, and 9 per cent is intermittently covered in the remaining area, including Alaska. Of the 1.8 billion acres at one time in the public domain, approximately 1.3 billion have been surveyed. In the vast literature about the frontier and agricultural history of the Upper Middle West the survey is taken for granted and is generally accepted as an advantage for settlement. For example, Frederick Jackson Turner, after extolling the Ordinance of 1787 in an article on the Middle West (*International Monthly*, December 1901), stated: "The Ordinance of 1785 is also worthy of attention . . . for under its provision almost all of the Middle West has been divided by the government surveyor into rectangles of sections and townships by whose lines the settler has been able easily and certainly to locate his farm and the forester his forty. In the local organization of the Middle West these lines have played in important part."

Turner's observation at least touches upon the persistence of the survey's influence on the "order" of the land, an order which is somewhat modified in the dissected country along the upper Mississippi by the soil conservation practices of the twentieth century. But, regardless of the region on which we focus, we cannot ignore the Ordinance of 1785 and the acts that followed it as a basic formative influence on the American landscape.

We must also touch upon European precedents that may have influenced the American system. Thus, because they were part of the tradition that settlers carried with them to the Hill Country, various settlement forms of the Eastern Seaboard are briefly discussed here. Nor can we ignore the thoughts of creative artists—the masters of form—in this study of the survey as the formative element of order. Pictures and visual experiences, then, are not merely incidental but are integrated with the text, for, as is so succinctly revealed by Rudolph Arnheim in his *Visual Thinking*, perception is an active concern of the mind.

Order Upon the Land deals with some of the characteristics inherent in rectangular systems and looks at the survey in the context of the rationalism of the eighteenth century. Then, after discussing early land ordinances, the book treats the emergence of the survey landscape topically. An attempt is made to bring the past alive as part of the present landscape. The landscape of the Upper Middle West, of course, has been affected by many other forces besides the original survey. But this book is not an essay on the general history of a region; it is an interpretation of one influence in a region's historical-geographical development.

The major part of my interpretation of the federal survey grows out of the reading of contemporary sources. Individual illustrations rather than summarizing statements are used, so that the presentation of details may bring an insight into reality that abstractions cannot convey. The focus on one visual component invites readers to direct their eyes to the geometry of the land. Perhaps some readers will look for themselves and compare examples presented here with others culled from their own empirical observations. The shock of recognition is a delightful experience and especially invigorating when one discovers something others have overlooked.

HILDEGARD BINDER JOHNSON

CONTENTS

FIGURES

PART I
THE ORIGIN OF THE RECTANGULAR SURVEY

1 SETTING AND DIRECTION

The European Approach to North America

The delineation and awareness of regions are continuing concerns of geographers; ordering the world around us by subdividing its geography into parts has a long Euro-American tradition. Historians and sociologists confidently acknowledge the legitimacy of American regionalism, and while geographers refine criteria for the definition of conceptual, such as functional, regions, others usually employ regional terms derived from traditional or subjective experiences of different landscapes. Their visual recognition depends most of all on scale, which in a way is a function of the speed with which a given area is canvassed.

On very large-scale maps the transition from one region to another is blurred, while distinct divisions between lowlands and mountains seem feasible on the small-scale maps of most atlases. Viewing North America and Europe from high altitudes makes it possible to recognize the over-all difference between the alignments of major physiographic features. The roughly north-south grain of major landforms in the United States begins with the eastern coastal plain and proceeds across the Appalachian Rangelands and Mississippi basin. It is intermittently maintained by the mountain chains of the Rockies, the axes of the interior basins, and the trend of the Sierra, the western valleys, and the coastal ranges. Many smaller regions do not fit this accordion-like setting, but this does not invalidate a general contrast with Europe, where the Eurasian plain stretches eastward from the lowlands of northern France, widening in Central Europe and Russia. The mountains of the Eurasian barrier begin in the west with the Pyrenees, compact into the Alps in the center, and fork away into the eastern European

3

and Asian ranges with major crests generally trending in an east-west direction. For northern and central Europeans, Mediterranean Europe is the South, the land of the sun beyond a formidable mountain barrier. No comparable image supports the American tradition of a North and a South, and its lack was expressed in words appropriate to our topic by Abraham Lincoln in his second annual message to Congress on December 1, 1862:

> There is no line straight or crooked, suitable for a national boundary on which to divide. Trace through from east to west, upon the line between the free and slave country, and we shall find that a little more than one-third of its length are rivers, easy to be crossed and populated or soon to be populated thickly on both sides; while nearly all its remaining length are merely surveyor's lines, over which people may walk back and forth without any consciousness of their presence.[1]

A fundamental phenomenon in the European occupation of the North American continent was the general advance of anthropogeographic patterns from east to west and thus not with, but against, the grain of physical geography. There were modifications of this direction, notably when Mississippi steamboats brought European immigrants from New Orleans directly into the heartland of America before the Civil War. There also were regional exceptions; for example, the history of settlement in the Southwest reflects migrations by three groups of people from different directions and at different times. But in general, the direction of migration from east to west corresponds to the progress from earlier to recent history in the United States. Thus the spatial and chronological correlation leads to a fairly linear structure of historical geographies of North America. Correspondingly, an eastern viewpoint is reflected in historical reports of the occupation of the continent, many of which were written in Europe. Such a linear and spatial directive does not exist for the historical geography of Europe, where migrations shift with the rise and fall of empires and become very complex.

Locational terms such as "Trans-Mississippi" or "100th Meridian" clearly imply one direction only and are not bi-directional. Bernard de Voto's "cismontane" rivers—the waters that drain the Alleghenies to the Atlantic Ocean—and G. Malcolm Lewis's "Cis-Rocky Mountain West" (an English geographer's concept of the Great Plains), imply a historically developed eastern stance. The one-directional feeling lives in the vernacular too: Americans go "back East" and "out West," and it seems insensible to reverse the combination. The future may bring a change in the symbolism for directional space now that a journal entitled *Cry California* is published in the state that today has a larger population than New York. In 1856 Walt Whitman envisioned a continent reaching from the Atlantic to the Pacific; that is, from east to west, but a century later when Woody Guthrie sang the words "from California to the New York Island," his perspective was in the other direction—from west to east.

Along the routes of exploration and expansion, men always encounter and perceive opportunities and obstacles in spatial, chronological sequence, and these become effective in a temporal order that is not interchangeable. The perceptions and experiences of those who crossed the Atlantic and of those who moved west after a sojourn along the eastern seaboard varied with their cultural preconditioning and the routes they took. For example, the French who came to the St. Lawrence expected a climate similar to that of Paris, which lies approximately on the same latitude. This preconception was rooted in ancient theories about climates as belt-like zones; the newcomers did not yet understand the role of land masses in producing continental climates along the eastern side of continents nor did they recognize the influence of the Gulf Stream. And the fur trade route favored by the French into the eighteenth century—along the Ottawa River via Lake Nipissing to Georgian Bay—was an outcome of the French upstream-approach to the St. Lawrence Valley and the Lachine rapids (the latter a name which reflected their hopes for a northwest passage to China). In the eighteenth century the French approached the Middle West both from the south (on the Missis- sippi) and the east (on the Illinois from Lake Michigan), a two-pronged approach that contributed to administrative indecisiveness on the part of the French in the Illinois Country. As late as 1748 the governors of Canada and Louisiana could be heard advancing reasons for ruling Illinois from Québec on the one hand or La Nouvelle Orléans on the other, and the Illinois country, which had become a granary for French Louisiana by the 1720s, remained undeveloped.

The French empire in North America consisted of widely spaced settle- ment clusters, which evolved along rivers. The exhilaration of the Gallic explorers and voyageurs when the height of land was reached, another portage completed, and the next river sighted has often been recorded. Reports from the British, however, sound different; they tell of ventures into mountain valleys on horseback, of marching convoys, of the endless crossing of rivers, of toting bundles across rushing waters, of finally following the traces to another gap. One of the problems the pioneer "woodsman" experi- enced is illustrated by a report to the Royal Society in London on the travels of two Englishmen in western Virginia in 1671:

> It has been generally found by our surveyors in the woods of America, as I
> have been told by some of them, and as it appears indeed from their Surveys
> compared with the Accounts of Travellers, that a true measured distance in a
> strait course is about one third the usual Distance computed by Travellers in
> the woods, where they have no strait Roads and no Distances to guide them.
> Accordingly we find from these Surveys of the Countrey, that it is about one
> hundred and forty Miles in a strait course from the Falls of Appomatox River
> to Wood River in Virginia, which is a little more than one third of the Distance
> computed by our Discoverers.[2]

The English were "not really barred by a wall of forested mountains," in the words of Ellen Churchill Semple. By the turn of the seventeenth century, fur traders from South Carolina had opened a land route to the forks of the Alabama River, following Indian trails up to the headwaters of the Savannah and down the Tennessee, thus circumventing the barriers to the south.[3] The Mohawk depression, which Captain Rooseboom crossed in the 1680s to reach the Great Lakes, was a physically unobstructed route.* The Wilderness Road through the Cumberland Gap to Kentucky, and the course of the National Road up the Susquehanna River to the Allegheny and the Forks of the Ohio had already been used by a Dutchman out of Albany in 1692.[4] All were serviceable routes to the west, but they were land routes, through forests, and none was direct. Movement was slow compared to travel by wagon through the more level Ohio country and by boat on the Ohio River; it was very slow compared to travel on the Erie Canal, which opened in 1825. At all times, British explorers, traders, and settlers interacted with the various Indian tribes in ways more complex than those of the French, whose main motive was the fur trade.

The experience of the Spanish colonists along the Rio Grande was very different from that of the French or the British—because, in Donald Meinig's words, "an important body of Indians were village agricultural societies."[5] The small Spanish share of any westward movement from the eastern seaboard was south of the Appalachians along the road from St. Augustine to Fort St. Marks (south of present-day Tallahassee), and it took place after the Spanish occupation of the coast had proceeded northward from Florida to Georgia. The string of Spanish missions in California also resulted from a generally northward coastal movement, although they were not founded in a direct south-to-north sequence.

Myths, images, maps both accurate and inaccurate, incidental information and enlightened guesswork, and at all times the availability of Indian trails played a role in determining the direction taken by individual scouts, explorers, and land agents in search of a site for settlement. The particular routes of individual travelers were not always directly west, but the over-all direction of the Anglo-American advance was. This direction left a legacy of regional labels derived from spatial perceptions in the United States.

The Three Northwests and the Upper Middle West

An unfortunate example of a misnomer is the European use of the term "Indian" in the Americas. To label the Caribbean islands the *West* Indies because they were reached in a westward voyage is as ethnocentric as

*It was considered difficult, however, because of the hostile Iroquois one was likely to encounter along the way.

declaring an area inhabited by a people alien to our way of life as a "wilderness inhabited by savages" and therefore not "settled." Equally disconcerting are the labels of Near, Middle, and Far East, which suggest that the American Middle West could have been a Middle East if the Russians had persevered and pushed eastward across the continent—perhaps from the Russian River in California.

The American Middle West—the heartland—is located in the central part of the Mississippi drainage basin. The term "heartland"—as symbolic a term for the Middle West as is "cradle of the nation" for New England—applies to a region which extends into twelve states, from Ohio in the east to a north-south line from the Dakotas to Missouri in the west; Iowa and Illinois represent the core of the heartland. The term "Middle West" expresses a spatial awareness which began with the term "Middle Colonies" for New York, New Jersey, and Pennsylvania, but the perception of a "middle" belt had faded by the time the Pacific was reached. Writing in the 1840s, American artist George Catlin provided amusing examples of the indiscriminate usage of the term "West" and concluded: "Few people even know the true definition of the term "West"; and where is its location?—phantom-like it flies before us as we travel, and on our way is continually gilded, before us, as we approach the setting sun."[6] One West, the Wild West, never had a location but was the show with which William Cody toured Europe and the United States in the late nineteenth century.

During the first decades of the nineteenth century the development of navigation on the Ohio and Mississippi rivers opened the heartland to the south as well as to the east. When the route via the Erie Canal was extended as far as Lake Michigan through steamboat navigation on the Great Lakes, and railroads rapidly complemented or replaced overland road travel, the east-west orientation of movement in the northern United States was reinforced, reflected in the evolution of three successive Northwests with three distinct spatial connotations: the Ohio Country, the Wisconsin and Iowa territories, and the Oregon Territory.

The first Northwest was the Ohio Country. Called the "Big Country" in the contemporary vernacular, the area was labeled the "Western Territory" in the Ordinance of 1785, and the "Territory Northwest of the Ohio" in the legislation of 1787, thus reflecting the spatial awareness of people in Virginia and the Carolinas who would travel to Kentucky and Boonesborough and the Ohio Country via the Wilderness Road and Cumberland Gap. The Northwest Ordinance of 1787 organized the "Northwest Territory," which included all the land south of the Great Lakes, north of the Ohio, east of the Mississippi, and west of Pennsylvania. After Ohio became a state in 1803, the first Northwest disappeared from the maps, but lived for a time thereafter in peoples' awareness as the "Old Northwest." Today it is a regional term in literature only.

The second and the "New Northwest" consisted of the Wisconsin Territory of 1836 and the Iowa Territory (which included much of the Dakotas) of 1838. In 1882 the president of a private college in St. Paul wrote of "building up a broad college in the vast North West Territory," and a number of journals using the term "Northwest"—the *Northwestern Miller*, *The Northwestern Reporter*, the *Northwestern Agriculturalist*, the *Northwestern Banker*, and *The Literary Northwest*—were published in the area. In 1972 the term lived on in telephone listings (179 in Minneapolis and 98 in St. Paul) of firms including "Northwest" or "Northwestern" in the company name; in advertisements for a beer "that made the Northwest famous"; and in the nightly announcement of a Twin Cities television station as "the Northwest Telecommunication center." Minnesota historians call their state the "Northern Gateway to the West," and in Minneapolis an area called the Gateway District dates back to the days when railroads made the city the entry-way to the Great Northwest, but colloquially the second Northwest has been replaced by "Upper Middle West," or "Midwest."

The third Northwest—the "Great Northwest"—was the Oregon Territory of 1848, later divided into Oregon, Washington, and Idaho. By 1900, the area had become the "Pacific Northwest" on maps and in national awareness. The term "Pacific Northwest" was probably originated by business enterprises and railroad interests in Portland in the 1880s,[7] for the Census division, which included Washington, Oregon, and California, was labeled simply as "Pacific."

In the twentieth century the Middle West, or Midwest, is defined in the *Dictionary of Americanisms* as the area north of the Ohio between the Alleghenies and the Rockies, but the definition does not include all of Missouri and eludes precise regional definition. The Middle West is more than a region; it stands for a way of life. Perhaps the term has been overused, an overuse that has prompted American scholars of regionalism to call it "the most American" of all regions, and an English devotee to the Middle West to comment that "Americans of all kinds are forever speaking of the Midwest and its attitude toward this or that problem."[8] "Middle West" and "Upper Middle West" are vernacular terms compared to the bookish terms of "Middle States," or *Midlands*, the title of a journal published in Iowa in the 1890s, or to "Middle Border," as in Hamlin Garland's autobiographical novel *A Son of the Middle Border* (1917). Also used less is "Upper Mississippi Hill Country"—the heart of the Upper Middle West. But the latter term had a distinct, even distinguished, international reputation in the mid-nineteenth century, when the Upper Mississippi Valley was the destination of fashionable tourists and was as popular as East Africa with its photo-safaris has been in recent years.[9]

Touring the Upper Mississippi

The period when the Upper Mississippi became famous in the United States and abroad coincides with the pioneer settlement in the region. Many who took "The Fashionable Tour on the Upper Mississippi" were amazed at the crowds lining the shores.[10] Others experienced the tour vicariously by panorama, the travelogue of the nineteenth century.

Panoramas were a series of hand-painted scenes on long, continuous canvases that were unwound from one cylindrical drum and rolled on to another before viewing audiences. In 1839 two panoramas showing the Upper Mississippi were in the show halls of the United States; three more were touring by 1849; and eight, possibly ten, displayed the beauty of the region by the end of the 1850s. Only one is partially preserved; all the others are lost, including the *Mammoth Panorama of the Mississippi* by Henry Lewis, which was the largest of all.[11] In 1853 and 1854 Lewis's panorama toured the large eastern cities, including Washington, where President Zachary Taylor saw it. It was also shown in Canada, and in London, the Hague, and Berlin; a newspaper in The Hague advertised it as "the finest trip you will ever make … a succession of picturesque views, superb towns, frightful rocks, woods, forests, fairylike scenes, matchless vistas, light effects." It was well received in Europe, better than in America—where in Lewis's words the market was "possibly overstock'd."

Figure 1-1. *Prairie at Montrose*, watercolor by Seth Eastman. *(Minnesota Historical Society)*

Some of the scenes in the *Mammoth Panorama* were probably similar to those in *The Valley of the Mississippi Illustrated,* a volume of Lewis's sketches and lithographs. Lewis was undoubtedly inspired by Seth Eastman (a soldier-artist stationed at Fort Snelling in the late 1840s), whose water-colors of Mississippi Valley scenes (Fig. 1-1) were artistically superior to his own rather romanticized work.[12] Strongly influenced by Emanuel Leutze (known for his painting *Washington Crossing the Delaware*) and the Düsseldorf School, Lewis perceived the American landscape with the eye of a European. An expert in fine art and literature would probably find a "socially significant mode of vision" in his portrayal of the Upper Mississippi, a portrayal painfully close to the picturesque "cottage art" of the eighteenth and nineteenth centuries.[13] His poor, toiling settlers and the neatly grouped Indians reflect what Ruskin would call a "debased form of contem-plation." An Indian cemetery near Red Wing's village, boatsmen and cot-tages at Cassville, Wisconsin, a neat stockade surrounded by toy-like houses at Prairie du Chien all reflect Lewis's sentimental perception of the environment.[14] Lewis's work also shows an affinity to calendar art, which has been recognized as the kitsch that releases the social and artistic feelings of the successful urban middle class—precisely the social group who took The Fashionable Tour, looked at panoramas, and constituted the market for the expensive travel books of the time.

Giacomo Beltrami, an Italian exile, was the first traveler to take the steamboat tour from St. Louis to Fort Snelling in 1823. And George Catlin in a letter written in 1835 at the Falls of St. Anthony, suggested and popularized the term "The Fashionable Tour." He advised:

> The traveller in ascending the river will see but little picturesque beauty in the landscape until he reaches Rock Island; and from that point he will find it growing gradually more interesting until he reaches Prairie du Chien; and from that place until he arrives at Lake Pepin every reach and turn in the river represents to the eye a more immense and magnificent scene of grandeur and beauty.[15]

In 1847 David Dale Owen, the state geologist of Wisconsin, also traveled the river, sounding a romantic note:

> The constant theme of remark, whilst travelling in the regions of the upper Mississippi occupied by lower magnesian limestone, was the picturesque character of the landscape, and especially the striking similarity which the rock exposure presents to that of ruined structures. The scenery on the Rhine, with its castellated heights, has been the frequent theme of remark and admiration by European travellers, yet it is doubtful whether, in actual beauty of landscape, it is not equalled by that of some of the streams that water

this region of the far west. It is certain that though the rock formations essentially differ, nature has here fashioned, on an extensive scale, and in advance of all civilization, remarkable and curious counterparts to the artificial landscape which has given celebrity to that part of the European continent.[16]

And in 1854, when the Chicago and Rock Island Railroad staged a huge excursion from Rock Island to the Falls of St. Anthony (including such personalities as former President Millard Fillmore), the New England novelist Catharine M. Sedgwick wrote:

> The bluffs, at some points, make the shore of the river, then they recede leaving a broad foreground of level prairie. They are planted, quite to their summits, with oaks mainly, and trees of other species, as (Andrew) Downing with his love of nature and study of art, might have planted them; now in long serpentine walks, and now in copses, and then so as to cover, with regular intervening clear spaces, the whole front of the declivity, producing the effect of a gigantic orchard. Midway on the bluff, you sometimes see a belt of rock, reminding one of the fragments of Roman walls on the Rhine, but still above and below it, the same bright green turf ... But the surpassingly beautiful marvels of all, are the mimic castles, or rather foundations of ruined castles, that surmount the pinnacles. These mere rocks of lime and sandstone so mock and haunt you with their resemblance to the feudal fortresses of the Old World, that you unconsciously wonder what has become of the Titan Race that built them.[17]

Miss Sedgwick saw resemblances between sharp rocky points and the *Aiguilles* of the Alps. Her pseudo-social awareness also was in the Euro-American tradition: "In returning from St. Anthony's to St. Paul, we all left our vehicle to follow the wheel plow as drawn by six noble oxen; who cleared the turf, and upheaved it for the first time for the sun and the hand of man to do their joint fructifying work upon it. The oxen (not the man) looked like the natural lords of the soil. It was the sublime of ploughing." Altogether she was reminded of the Rhine more than of the Hudson.

This description of the Upper Mississippi Country invites comparison with Tombleson's *View of the Rhine* (1852), an illustrated tour book:

> By our numerous engraved delineations, we shall endeavour to familiarize with the eye when present, and with the recollection when removed, all the beauties and classic interest with which the far-famed river abounds—scenery, which in uniting the romantic and picturesque with the sublime and beautiful, creates a degree of enthusiasm in the mind and feelings of the observer, either as Artist or Tourist; raising and exalting the imagination, from the contemplation of the sublimation of Nature, even to Nature's God.[18]

The Tombleson engravings of the Rhine scenes and Lewis's paintings of the Mississippi Valley show a sameness—in the vertical exaggeration of hills and mountains, the sharply contoured profiles of bluffs and valleys, the grandeur of single-stand trees, and the static reflections of objects in the water. Light and shadow effects are strong. Only foreground figures differ—Indians and tents, peasants and inns, boatsmen, a contemplative hunter. Other American painters of the Düsseldorf School also contributed to the contemporary image of the American landscape, and the Rhine, to which the Hudson and Ohio were likened in literature, became an archetype to be emulated. There were also primitive painters, such as the Austrian Franz Hoelzhuber, whose paintings of the Mississippi Country are supposedly "faithful" renderings of the area in the 1850s.[19] Faithful, indeed, to the cultural biases created by approaching the Upper Mississippi from the eastern seaboard and from Europe!

The appeal of a landscape or so-called scenic beauty is a function of culture, and in the nineteenth century a viewer's responses to reality were often preconditioned by landscape paintings, just as they might be preconditioned today by photographs, television, and films. The observant English traveler Fredrick Marryat wrote that the bluffs along the Mississippi near Prairie du Chien reminded him "very much of Glover's landscapes of the mountainous parts of Scotland and Wales"— not of Scotland and Wales themselves.[20] The influence of European styles on contemporary American illustrations, which were often produced by European immigrant printers in this country, affected to a considerable extent the American image of the Middle West in the nineteenth century.

By the grace of its geographical setting, the Upper Mississippi Valley became even before the Civil War what Vincent Scully calls a "psychological landscape"—just as Greece and Italy had been for more than 200 years.[21] The region still has "geographical individuality," to quote Albert Demangeon, a French master of regional monographs. The region evokes a positive response, largely through its closeness to the Great River, which nowhere seems to be far away, and through its strong relative relief.[22]

The physical geography of the dissected upland in our region has been compared to the rugged plateau of West Virginia and Kentucky. Its central part comprises the so-called "Driftless Area," which is largely in Wisconsin with a small extension into southeastern Minnesota and northeastern Iowa.

The dissected upland begins south of Hastings in Minnesota opposite the mouth of the St. Croix River. The country gradually becomes more rugged, with valleys cut to a depth of as much as 300 feet. These valleys are now followed by the Zumbro, Whitewater, and Rollingstone rivers in Minnesota and by the Wisconsin, Black, Trempealeau, and Chippewa rivers in Wisconsin. Interfluves in the heart of the area are often narrow saddles between short valleys; to the south they are wide ridges from which the uplands roll away. On a map the Upper Mississippi Hill Country, or the "Hill Country" is oval in shape with the south-southeast flowing Mississippi as its axis and with its greatest east-west width (130 to 140 miles) in the latitude of Madison, Wisconsin (Fig. 1-2).

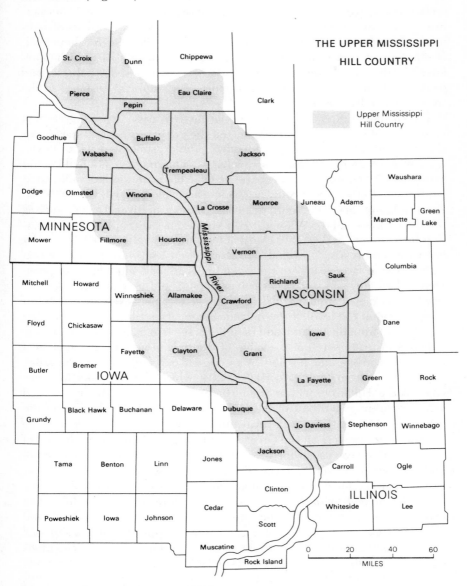

Figure 1-2. The Upper Mississippi Hill Country

Depending on the direction of travel, two rather different impressions can be gained from driving across the Hill Country. Side roads offer the greatest variety. Beginning in the northeast, where the wet prairie and forest of the upland have not been entirely drained, one gradually descends along straight section roads, then on curving roads that descend more rapidly—perhaps through narrow wooded gullies along hidden creeks and past cuts of sedimentary rocks—to join, after more curves, a main valley. Such valleys lead, at times surprisingly abruptly, to the Mississippi's floodplain, which is followed by the Great River Road. From the west, where soils are better and drainage of the wet prairie has been more successful, the distance of the river is generally shorter.

The changing water level of the glacial River Warren (whose channel is now followed by the Mississippi) affected the gradient of its tributaries. So the tributary valleys developed individual profiles, some with wide alluvial terraces and others with only narrow bands of lateral deposition along the valley flanks. These differences are reflected in the many kinds of valleys that cut through the dissected country.[23] Some are wide and flat, like the Rush River in Minnesota or the south side of the Wisconsin River. Others, such as the Upper Iowa and the Whitewater in Minnesota, have entrenched meanders beneath rock-walled cliffs. Most of the tributary valleys are followed by good surfaced roads. Graveled side roads often lead into smaller hidden valleys; there, farmsteads are squeezed between road and hillside or pocketed at the valley end, and only small patches of field are cultivated. A short climb up a ridge or around a hill brings into view the next valley or leads to a wider ridge on the level of the upland. Some farmsteads sit on spurs that finger down from the upland, and their fields seem to hang down the slopes. Other farmsteads perch at the edge of the upland and are reached by a section road on one side, possibly by a steep and curving road from the valley below. Views from Interstate Highway 94, which skirts the northeastern edge of the Hill Country, or from Highway ·14 between Rochester and Winona barely give a hint of the variety of field and farm layouts in the valleys. A side excursion well repays the effort.

Observant travelers on the Great River Road (which follows both sides of the Mississippi) can construct imaginary lines connecting the heights of the bluffs on either side of the river. The opposite side will look more like an undistinguished level, even a monotonous rise, above the valley; and along the road, the cliffs with their rock outcrops appear as individual hills. The expanse of water diminishes the impression of the relief of the land, and swamps, woods, and stretches of stagnant water trapped by railway and road embankments almost hide the channels of great tributary rivers. The bluffs and the labyrinth of lakes and channels in the Mississippi floodplain combine to make one forget that a rectangular survey system was imposed on this land.

In the mid-nineteenth century the Upper Mississippi River consisted of a series of deep pools separated by shoals and rapids. Above St. Louis, the Lower Rapids (Des Moines River Rapids) and the Upper Rapids (Rock River Rapids) were serious impediments to navigation; even so, seven steamboats toured between St. Louis and St. Paul, the upper terminal for navigation. After 1854, however, when the Rock Island Railroad reached the Mississippi, tourists coming from Chicago could bypass the Upper Rapids.

At times more tourists than immigrants were aboard the riverboats, but during the 1840s and 1850s thousands of settlers converged on the Upper Mississippi by various routes. From New York they moved up the Hudson to Albany, where they were joined by New Englanders. Then they proceeded by the Erie Canal and railroads to Dunleith (East Dubuque). From Pennsylvania and the port of Baltimore they traveled by railroad to Columbia, Pennsylvania, then by canal boat along rivers and portages to Pittsburgh, and thence down the Ohio (along which land seekers from Ohio, Indiana, and Illinois might embark) to St. Louis. Many immigrants from England and Germany landed in New Orleans; usually their first impression of the American landscape was when they stepped off the riverboat in the Middle West. From the eighty-five towns, villages, and landing places between St. Louis and Fort Snelling listed in Lloyd's *Steamboat Directory* of 1856 the land seekers fanned out into the Upper Mississippi Country. When the author of the *Minnesota Handbook* of 1856-57 took the "Fashionable Tour" on the steamboat *Northern Belle,* he saw "hundreds of persons whose beds covered almost every foot on the cabin floor," and "mused upon the various situations and climates and nations these people had left."[24] The lake port of Milwaukee and railroads between Milwaukee and Chicago and the Twin Cities and Iowa became more important for immigration to the Upper Middle West only after the Civil War.

The Westward Movement and Environmental Perception

The environment from which settlers and travelers alike came affected their perception of the new surroundings. In time what at first was new and unique became familiar and accepted. Most of the newcomers did not keep diaries, and those who did report their journeys often repeated what they had heard, not what they actually observed. An individual's observations were affected by his national origin, level of education, and economic status as well as incidental contacts, and hazardous encounters.[25]

In travel descriptions, newspapers, diaries, and letters the absence of comments on the rectangular survey system is noteworthy, particularly since foreign-born writers made frequent comparisons on other subjects. Just one example: Friedrich Münch, a distinguished German writer and journalist living in St. Louis, expressed shock over the appearance of American churches, which he found little different from residences. He also found violets without scent and colorful birds which "hardly please the ear by any song." The American familiarity with rifles he found remarkable: "Hunting in Germany was still an aristocratic pastime only."[26] But still he did not compare the settlement system with that in his homeland, although it differed drastically. My rather wide sampling of German-American litera- ture of the nineteenth century (which includes the eleven-volume German-American encyclopedia, compiled "with special consideration for the needs of Germans living in America")[27] yields no specific reactions to the U.S. survey system. It would appear that the rules under which immigrants claimed, bought, and settled their new land were simply taken for granted.

The quality of the land was the main concern of the immigrants. Adver- tisements aimed at the foreign-born tried to invoke familiar images; for example, the head of the land department of the Burlington Railroad sug- gested that lands in Iowa should be advertised as comparable to those in Hungary. He also noted that for a European, "Corn and cattle offer no special attraction" but that the "promise of the crops with which he is familiar, grapes, rye, barley, wheat would stir him."[28] An abundance of such advertising has led to the notion that foreign-born settlers selected land which reminded them of their homeland or which they had been led to believe would do so. But to verify this notion the geography of the actual place of origin of each settler would have to be identified and compared with the American location he had selected—or found himself stranded in.

Contemporary historians described the land using terms from surveyors' notes, such as "rolling prairie with oak openings." Soils were similarly identified as "alluvial bottoms," qualified perhaps by "subject to inundation" or "very fertile," or by a reference to texture as in "sandy loam," "rich loam," or "black loam with a slight mixture of sand." Surveyors classified soils in their notes as being first, second, and third class, based on a quick judgment.

Good land was "well-watered" and good timber, such as oak, sugar beech, hickory, or black walnut was a sign of fertility; swamps were to be avoided because of poor drainage and because they caused various fevers. The vocabulary stemmed from the humid eastern wood culture of the westward-moving American pioneer, who needed lumber for fuel, housing, fencing, and—often overlooked—for maintenance of roads, miserable as they were. The carry-over of the eastern wood culture endures in many Middle Western single-family dwellings, which are of wood-frame construc- tion with wood-burning fireplaces.

The treeless prairie that settlers encountered in the westward movement has become an intriguing subject in historical geography. Prairies, earlier called meadows, were but small patches in the woods in Ohio, larger in Indiana, and extensive in Illinois. The mixed prairie and forest land in southern Wisconsin and Minnesota was bordered by the "Big Woods" toward the north and by a transitional zone of prairies with some oak openings toward the west. Further west where the famed tall-grass prairies took over, wood was found only along the watercourses. The origin of the prairies east of the Mississippi is still debated, and correlations with Indian burnings or rainfall conditions are not always conclusive. How observers reacted to and in what sequence settlers elected prairie or forest land has engaged much scholarly effort.

The English immigrants were especially apt to enjoy the park-like appearance of the prairie. Morris Birkbeck, one of the founders of the English settlements on the Wabash, wrote in 1818:

> The view of that noble expanse was like the opening of bright day upon the gloom of night, to us who had been so long buried in deep forests. It is a feeling of confinement, which begins to damp the spirits, from this complete exclusion of distant objects. To travel day after day, among trees of a hundred feet high, without a glimpse of the surrounding country, is oppressive to a degree which those cannot conceive who have not experienced it; and it must depress the spirits of the solitary settler to pass years in this state.... In a hilly country a little more range of view may occasionally be obtained; and a river is a stream of light as well as of water, which feasts the eye with a delight inconceivable to the inhabitants of open country. [29]

Birkbeck, who was certain that diseases were "not attached to the climate but local situations," also lamented that Americans settled in the vicinity of rivers on account of "advantages of navigation and machinery as well as the fertility of soil having generally suspended a proper solicitude about health." Only in passing did he mention that the land was surveyed by townships and sections and that he planned to sell subdivisions of 320, 160, and 80 acres. Flowers, his partner, also was intrigued by the magnificence of park scenery and explained that his individual preferences for prairie, forest, or river bottoms came about through cultural conditioning. Heavy timber and rich land, he found, were "the delight of Americans and dread of Europeans, who are incapable of clearing off timber to advantage.... The Americans, by pushing onward and onward for almost two generations had a training in handling the axe and opening farms, and from experience, bestowing their labor in the most appropriate manner, which we, from our inexperience, often did not. Fresh from the old country, teeming with the conveniences of civilized life, at once in a wilderness with all our inexperience, our losses were large from misplaced labor."[30]

The settlement of the prairie lands in Illinois was slightly delayed by lack of timber for fuel, fences, and building; by greater expenses for digging wells; by poor drainage; and by the need for a new plowing technology. The edges of the prairies were usually settled first; the central area of the territory, consisting of much wet prairie and being less accessible by roads, was settled later.[31] Settlers from the East thus combined the best of two environments: a familiar forest for wood supply and fertile virgin land that needed no clearing. Settling the periphery first and then moving in toward the center was also the usual sequence of claiming land in mixed dry prairie and forest country. The wet prairies needed a new technology, drainage ditches at first and then tiling.

No attempt was made by legislators to grant prairie settlers the right to buy only five or ten acres of woodland separately (but within hauling distance of their farms) at government prices. Nor was such an adjustment suggested in contemporary literature when land was being claimed in the Upper Mississippi Country. It is certain that many settlers helped themselves to free wood from land that was still in the public domain or in the hands of absentee owners.

Information on climatic conditions was restricted to precipitation, the dates of the first and last killing frosts, extreme winter and summer temperatures, and the frequency of heavy thunderstorms (which invariably were frightening to European immigrants). The average annual rainfall, no matter how small the number of years for which precipitation was recorded, was all that was known. But the connection between a cleaned-tilled row crop, and erosion-causing surface runoff after heavy downpours was not generally realized. To the many New Englanders who moved west—farmers used to worn-out, thin topsoils—the soil of the new Northwest was thick and fertile beyond their expectations, and the term "inexhaustible" crept into literature and the vernacular—even into teaching at land-grant colleges at the end of the century.

The westward-moving settlers moved from the tall-grass prairie of Iowa to areas of needlegrass and wheatgrass. Trees, no longer mostly hickory and oak but willows, cottonwood, and basswood, grew only along the river courses, and lone trees became landmarks for trekkers. Such was the "Lone Elm" by the Platte River, described as a "very poor tree" by Adolph Wislizenus, scientist to a military survey carried out in 1846. Annual averages for rainfall became less meaningful. The agricultural potential of land was judged by the appearance of the precipitation, which changed with annual variability and seasonal distribution. Thus observers expressed widely differing views about the West, ranging from desert to garden, and scholarly debates on the images invoked by the Great Plains have continued to the present and will not soon subside.[32]

The division between East and West has been symbolized by the 100th meridian, although it is well understood that no fixed north-south line divides the humid East from the arid West. The suitability of the U.S. survey system for land west of the 100th meridian was seriously questioned for the first time in 1878 by Major John Wesley Powell, the explorer of the Colorado. In his *Report on the Lands of the Colorado* (1878), Powell pleaded for adjustment of land laws to fit geographical conditions, explaining that in a region where water, not land, was the major resource, different regulations were essential for survival. [33]

The invariably rectangular pattern of holdings, Powell said, would have to be replaced by the organization of pasturage districts, where the inhabitants would reside "grouped to the greatest possible extent." This settlement form might be "practically accomplished by making pasturage farms conform to topographic features in such a manner to give the greatest possible number of water fronts." He asked for "a system less arbitrary than that of the rectangular survey [then] in vogue." When "lands are surveyed in regular tracts as square miles or townships, all the water sufficient for a number of pasturage farms may fall entirely within one division," he noted, adding that "the people settling on these lands should be allowed the privilege of dividing the lands into such tracts as may be most available for such purposes, and they should not be hampered with the present arbitrary system of dividing the lands into rectangular tracts." Powell also declared that in arid land a quarter section for a family was totally insufficient as a unit to sustain a farmer or a cattlebreeder, and that the government should allow four sections to each settler. [34] This part of the report has generally received more attention than his suggestion that the rectangularity of the survey be avoided in the arid lands. Powell's insight was unequaled, but Congress did not act upon his report. Any important land legislation reflecting adjustment to the arid West had to wait until the Taylor Grazing Act of 1934 was passed.

At the time that Powell warned against the unsuitability of the U.S. survey in the arid West, surveying had been started independently along the Pacific Coast, although much of the intervening western country was as yet not surveyed. Surveyors-general were appointed for Oregon in 1850, California in 1851, and Washington in 1854.

The process of settling the Upper Mississippi Country was greatly accelerated by steamboats and railroads. Steamboat arrivals at Chicago increased from 176 to 5060 between 1834 and 1854. After 1839 the Galena stagecoach maintained regular service to Chicago, which had its railroad connection with the Atlantic seaboard by 1852. From Chicago the railroad reached Rock Island in 1854; the Illinois Central Railroad reached Dunleith, opposite Dubuque, in 1855; and the Burlington Railroad reached Quincy in 1856. Milwaukee was connected with Prairie du Chien in 1857, with La Crosse in 1858, and with St. Paul, after some delay due to the Civil War, in 1867.

The development of transportation depended just as much on the investment of private capital and public funds as on technological progress. Extraordinary expenditures went into speculative enterprises, particularly in land. Speculation in public lands peaked in 1818 - 19, in 1836, and again in 1858. Upon the urging of Congress, in turn spurred on by eastern capitalists, land surveys were carried out rapidly, to stay ahead of the settlers. By the end of the 1850s all of Upper Mississippi County had been surveyed, and most of its land offices had moved further west or north. During 1855, when three ferries operated across the Mississippi around the clock at Prairie du Chien, 325 million acres of land were taken up in Iowa alone.[35]

The many land agents, who often had been surveyors or registers and receivers at land offices, worked from towns such as Burlington, Blooming-ton, and Davenport, advertising in local as well as eastern newspapers. They could not have operated with a survey system in which land parcels were identified ambiguously. Simple identification made possible the easy trans-fer of land and thus land speculation and sales. Thus another potent force contributing to the speed of the westward movement was the rectangular survey. Further contributing to a psychology that perceived land as a standardized commodity identifiable by simple plane geometry was the warrant system; through it members of the military were awarded scrip which entitled them to acquire from 40 to 160 acres of land.

The decision-makers of 1785 could not foresee the extent to which the rectangular survey would be employed through space and time. Their experiences were restricted to the eastern seaboard, and they were influ-enced by traditions of which they might not always have been aware and that are sometimes hard to trace. Last, they also were men of the eighteenth century, the century of "rationalism and enlightenment." For a better appreciation of the United States land survey as an American accomplish-ment of continental proportions we should compare it with historical prece-dents and other systems of land assignment.

2 TRADITIONS OF LAND ASSIGNMENT

Settlement Forms in French Canada and the British Colonies

Pioneer settlements in colonial North America can be grouped under four general forms: (1) Systematic settlement patterns with field layouts generally associated with direct accessibility to rivers and roads; (2) Clustered villages with house lots and fields in separate locations; (3) Irregularly shaped and often large landholdings, with private docks and residences in interfluvial locations; and (4) Regular, that is, rectangularly shaped and planned, town-sites and settlements, which invite comparison as "colonial precedents" to the survey system that developed after 1785.[1]

Patterns of settlement are visual statements on the land and often reveal less of their present functionalism than of the genetic aspect which brought them into being. In Western societies the first step toward control of an environment usually is the assigning of tracts as grants of property—done by drawing lines on paper, although little may be known about the tract that is to be colonized. The desire of governments to attain as complete an occupancy of their territories as possible leads to assignments of land that are rectilinear and adjacent. But the delineation of land grants and the use of technology are dependent on accessibility, which in North America in the beginning stages of colonization was provided by rivers.

Accessibility to the St. Lawrence River, the main artery of transportation in New France, was the consideration when land grants were drawn on maps in Paris; all early seigneuries fronted the river. For the patroons along the Hudson and for planters in Virginia and the Carolinas, straight lines drawn inland from points along the waterfront designated the land grants on maps drawn in Amsterdam and London. But, while the lines were precisely placed on those documents, they were vague in reality and often not surveyed. Many became buried under subsequent subdivisions, roads, and urbanization. The lines for the seigneuries remained mainly on paper, but the riparian long-lot, or *rang,* system in the older parts of Lower Canada characterizes the rural settlement of French Canada and is strikingly real. Long lots can be seen from Highway 15B out of Québec toward Montmorency Falls, particularly at Beauport, the oldest region of settlement around the Côte de Beaupré. They are also perpetuated in the street alignment of towns and in urban subdivisions, which take the form of elongated strips on modern road maps.[2]

But the best view of a long-lot landscape is from the air between Montréal and Québec, where the lots fronting the St. Lawrence predominate. At times they meet at sharp angles with other long-lot systems oriented toward tributaries of the St. Lawrence. Roads lined at irregular intervals with houses, rows of dark hedges and shrubs bordering the fields, and short, often narrow rectangles of woodland distinctly reveal the pattern of the rang. The long-lot landscape is unique to North America and is very different from that of the American rectangular survey. But both systems are remarkable in that their visibility has become greater with the passage of time.

The origin of the rang is still debated, "a dilemma between the question of an importation or an invention in the region of new settlement."[3] In Canada there was no Indian model, and similarities with medieval French settlement patterns do not prove origin. It is comparable to the German *Waldhufendorf,* the Czech *chota,* and the Polish *jan,* all long-lot forest villages. Linear spacing of houses along a road, canal, or dike, with long, narrow fields stretching behind, is also characteristic of parts of Holland and Friesia, where the pattern derives from the drainage of moors and former seashores. Like its European counterparts, the rang offers the advantage of including in one farm land of different qualities; for example, in that area of Québec where the bottomland is not very wide, a rang often includes terrace land, the talus of slopes, and wooded bluffs.

In Québec the proportion of long-lots was on the average ten arpents (one arpent=192 feet.) in length to one in width; but occasionally they were extraordinarily long and narrow, and the ratio of one hundred to one is documented.[4] Houses were thus closely spaced, especially after the land was further subdivided.

The first rang directly facing the river was by no means fully settled before a second rang developed behind it, along the road connecting the new farms. Houses often stood at an angle on the connecting road, being oriented toward the line of the riverfront, from which the first farmstead (roture) had been surveyed.* Today the siting of houses may be seen to advantage along the oldest highway of French Canada, the Rue Royale.

*North of Québec, however, there is a departure from the system. The linear and originally

By the mid-1700s it had become apparent that farms would soon extend into the less-fertile uplands. It was also apparent that subdivision of the land into ever-narrowing strips would be uneconomical, and in 1745 Louis XV issued an ordinance that a roture could be no narrower than 1½ by 30 to 40 arpents.⁶ As long as the French Canadian farmers had additional income (such as logging) and were devoted to their neighborhoods, the system of long lots, even if impractical, was continued.

The French did not come to Canada in groups from the same villages or regions in France. In the New World they formed new parishes, and their religious and communal life became associated with the rang system. When the fur trade no longer provided employment for the farmers, every acre of an old roture was brought into service, and new long-lot farms were cleared—even on the less fertile uplands. Boundaries were carefully observed, accentuated by shrubs and fences *(clotures)*, which became a hindrance to the enlargement or consolidation of the narrow lots. The parallel with British enclosures is self-evident.

During the nineteenth century many French Canadians left their farms to seek work elsewhere. But some stayed on the land, and those people, hesitant and financially unable to mechanize their agriculture, adhered to their old ways and to their long lots as an expression of cultural identity. "The *rang*," according to geographer Deffontaines, "constituted the primary social unity."⁷ Many farmers, particularly those around urban centers, learned to specialize—64 per cent of commercial farms in Québec were dairy farms in 1971—but they still remained culturally tied to the long-lot system. In the words of Louis Trotier, the French Canadian geographer: "The rural French Canadian today thinks in terms of the *rang*." Cultural consciousness has been further intensified by affluent urban Québecois, who pay high prices for farmhouses (preferably built of limestone) with the long lot as an indispensable accoutrement of genuine French Canadian rural culture.

The genesis of the long-lot landscape has been described here because of an interesting dichotomy: it has been perpetuated and visibly intensified largely through cultural identification and the technological retardation of agriculture; it has become an expression of urbanites' prestige as well. In contrast, as we shall see later, the landscape of the rectangular survey also became visually intensified, but through exactly opposite forces: the assimilation of people of different cultural backgrounds accompanied by their dedication to increasing application of technology to the land.

The French Canadians took the long-lot idea with them to the Red River and the Assiniboine, north and south of Winnipeg. Eighteenth-century maps show rangs along the Rivière du Detroit and Lac St-Clair; today the old

open spacing of houses made defense against the Iroquois difficult, and, under the order of Intendant Talon, the villages of Charlesbourg and Bourg Royale were built as compact units.⁵

alignments are recognizable when one flies east from Detroit. When the Clark grant of 1784 was laid out, surveyors found long lots stretching away from the Wabash River around Vincennes in Indiana. The claims of earlier French settlers were honored, and, while some lots were consolidated into larger fields, the tilting of the axis is apparent from the air. Long lots also prevailed in southern Louisiana along the Mississippi. In Québec's eastern townships around Sherbrooke, they intermingle with squarish fields laid out first by immigrants from New England and later by Canadian surveyors. And in the Saguenay River country, cleared less than 100 years ago, there are narrow lots stretching down to the shore of Lac Saint Jean.

But in the nineteenth-century Middle West the French regime left only scattered testimony to the long-lot system. Some street alignments in St. Louis can be traced back to French river lots. Long lots were laid out around Kaskaskia on the Illinois side of the Mississippi; while the lot lines were carefully drawn on an 1839 map for prospective immigrants, the lots today are not impressive in the landscape.[8] At St. Genevieve in Missouri, there were long lots but they were almost literally flooded away in 1785.[9] And before 1800 the French had claimed narrow river lots at Prairie du Chien and also at Green Bay.[10] Claims, deriving in part from the long-lot system, were being settled as late as 1863 through special acts of Congress.[11] By that time, only place-names remained from the French legacy in the Upper Mississippi Country.

The manors along the Hudson River granted to "Patroons, Masters and Private Individuals" by the Dutch West India Company "the better to people their lands," also were intended to have riverine locations. But the patroonships differed from the seigneuries: in New Netherlands it was permitted "to extend their limits four leagues along the shore, or on one side of a navigable river, or two leagues on each side of a river."[12] Indeed, the patroonship of Rensselaer around Fort Orange extended into the hinterland on both sides of the Hudson. Yet no distinctive settlement pattern is associated with these early grants. The Dutch lived in scattered locations by rivers "as each found most convenient," according to a French observer in 1646.[13] New Englanders, who came early to New Netherlands, also settled separately, but close to the Indians for easier trade—much to the Indians' annoyance since the cattle of the white man often broke into their cornfields.[14]

On a sketch of Manhattan by Jaspar Dankaert during his visit from 1679 to 1680, houses were sited on higher land or a terrace, and fenced fields stretched down to the water.[15] Dankaert, a member of the sect founded by the French-born reformer Jean de Labadie, had in 1679 founded a Labadist colony near New Castle, Maryland. "Bohemian Manor" extended over 3750 acres and four "necks of land"; to the delight of Dankaert, it was inaccessible by road and thus could not be "resorted to by everyone, especially by these miserable Quakers."[16] The reformers, who became tobacco planters and also used slave labor, later subdivided their tract with each division accessible from an estuary or a river.

The frequency of riverine location of colonial plantations in the South has been called "unusually striking."[17] Farmsteads in the Middle Colonies also were as close to rivers as possible; and so-called roads in the region, winding through the woods and of uncertain direction, were a constant complaint of travelers. Paths and traces connected the separate farmsteads in New Jersey, Pennsylvania, and Delaware, and farther to the south, the dispersed plantations. The remnants of Indian clearings and scattered patches of land cleared by the colonists resulted in an irregular distribution of fields, stemming from what came to be called "indiscriminate location." The term, however, was inappropriate since the selector of a site was in fact usually rather discriminating—claiming and possibly bounding only that land which he really desired, while totally ignoring systematic shapes and contiguity with neighboring properties. A map in the New Jersey Patent of 1664 contains the note that "due to vagueness of recorded data, boundaries can be considered only approximate." The scattering of holdings, some with overlapping boundary claims, particularly in Virginia, was indeed "uncontrolled and chaotic,"[18] when compared with the orderly lineup of long, narrow fields in colonial river towns such as Wethersfield in Connecticut, Springfield in Massachusetts, and Ellsworth in Maine.

The most orderly and controlled settlement form along the eastern seaboard was created by the town proprietors in New England. After 1641, towns in Massachusetts and their bounded acres had to be laid out within one year after land had been granted for settlement. In these towns, settlers themselves had little choice of location. It was ordered "that no man shall set his dwelling house above the distance of half a mile or a mile at the furthest, from the meeting of the Congregation, where the Church does usually assemble." All farmers were assigned tracts of meadowland and shared in the use of woodland; each had a small lot facing the commons.[19] But such order in settlement was no longer maintained when religious control became less stringent and the fear of Indian attacks abated. Home lots became larger—as large as sixty acres—and their short sides usually fronted winding roads, which resulted in a pleasant blend of the uncertain rectangularity of properties and fields and the adjustment of roads to topography. Land holdings were assigned and measured by the metes-and-bounds system with legal descriptions such as the following one for a ten-acre tract:

> At the northeast corner with a maple tree between him (Captain West) and Abraham Masters, from that westerly 30 poles* to a hemlock tree between him (Captain West) and Abraham Masters, from that southerly westerly 39 poles to Morgan's Stump, from that southeasterly 44 poles on said West's farm line to a black oak, and from that 66 poles northwestward to the first point."[20]

*A pole was 16½ ft. long; the measuring was done at times by pacing.

The metes-and-bounds system, which was the rule in all British colonies, was discontinued after the American survey became the law. The term itself still indicates measurement as such.

Examples of the fourth general form of settlement, rectangular town plats, have been called precedents for our national land system.[21] Squares for holdings of various sizes appear in many places—on eighteenth-century maps of New York along the Upper West Branch of the Hudson River and along the Schenectady; on field plans as far north as Meredith, New Hampshire, and as far south as Ebenezer, Georgia. An exactly square 640-acre tract is reported to have been surveyed as early as 1666 in Massachusetts. Nor is rectangularity in town plans unique to any one ethnic or cultural group. A Dutch surveyor laid out the grid plan of 1664 for Bergen between the Hackensack and the Hudson.[22] Plymouth village, with its homes and courtyards "arranged in very good order" according to Governor Bradford, was an enterprise of the English, and the original plan of New Orleans is reminiscent of French *bastide* towns such as Monpazier. New Haven's plan of 1638 may derive from Vitruvius, the author of the *Ten Books on Architecture*. The town's nine squares with an open central square also bear a striking resemblance to the legendary plan of Mencius for the nine-square well-field system in China. (The simplest contiguous field form, one which combines the principles of rectangularity, centrality, and equality, consists of nine squares.) The ingenuity of designs employed by various planners for regular settlements may be studied with pleasure in *The Making of Urban America* by John W. Reps, who wisely notes "man's almost instinctive use of geometry in laying out new towns when speed and simplicity are dominant requirements."[23]

When studying historical town plans, one must keep in mind the narrow line between utopian planning and planning for real locations. One of the most widely republished plans was Robert Montgomery's "Margravate of Azilia" (1717) for South Carolina. It consisted of 116 squares, each 640 acres, with four squares symmetrically arranged as forested parks.[24] Although seriously intended, Montgomery's plan was utopian in its extreme symmetry and was never carried out. In colonial Georgia, New Ebenezer was started on a regular plan which included open spaces, town lots, garden lots, and farm lots. The minister of New Ebenezer wrote in 1734 that "all houses and gardens are laid out in mathematical equality which will make a fine show when they come to perfection." But they never did, and New Ebenezer no longer exists. Savannah survived with a gridiron plan endorsed by General Oglethorpe, the planner of that colony for the poor. Its squares have maintained their pleasant individual identities to the present. A widely reprinted oblique view of Savannah executed by Peter Gordon in 1734 (Fig. 2-1) appeared on the cover of the catalogue for the Wilderness Exhibition of the National Endowment for the Arts (1971). It is thought-provoking that

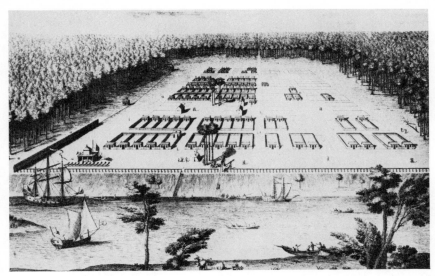

Figure 2-1. Peter Gordon, *A View of Savannah* 1734. A prototype of rational planning and colonization, Oglethorpe's plan shows a grid-pattern city with four squares in the process of being walled against the wilderness. Trees in the dense forest are as uniformly spaced as are lots and houses. (*The New York Public Library*)

this print, one of a wide variety of illustrations representing the American wilderness, was chosen to symbolize so prestigious an exhibition. Gordon's view shows a gridiron plan with four symmetrically placed open squares, and wide streets lined with totally uniform houses. The future town is set squarely against the thick forest in the background. The initial conquest of the wilderness, by right-minded order indeed!

Communitarian colonies are often associated with utopian, or "regular," planning. Moravian settlements such as Bethlehem, Lebanon, Lititz, and Emmaus in Pennsylvania are examples (they later became urban places, however, and today the regularity of the fields surrounding them is hard to visualize).[25] The plan most beloved by Americans is probably that of William Penn's colony in Pennsylvania with its regularly laid out town of Philadelphia.[26] He also laid out Newton and Wrightstown in Bucks County with village squares and equally regular land assignments. But painstaking probing reveals that the groups of contiguous lots were not settled in an orderly way and that squatting by "discriminating" settlers became a widespread practice. Farmsteads became widely dispersed, and any regularity of fields resulted from self-interested practices and property bounding rather than from utopian planning. People simply preferred to live on their own farms rather than in compact villages. The dispersed farmstead with immediately accessible land was the cheapest method of production and by the end of the eighteenth century, the agricultural village had become an anachronism.[27] One could not waste the most precious commodity, labor, in an environment where land was surplus and labor scarce.

When in the early nineteenth century surveyors extended their measurements into the territory of the Louisiana Purchase, they met with square land claims (Spanish *sitios*) in western Louisiana. Generally one league square (4428 acres), these land divisions merged with those of the U.S. Survey only when they were strictly north-south oriented.[28] When tilted, usually for orientation toward a watercourse, the sitio field layout runs in a different direction, which is strikingly apparent from the air. Sitios and the gridiron pattern of Spanish colonial cities have led investigators to look for connections between the rectangularity of the Spanish cities and Roman models, although the American Indian influence, at least for the square plaza, cannot be ruled out.[29] The striking parallels to Roman mensuration cannot be neglected in seeking origins for the American rectangular land survey.

Roman Centuriation—A European Precedent

Air photo interpretation has aroused new interest in ancient Roman centuriation, a cadastral system later praised by Pliny and Vitruvius and more recently the subject of thorough study among European classicists.[30] The basic unit of this field system was the *centuria*, which consisted of 100 square *heredia*, or roundly 132 acres.[31] These 100 units were allotted to a *curia* (100 families). Each centuria was laid out by the measurers of fields, called *agrimensores*, with the help of a cross-staff. At its center, a north-south running axis, the *cardo maximus*, intersected an east-west running line, the *decumanus maximus*, dividing the surveyed area into four quarters. Inscriptions on stone markers reveal standard labels for the sections: left rear for the northwest, left front for the northeast, right rear for the southwest, and right front for the southeast quarter.[32] These labels reveal the ancient origin of the center, namely the point at which an augur stood facing east with the northeast and southeast quarters in front of him.

We now begin to recognize another aspect, the original connection of the Roman system with the religious meaning of the center. To clarify the religious symbolism we must distinguish between two derivations from Latin: square, from *quadra* (also *quadrum* leading to *quadratum*), and quarter, from *quartarius*, or the fourth part, as in "quartering" a circle. The first implies a form in equilibrium and has a static meaning in ancient cosmology. The second has dynamic meaning in cosmological schemes. The quartering of the circular horizon by the augur who stood at its center facing east was the religious act by which stability—the orderly delimitation of fields by agrimensores—would be achieved.[33]

By imperial times surveying was becoming scientifically refined (although surveyors are reported to have been greatly pleased when a centuria cross-point coincided with the actual crossing of two thoroughfares in a new settlement). *Via praetoria* and *via principalis* had replaced the earlier names for the crossroads, but the surveyors' old insignia were still engraved on the markers. For example, DDVK meant *dextra decumanum ultra* (u rendered by v) *kardinem;* that is, the augur stood to right of the decumanus and before the cardo. The old and revealing word for the crosspoint, *umbilicus* (navel, or center of the world), was also kept in use. But, with the exception of religious practice, Roman surveying was not put into practice without regard for the lay of the land. For instance, north of Zara in Dalmatia is a well-preserved country road system based on a decumanus maximus that does not run strictly east-west.[34] Straight north-south orientation occurred only in plains—in Lombardia, south of the Po River between the Adriatic and the Appennine chain, south of Naples, and in some Roman colonies in Africa.[35] Elsewhere the direction of the axis was often adjusted to the terrain.*

The main roads in a *limitatio* (surveyed area) which followed the de-cumanus maximus and the cardo maximus were 40 feet wide. Every fifth field line *(quintarius)* became a public road 12 feet wide, and the lanes in between were 8 feet wide. The field pattern, which was as precise as that of the roads, has persisted to the present and is impressive from both the air and the ground. One can see it well in driving from Venice to the Abbey of Pomposa, around Ravenna, and between Ravenna and Rimini. Straight roads and right-angle turns on the very level land give a formal appearance to the landscape, and, in spite of different human artifacts and a smaller scale, one might well experience a "shock of recognition."** The evenly sized fields are rectangular and on the same north-south axis as the American survey. Another and more kaleidoscopic view of a landscape that still reflects cen-turiation may be seen along the *Autostrada* between Verona and Padua.

Centurialism was never conceived of as unconditionally continuous but began, so to speak, anew from each crosspoint. Thus Italian landscapes deriving from the Roman system vary according to natural regions.

The American survey, however, paid no attention to natural regions. Scholars have been intrigued by the possibility that the idea of the American survey was not originally American but could have been derived from the

*Surveyors sighted the decumanus maximus not necessarily due east, but toward the point of the rising sun, which, of course, changed with various dates. Thus, because survey dates might have been selected to commemorate the foundation of a settlement or to honor a divinity, it is difficult to determine if the axis of a limitatio was tilted because of surface configuration or for cultural reasons.

**The Shock of Recognition* was the title of an exhibit and catalogue dedicated to the influence of sixteenth-century Dutch landscape painting on English nineteenth-century landscape painting (The Tate Gallery, London, 1968).

Roman system, perhaps directly, perhaps via Holland where rectangularity is the most striking feature of the landscape. However, it should be noted that no straight north-south and east-west field lines prevail in Holland, either. It is indeed puzzling that Thomas Jefferson should have proposed a subdivision of "hundreds" into hundred square miles (as we shall discuss later) as the basis for the U.S. survey. But so far, diligent research has not been able to prove that Roman centuriation provided him with a direct model.

The Roman system, then, could be considered as a precedent to the American survey, the difference being that the coordinates in the latter system, crossing at what surveyors call the "initial point," always run north-south and east-west with complete disregard of the terrain. This unconditional rule makes it possible for the survey to be continuous not only in concept but in practice over thousands of square miles—the most extensive uninterrupted cadastral system in the world. The regionalism that does exist is largely due to the existence of private claims and property lines established before the survey. These claims had to be respected even if they did not fit parallels and meridians.

Assigning land by coordinate systems and planning cities on a rectangular grid are ancient and pervasive practices.[36] The Egyptian character for a land district is a grid; so is the Chinese character for the nine-field or well system (which was probably never developed). The grid pattern is the simplest form for equal assignment of land, taxation, design of irrigation canals, and so forth; in short, for initiating man's control of land wherever it is flat and fairly uniform in quality. A certain similarity between Western (Nordic) and Greco-Roman plans, and Eastern (Indian, Chinese, Korean, and Japanese) rectangular patterns in land and city planning[37] brings us closer to understanding what people in many different parts of the world believe: the circle, with its central point designated by a vertical axis and its easy quarterability, is sacred. The square, the most easily defined and practical form representing a defined horizontal area, is a secular equivalent and archetype.[38]

Similarities also exist between geometrical figures and arithmetic numbers. Consider the story of how Socrates elicits from Meno's slave the desired answers regarding a square space by drawing figures in the dust—two-by-two and three-by-three squares.[39] In many places, it is thought that counting developed from one-plus-two plus three-plus-four to ten.* The sizes of plats and proportions of subdivisions vary in colonial plans, but they usually have a central square or a central crosspoint (Fig. 2-2). But multiples of four and nine and ten are standard, and utopian numerology is

---

*Of 307 numbering systems among primitive American peoples, 146 were found to be decimal[40] and may have developed in this way.

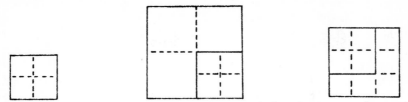

Socrates drew these lines in the dust to elicit from Meno's slave the answer to the question "How long is the side of a square with double the area of a given square?"

Geometric progression leading to a square field, a central point, and a central square.

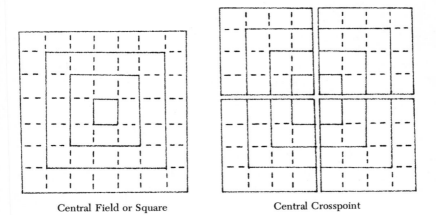

Central Field or Square   Central Crosspoint

Figure 2-2. Archetypes in field divisions and grid town planning.

usually of the simplest kind, such as the six-by-six square block in Amourotum in Thomas More's *Utopia*.

French and English Boundary Claims in North America

The search for the historical origin of the rectangular pattern is losing its appeal. When William Pattison suggests, regarding the claims of invention or derivation of the American survey, "that the issue of origins is likely to be more entertaining than instructive,"[41] he is not only voicing the opinion of

many geographers but that of scholars from other fields as well. Joseph
Needham recognized the pitfalls of the belief that "everything must have
had only one origin" and warned that "convergence need not mean independent invention of a high order. It may only mean that when presented
with the same rather simple problems people in different parts of the world
solved them in the same way."[42] The advice of an anthropologist, John H.
Rowe, is not to let "the assumptions of the diffusionists undermine the very
foundations of comparative study."[43] Let us now take a comparative, short
look at two different ways of defining colonial boundaries in North America.

The French and English followed different routes in exploring North
America, which has led to speculation about the influence of the physical
environment on the fate of their empires in the New World. The French are
said to have been able to move quickly inland by way of the great rivers,
particularly the St. Lawrence, while the British are said to have been
blocked by "a wall of forested mountains."[44] The way in which the French
and British perceived the vast stretches of the unknown continent and came
to define their territorial claims may well have been affected by the different
approaches open to them.

Samuel de Champlain, who founded Québec in 1608, navigated the St.
Lawrence upstream and then ascended the Ottawa River, continuing to
Lake Nipissing and Lake Huron. His maps, excellent for his time, show the
enormous, unknown interior threaded by rivers. Talon, the first Intendant
of Canada, reported in 1665 to Colbert in Paris that accessibility to the large
area of New France was "through the St. Lawrence and the rivers which flow
into it." At Sault St. Marie in 1671, Sieur de Saint-Lusson took possession of
"the Sainte Marie du Sault, also Lake Huron and Lake Superior, the Island
of Caientoton (Manitoulin) and of all other countries, rivers, lakes and their
tributaries contiguous and adjacent thereto, those discovered and to be
discovered." Jacques Marquette noted in his diary when he arrived at the
portage between the Fox and the Wisconsin rivers in 1673 that he was
leaving the waters flowing to Québec, 400 to 500 leagues away, in order "to
float on those which would take him to strange lands." The grant issued by
Louis XIV in 1702 to Antoine Crozatte for the development of trade in
Louisiana defined the area as "of the St. Louis River (Mississippi) up to the
Illinois, of the River St. Phillippe (Missouri) and of the St. Jerome (Wabash)
"with all countries, territories and lakes in this region and with the rivers that
flow directly or indirectly into the St. Louis River in this area." In his
memoirs (1750) Count de la Galissonnière urged that the divide (les eaux
pendantes) between the Atlantic coast and the Gulf become the boundary
between the French and British lands.[45]

The terminology of the French claims reflects the approach of traders and
voyageurs; they used the concept of drainage basins in their political geography. The English made equally extensive claims but they formulated them

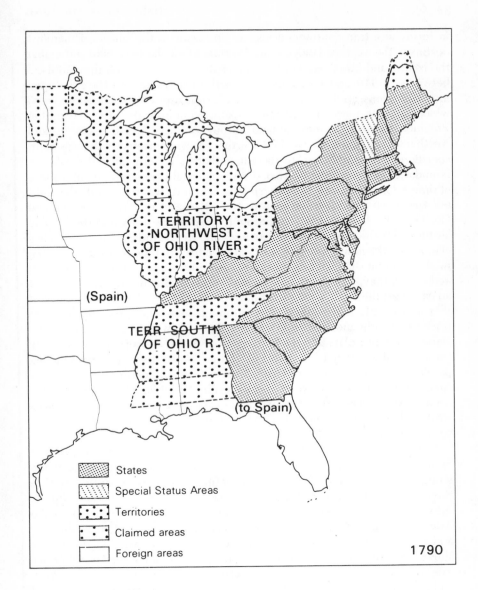

Figure 2-3. Territorial Organization, 1790.

in terms of a transcontinental vision, precursor of the image of manifest destiny in the westward movement. Virginia's first charter (1606) stated that the colony and other parts of land along the seacoast and on the mainland between the 34th and 45th degrees of northerly latitude could be developed into habitations. In the colony's second charter, capes were named between which "all that Space and Circuit of Land, lying from the Sea Coast of the Precinct aforesaid, up into the land, throughout from Sea to Sea, West and Northwest" was granted. The first charter of Massachusetts (1629), was more specific about points close to the coast; that is, it designated the colony's boundaries as three miles north of the Merrimac River and three miles south of the St. Charles River; from there Massachusetts was to extend "throughout the mayne Landes there, from the Atlantick and Westerne Sea and Ocean of the Easte Parte, to the South Sea on the Weste Parte."[46] The latitudinal boundaries of several colonies and the boundaries along parallels claimed by the newly independent states go back to these early grants. One might detect a slight degree of empiricism in the initial English approach and vision: they knew, with France making claims further to the north, that an east-west line of division might have to be acknowledged. The argument that it is simply more convenient, although somewhat presumptuous, to refer to latitude and longitude when little is known of the territory to be claimed is more plausible. Colonizers from Western Europe, particularly from England, often drew political and administrative boundaries along parallels and meridians over large areas in overseas territories, notably in Africa and Australia. An example of a meridian used for a boundary early in colonial America is the charter for Maryland of 1632, which fixed the colony's western boundary as a meridian line running "through the head of the first spring of the Potomac River."[47]

In the Treaty of Paris (1783) the first southern boundary of the United States was defined as it appeared on John Mitchell's map of 1755. It ran straight east from a point in the middle of the Mississippi at latitude 31°N to the middle of the Apalachicola River, along that river to its junction with the Flint River, and "thence straight to the head of St. Mary's river to the Atlantic Ocean." This boundary was inaccurately defined geographically, and the courses of the rivers were not completely known. But the Treaty shows how statesmen persisted in using parallels for boundaries. Other examples are the boundary between Canada and Vermont and New York and the boundary along the 49th parallel between Canada and the United States. The same feature is very obvious on later American territorial and state boundaries (Fig. 2-4).

During the period when Spanish sovereignty over North America west of the Mississippi was recognized, the states along the eastern seaboard extended their claims only as far as the Mississippi, abandoning the earlier vision of occupying the land from sea to sea (Fig. 2-3). The claims remained

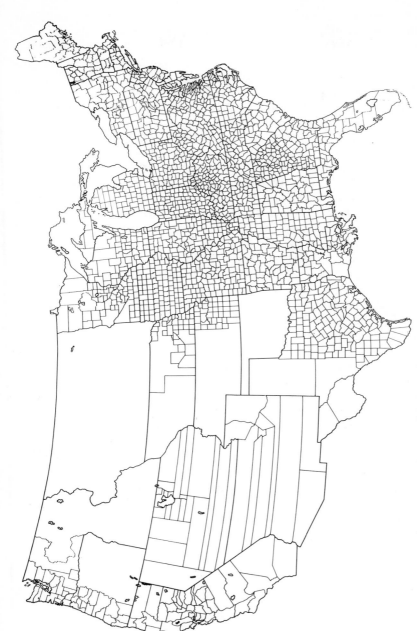

Figure 2-4. County boundaries in the United States, 1860.

defined by parallels, such as those made by Massachusetts for land between 41° and 42°2′N and by Connecticut for land between 44°2′ and 44°15′N. The shape of the state of Tennessee is the result of an erstwhile transcontinental vision transformed by necessity into a westward-to-the-Mississippi one. How this tradition of territorial assignment by parallels continued is illustrated by Figure 2-4, an 1860 map of county boundaries in the United States. The less men knew about the land, the straighter were the lines they drew—right across rivers and mountains.

A successful surveying of a parallel was completed in 1767 by the English engineers Charles Mason and Jeremiah Dixon for the boundary between Pennsylvania and Maryland. And by the late 1700s parts of lower Canada had already been accurately surveyed under instructions from the Crown (1763), which also directed that townships of a convenient size were to be laid out and that the specific agricultural capabilities of the land were to be described. In 1783 the British Crown directed the governor of Québec to survey new lands to be granted to disbanded soldiers and to loyalists who wished to emigrate from the United States to Québec. He ordered that townships in what is now Ontario be subdivided into 120-acre lots, noting that a township of thirty-six square miles was the best, "as the People to be settled there are most used to it, and they [the townships] will best answer the Proportion of Land I propose to grant to each family." The resulting townships, known as "the single-front system" in Canadian surveys until 1818, were rectangular (as were the lots) and faced Lake Ontario. They were not on a non-varying grid. [48]

The thirty-six-square-mile township goes back to medieval England, when such an area was the limit for convenient marketing with horse and wagon. Township size is also tied to non-mechanical agricultural technology, which continued to prevail in the New World among settlers when other medieval customs were dying out. The feudal open-field system, fragmentation of holdings, compact villages, and fair distribution of land according to different quality—to name a few—had been outdated by the mid-1700s. The desire for assured ownership of separate property parcels required simple and accurate descriptions of landholdings, and the Ordinance of 1785 was a plan in support of such possessive individualism.

3 NEW LAND ASSIGNMENT THROUGH THE LAND ORDINANCES

Individual Property and Common Fields

"As much land as a Man Tills, Plants, Improves, Cultivates, and can use the Product of, so much is his Property. He by his Labor does, as it were, enclose it from the Commons." So wrote John Locke in *Treatises* of government.[1] During the late seventeenth and throughout the eighteenth century the trend was indeed away from dispersed fields and land communally used for grazing and wood supply to compact holdings and clearly delimited individual property—in America as well as in England.

In the British Isles, estates were slowly expanding in connection with sheep and wool production.[2] Amelioration projects, which included the introduction of new crops, better grasses, and a different field rotation linked to the growing of grain and raising of livestock were introduced. Customary field practices began to disappear, and properties were re-surveyed: the precise location of field boundaries had become important. The need for accurate surveying created a new profession during the second half of the eighteenth century in England and Scotland: the surveyor, who often had been a teacher of mathematics, also became a planner. "Before him he saw an open fragmented scene, half moorland, but he visualized an ordered, geometrical fenced landscape."[3]

In the spirit of economic progress, the enclosure movement in England was geared toward the assurance of property lines as well as the elimination of wasteland. Through more than 2000 enclosure acts between 1714 and 1801, about six million acres were assigned anew, and common fields and common "wastes" almost disappeared. In the Scottish lowlands, fields acquired a somewhat geometrical appearance. The *General Report of the*

Agricultural State and Political Circumstances in Scotland of 1814 mentioned as advantages of enclosures increased yields, protection of cattle, and
the "opportunity to appropriate many waste spots, and otherwise useless
corners, for plantations which after a few years, will render the contiguous
farms more valuable."[4] Occupancy of cottages, the report explained, gave
"no right to keep cows on these wastes." The last point raises the controver-
sial idea of "communal" holdings and other usage rights as a possible tradition in Western civilization, which could have but did not surface in the
debates on land legislation in the United States.

COMMUNAL LAND USE

Many historians of the nineteenth century, largely under the influence of
romanticism, accorded an almost mystical role to communal land use, starting a long-standing controversy. French scholars, notably Fustel de
Coulange, pointed out that the lords of the manor were the actual owners of
the land, and that when villagers used it for grazing, wood gathering, or
other purposes, it was always tied to the condition that the villagers were
property owners themselves.[5] Prodigious contemporary literature on European village communities reveals that in communal land management,
economic, technological, and geographic forces of particular local character
play a far more important part than any commonly held cultural tradition of
communal land holdings.

In colonial America, communal use of land probably did not derive from
English or other Western European traditions. It usually existed not so
much by assignment as by opportunity. And often it was motivated by a new
world ideological solidarity, usually religious sectarianism. Examples were
the 500 acres at Bethlehem, Pennsylvania, bought by the Moravians in the
eighteenth century, and the Rappite colonies in Butler County, Pennsylvania and at New Harmony, Indiana. But few land seekers in the Northwest
Territory were members of coordinated groups, and it is fair to say, as one
observer has noted, that "their influence upon the life and thought of the
American people in the eighteenth century was inconsiderable."[6] The
Moravian settlements, for example, were known primarily because of their
planning of cohesive towns with outlying lots. Their communal rural
economy, which was fairly short-lived, had been replaced by a system of
controlled private enterprise by the end of the 1760s.[7]

In New England commonly held land existed in the beginning stages of
town settlement. Each villager had a house lot, a number of fields owned
outright, and rights to graze livestock or collect wood from unallocated
commonly held land. These commons as well as completely idle land were
later subdivided and allocated to individuals.

INDIVIDUAL FARMSTEADS

It is often difficult to make a sharp distinction between separate farmsteads and villages that are not closely clustered, but the concept of a continuum from dispersed to nucleated settlements might be serviceable. New settlements were often planned as villages and towns with "proportionate ownership in town and country," in William Penn's words. But soon—in Pennsylvania as well as in New England—residents of the originally clustered village settlements began to move out to their fields, and by the eighteenth century, individual farmsteads were separate from the original village or town. The obvious advantages were that a farm family could live on the land they worked and that hogs and livestock could be grazed over larger areas, still close to home, while the farming operation was integrated around the residence. At the risk of over-simplification it may be said that the general trend throughout the colonies' was from more compact to more dispersed settlement during the eighteenth century.

The way of life represented by the separate farmstead has endured; the Ordinance of 1785 took it for its model. That the separate farmstead was considered the norm was confirmed by the Pre-emption Act of 1841, which required settlers to establish residence on their own tracts of land in order to secure patent. The American pioneer with his possessive individualism had become accustomed to live on his property, which, at least on paper, was clearly bounded. The Ordinance of 1785 was the first legislative act of many designed to insure—in the words of Thomas Jefferson—that "as few as possible shall be without a little portion of land."

In 1785 Jefferson recorded his impressions of the enormous park at Versailles, which covered an area one-fourth that of Paris and, together with the formal layout of the gardens close to the palace, allowed for many activities, including the enjoyment of nature. He wrote of talking to a French day-laborer, a conversation that led him into a "train of reflections on that unequal division of property which occasions the numberless instances of wretchedness ... in France which still has much uncultivated land." He continued:

> These lands are undisturbed only for the sake of game. It should seem then that it must be because of the enormous wealth of the proprietors which places them above attention to the increase of their revenue by permitting these lands to be labored. I am conscious that an equal division of property is impracticable ... . But it is not too soon to provide by every possible means that as few as possible shall be without a little portion of land. The small landholders are the most precious part of a state.[8]

When Jefferson wrote this letter at Fontainebleau he was Minister to France and no longer could play a role in legislating an ordinance that would assure the easy transfer of public land into private ownership, providing for each tract unambiguous identification and quantitative areal measurement. But he was the spirit behind the preparatory work for the Ordinance of 1785 in that he drafted a proposal for a land ordinance in 1784.

The Ordinances of 1784 and 1785

In 1784 the Continental Congress appointed Jefferson chairman of a committee to devise a plan for the temporary government of the Western Territory. The Ordinance of 1784 established that plan as well as one for the admission of new states into the Union, calling for constitutional conventions to establish permanent governments when the population of any territory reached 20,000. Jefferson's first draft (March 1784) also proposed a system for establishing boundaries of the new states:

> the territory ceded or to be ceded by Individual States to the United States whensoever the same ... shall be formed into distinct States bounded in the following manner as nearly as such cessions will admit, that is to say Northwardly & Southwardly by parallels of latitude so that each state shall comprehend from South to North two degrees of latitude beginning to count from the completion of thirty-one degrees North of the equator, but any territory Northwardly of the 47 degree shall make part of the state—next below, the Eastwardly & Westwardly they shall be bounded, those on the Mississippi by that river on one side and the meridian of the lowest point of the rapids of Ohio on the other; and those adjoining on the East by the same meridian on their Western side, and on their eastern by the meridian of the western cape of the mouth of the Great Kanhaway. And the territory eastward of this last meridian between the Ohio, Lake Erie & Pennsylvania shall be one state."[9]

Jefferson proposed states not only in the Western Territory but also south of the Ohio. The names he chose for the states were fanciful, and it is impossible to reconcile the wording of his documents with geographical features on modern maps. He did, however, draw a map (Fig. 3-1) which shows fourteen future states. Stippled lines were used for the parallels which separate existing states from northern Pennsylvania to South Carolina, and solid lines for the proposed three meridians and parallels. Nine states were outlined for the Western Territory. Aside from latitudinal and longitudinal lines, stretches of the Ohio and the Mississippi were to serve as river boundaries. The sketch, a pictorialization of the usage of grid-line boundaries in the East, was a portent for the future.[10] In the nineteenth century the boundary between Wisconsin and Illinois was run along the parallel of 42° 30'N between Lake Michigan and the Mississippi. And west of the Mississippi the parallel of 43° 30'N became the boundary between Iowa and Minnesota. As a boundary, the centerline of the Missis-

Figure 3-1. The Jefferson-Hartley Map (1783) with fourteen states proposed by Thomas Jefferson. (*The William L. Clements Library*)

sippi channel divides Minnesota and Wisconsin, Iowa and Wisconsin, and Illinois and Iowa, and continues downstream to Louisiana as a boundary between states.

Jefferson's plan was not fully realized. The idea of designating the boundaries of states in advance was resisted, among others, by George Washington, who had surveying experience and appreciated the difficulties of laying out large divisions over an area still subject to interference by the Indians. Washington also wanted to promote contiguous settlement and to discourage wide dispersal of squatters. There was criticism that Jefferson's plan contained too many states, and that some of them had no access to major rivers, while others seemed inconveniently divided by rivers. The Ordinance of 1787, which superseded the Ordinance of 1784, provided for no fewer than three and no more than five states in the Western Territory and for two meridians only, which later were to become the eastern and western boundaries of Indiana. It also contained a provision for a parallel of latitude to be drawn through the southernmost bend of Lake Michigan. This parallel never became a boundary between states, but other parallels did: between Michigan and Ohio, Michigan and Indiana, and Wisconsin and Illinois.

Jefferson, as chairman of the same committee, also submitted a draft of "An Ordinance establishing a Land Office for the United States," read for the first time in Congress on May 7, 1784.[11] The plan proposed to run straight north-south lines every tenth mile and to divide the Western Territory into squares of 100 geographical miles. These two concepts—a non-varying grid and square subdivisions— became basic to American land measurement.

We know that one member of Jefferson's committee claimed to be the originator of the plan. On July 5, 1784 Hugh Williamson wrote to Governor Martin of North Carolina:

> the plan for laying off and settling the Western Territory ... has not been agreed to in Congress, but is put on the Journals that the public may consider it before the next meeting. This being our sheet anchor is to oblige the Surveyors to account for the land by parallels dotts & meridians. However as I happen to have suggested the plan to the Committee it is more than probable that I may have parental prejudices in its favor. It has at least the merit of being original.[12]

Williamson, a mathematician and astronomer who was born in Pennsylvania, had taken a doctoral degree at Utrecht in Holland—the country with the most impressive rectangular landscape in northwestern Europe today. There is no reason to doubt that he could have conceived of square divisions of land along cardinal directions without being influenced by other systems of rectangular land divisions, such as Roman centuriation.

It is certain that it was Jefferson's idea to measure the land by geographical miles and that the subdivisions were to be "hundreds." He favored the decimal system over traditional measurements and in 1790 took part in the currency reform which established 100 cents to the dollar. Jefferson also intended to correct the traditional length of Gunter's chain of 66 feet, which had been used in surveying in England and America since 1620. Under traditional measurement the square mile contained 640 acres; under the reformed length it would be 1000 acres. By 1790 Jefferson doubted the usefulness of the geographical mile as a more certain measurement, but otherwise he continued to favor the decimal system.

A square mile with 1000 acres might have been more suitable than the 640 acres that was traditional when Jefferson proposed grants for officers and soldiers—1100 acres for a major-general, 850 for a brigadier, 500 for a colonel, 450 for an ensign, and 100 for a non-commissioned officer or soldier.[13] These liberal sizes derived from grants approved by Congress in 1776 and 1780 for men who had engaged in military service for the United States. After the Revolution, Americans began to think increasingly of large holdings, and by 1784 Washington found that in the Ohio Country, speculators "talked with as much facility of fifty, one hundred and even five thousand acres, as a gentlemen would formerly do of one thousand."

Jefferson's "hundreds" were designated by numbers from 1 to 100 "beginning at the northwestern lot of the hundred and applying the numbers from 1 to 10 to the lots in the first row from west to east and so on. The surveyors shall pay due & constant attention to the variation of the magnetic meridian, & shall run & note all lines by the true meridian, certifying with every plat what was the variation at the time of running the lines thereon noted." One can visualize a planner numbering the lots from left to right on grid paper. But in the field, surveyors probably would have proceeded from east to west; that is, in the direction of their extended lines, once the hundreds had been established with reference to the coordinates of parallels and meridians.

The draft stipulated that those hundreds which were most in demand would be surveyed first. This was in keeping with the practice in southern states, where land was selected before it was surveyed. However, it differed from the so-called "indiscriminate location" in that every piece of land selected would be bounded as a square lot and could thus easily include undesired land and exclude desired land. Selection was to be made under a warrant system that included payment of fees to the surveyors, who were to be appointed by Congress; licensing them for their qualifications was not stipulated. Such selection, of course, could have led to scattered subdivisions.

The proposal also contained instructions for surveyors, which were later incorporated in laws concerning the disposal of public lands. These laws dealt largely with the use of the compass, marking trees by "blazes," measuring by chain, and "describing the land on a plat marking water courses, mountains & other remarkable and permanent things." There was also a stipulation that stemmed from legal and administrative considerations: "Different lots adjoining side by side within the same hundred, may be included & passed by the same grant; but separate lots and lots in different hundreds, as also different hundreds shall be passed by different grants." This meant that one person could acquire several pieces of land in separate locations but that no separate pieces could be held by the same owner under a unified legal tender or description. The stipulation also reflected an awareness of the desirability of contiguity in landholdings.

At the time Jefferson made his proposals, he also urged the clarification of the cessions of the western lands claimed by the different states and the reduction of arrears of interest on the national debt. In 1784 it was a major concern that "the monies arising from the sale of warrants shall be applied to the sinking such part of the principal of the National debt as Congress shall from time to time direct & to no other purpose whatsoever." The national debt was even more pressing in 1785, when "An Ordinance for ascertaining the mode of disposing of lands in the western territory" was passed.[14]

In April 1785 the draft of the Ordinance of 1784 was again brought before Congress, and a new committee chaired by William Grayson of Virginia offered several amendments. The first substituted the statute mile for the geographical mile, and the seven-mile square for Jefferson's ten-mile square, or hundred. It also stipulated that these forty-nine square miles (townships) were to be subdivided into parcels of 320 acres. Military bounty lands in New York had been laid out by seven-mile squares in 1781, and Washington had later pointed out that small amounts of land at a reasonable price should be made available by "progressive seating," meaning contiguous settlement. And Grayson, in a letter to Washington, had expressed his preference for clear division by squares as the most economical method of surveying. He also hoped that settlement by townships would create neighborhoods of people with the same religion. Further amendments stipulated that the lands were to be surveyed prior to sale and that a description of the land was to be made available. Outright sale instead of the cumbersome warrant system was proposed to make land purchases possible for buyers who were not able to select a tract on the spot. Sale would be at auctions, with a minimum price of one dollar per acre—poorer people would be expected to band together for the purchase of a township; rich speculators would not be attracted because the price was rather high. The sale was to be undertaken by land offices in different states. Washington, upon Grayson's request, commented on the amended report and accepted the idea of the sale of a whole "township planting"—a system that appeared to him to have been advantageous in New England in the past. He objected, however, to sales of land through the states in their respective land cessions.

Further deliberations on the amended report reduced the seven-mile square to a six-mile square and provided a compromise between southern and New England practices by a system of alternation: "The township or fractional part of a township No. 1, in the first range, shall be sold entire; and No. 2, in the same range, by lots, in alternate order through the whole of the first range. The township or fractional part of a township No. 1 in the second range shall be sold by lots; and No. 2, in the same range, entire; and so in alternate order. . . ." Lot sixteen was reserved for the maintenance of a public school in each township. The lots numbered 8, 11, 26, and 29 were to be reserved for the United States—the purpose of which was not stated. The numbering of the subdivisions (the thirty-six square miles) was to begin at the succeeding range of lots with consecutive numbering, as shown on Figure 3-2. This made eight numbering sequences possible. The stipulations when transferred to paper produce a schema reminiscent of utopian plans.

One of the provisions of the Ordinance of 1785 was that surveyors, appointed from each state and directed by a geographer, would divide the territory into townships, and that the price for surveying a township (estimated at $36) was to be paid by the purchasers. The survey was to begin where the extension of the southern boundary of Pennsylvania met the Ohio

River and to run from the river directly north toward Lake Erie. Townships were to be numbered from one upward from south to north, and ranges for the townships were to proceed from east to west until seven ranges were completed. The lines running due north and south and others crossing at right angles "as near as can be" were "to depart from this rule no further than particular circumstances required."

The villages of Gnadenhutten, Schoenbrun, and Salem on the Muskingum River were to be reserved for the use of "Christian Indians, who were formerly settled there or the remains of that society, as may, in the judgment of the geographer, be sufficient for them to cultivate." This referred to

1	2	3	4	5	6
12	11	10	9	8	7
13	14	15	16	17	18
24	23	22	21	20	19
25	26	27	28	29	30
36	35	34	33	32	31

1	12	13	24	25	36
2	11	14	23	26	35
3	10	15	22	27	34
4	9	16	21	28	33
5	8	17	20	29	32
6	7	18	19	30	31

36	25	24	13	12	1
35	26	23	14	11	2
34	27	22	15	10	3
33	28	21	16	9	4
30	29	20	17	8	5
31	30	19	18	7	6

6	5	4	3	2	1
7	8	9	10	11	12
18	17	16	15	14	13
19	20	21	22	23	24
30	29	28	27	26	25
31	32	33	34	35	36

6	7	18	19	30	31
5	8	17	20	29	32
4	9	16	21	28	33
3	10	15	22	27	34
2	11	14	23	26	35
1	12	13	24	25	36

36	35	34	33	32	31
25	26	27	28	29	30
24	23	22	21	20	19
13	14	15	16	17	18
12	11	10	9	8	7
1	2	3	4	5	6

31	32	33	34	35	36
30	29	28	27	26	25
19	20	21	22	23	24
18	17	16	15	14	13
7	8	9	10	11	12
6	5	4	3	2	1

31	30	19	18	7	6
32	29	20	17	8	5
33	28	21	16	9	4
34	27	22	15	10	3
35	26	23	14	11	2
36	25	24	13	12	1

Figure 3-2. Township numbering systems. According to the Ordinance of May 20, 1785, townships of 36 square miles, sold entire, alternated with townships divided into 640-acre lots. The sequence of numbering was undetermined. Lots numbered 8, 11, 26, and 29 were reserved by the United States and appear in the same symmetrical location under the eight possible numbering systems. Lot 16 was set aside as school land.

villages in what is now Tuscarawas County, Ohio, by German sectarian missionaries from Pennsylvania. In 1782 ninety-six christianized Indians in these villages were massacred by the British after they took the German colonists into captivity.

The wording of these stipulations occupied about half of the 1785 report; the other half contained the forms and wording of certificates by which land could be acquired from the land offices. The Ordinance was designed for a part of eastern Ohio which was but slightly known, the area of the Seven Ranges. But it could have covered the territory ceded by individual states to the United States by wording and the western territory by its title. The word "section" had not yet appeared. A suggestion by George Washington that township lots of one square mile be divided into halves of 320 acres was not included. Nor was there any reference to the survey of state boundaries. Carried over from Jefferson's proposal of 1784 was the adherence to cardinal direction and the square form of divisions and subdivisions.

For the surveying of square townships and the division into thirty-six lots for each township there are several earlier suggestions or precedents. In an essay written in 1781 Pelitiah Webster suggested townships of six, eight, or ten miles square.[15] In 1783 General Putnam petitioned George Washington for a land grant in the Western Territory for officers who were in the process of disbanding; the grant was to be divided into six-mile square townships. In 1784 Putnam surveyed seven townships along the northeastern boundary of the United States in what is now Maine between the southern end of the St. Croix River and its estuary and the Cobscook River. The tract, which was completely bounded by water, was subdivided into straight-lined townships but tilted on a northwest-southeast axis so as to conform to the direction of the water courses. Through such a layout some adjustment to natural conditions was attained.

This was also the purpose of a motion made by Congressman Nathan Dane in May 1786. He referred to the lands in the lobe between the Scioto River and the large bend of the Ohio to the east, which were to be surveyed first under the Ordinance, suggesting that "due regard be had to the natural boundaries of Townships in those particular cases wherein a rigid adherence to Lines running East and West, North and South, as boundaries would manifestly prejudice the sales and future conditions of said townships."[16] But adherence to the non-varying grid was not abandoned.

JAPAN'S *JORI* SYSTEM

The cultivated landscape that evolves under a non-varying square grid is different from that which develops under a grid that tilts in accordance with natural features, such as slopes. The *jori* system in Japan offers an informative comparison. It is named after its coordinates *Jo* and *Ri*, with thirty-six sections (*cho*) located in a square-shaped parcel called a *Ri*. The latter is comparable to an American township. The sequences by which the thirty-six *cho* are numbered are also markedly similar to those of the American survey. This cadastral system was introduced to Japan during the seventh century through the Taika land reform in the Nara basin. There, land parcels are strictly aligned along a north-south axis; the main road runs through the middle of the basin from the center of the old capital of Kyushu at its northern end. This particular alignment—the ideal jori system in the eyes of Japanese geographers—prevailed throughout the Kinki district, *Kinki* meaning literally, "the vicinity of the capital." In other parts of Japan the *jori* system was not laid out ideally but adjusted to the topography. In Hokkaido, where American advisors to the ministry for colonial development introduced the American survey after the Meiji reform in the nineteenth century, modifications also occurred. Around Sapporo and in the city itself, a rigid north-south grid prevails; but in the Kamikara basin in inland Hokkaido, to mention one example, the grid pattern is tilted for the city of Asahigawa, and east, north, and south of it the coordinates, which determine the layout for the square fields, run in at least five directions. There are many other examples of adjustment to slopes, ridge roads, and waterways, all visible from various vantage points. The units of measurement and the resulting parcels of land are often smaller, but there are areas with large fields where the similarity to the landscape of the American survey is great. Still, the experience of the formal order of the landscape with all its rectangularity is different, even if the platting of the *jori* system on paper is strikingly similar to the American survey.[17]

SURVEYING UNDER THE ORDINANCE

The American plan to dispose of land by square tracts stacked continuously in north-south direction over large areas raises the question of the dichotomy between the convergence of the true meridians and the original design of square townships, be they Thomas Jefferson's hundreds or the thirty-six-square-mile tracts established by the Ordinance of 1785. Several contemporaries understood the problem and it was clearly pointed out by one Colonel Timothy Pickering in a letter to Rufus King, Ordinance committee member from Massachusetts:

> It seems to me it will be found impracticable. Each hundred is to be ten miles square, and each mile to consist of six thousand and eighty-six feet; yet the lines marking the eastern and western boundaries are to be true meridian lines: but meridian lines converge as you increase latitude; and to such a degree that if you take any meridian, say, at the thirty-ninth degree of latitude, and on that parallel set off ten geographical miles (equal to sixty

thousand, eight hundred and sixty feet) from such meridian, and then proceed northward to the forty-first degree of latitude, and there from the same meridian set off the like number of ten geographical miles, their extremity will be about eighteen hundred feet beyond the meridian of the like extremity at the parallel of thirty-nine degrees. I am aware that mathematical accuracy in actual surveys may not be expected; but a difference of six hundred yards in ten miles must surely produce material errors.[18]

In surveying, the practical solution of the dichotomy came later, not specified in laws but contained in practical rules for surveyors.

Surveying under the Land Ordinance of 1785 began in September of the same year on the so-called Seven Ranges and was carried on by eight surveyors, each from a different state. The work was not well executed. Surveyors were released from correcting the north-south running compass lines to run along true meridians after Congress repealed, on May 12, 1786, the paragraph that "the geographer and surveyor shall pay the utmost attention to the variation of the magnetic needle," for the reason that it "would greatly delay" the survey of the Seven Ranges. Nor was the work standardized; each surveyor worked a little differently. After nearly two years of effort only four ranges of townships were ready for sale. Further the survey had proved costly and land auctions did not produce the income Congress had expected. When the first Congress under the Constitution assembled in March 1789, the Ordinance of 1785 was allowed to lapse and with it land legislation. The ideas of the Founding Fathers endured when the rectangular system was re-established through the Act of 1796, which contained a few modifications of that of 1785 but kept the latter's essential features.

The landscape that resulted in the area of the Seven Ranges, which can be considered the cradle of the rectangular survey, reflects far more the influence of various natural features than the rigor of a geometric system. Aside from the Seven Ranges there were large tracts in Ohio claimed before 1796—the Ohio Company lands, the United States Military Reserve, the Miami Purchase, and the Virginia Military District.[19] Between the latter and the Ohio Company lands lies the large area surveyed after 1796, but not strictly drawn from south to north along meridians. Thus lands in Ohio have been surveyed under at least six different systems, and the state exhibits a peculiar regionalism resulting from a variety of cadastral surveys found nowhere else. In Ohio much experimenting took place, producing a fine opportunity for comparing landscape features that evolve under different systems. This opportunity has been used admirably by Norman Thrower in his intensive study of contrasting cadastral surveys in northwestern Ohio.[20] He analyzes in detail two relatively homogeneous areas of 100 square miles each. The first is in the Virginia Military District, surveyed under the metes-

and bounds system which he calls, very suitably, the "unsystematic" survey; it is not totally without rectangular parcels. The second area comprises parts of Hancock and Hardin counties north of the Greenville Treaty line in northwestern Ohio, where the systematic, or rectangular, federal survey prevailed.

PART II
THE SURVEY OF THE UPPER MISSISSIPPI COUNTRY

4 IMPLEMENTATION OF THE SURVEY

Federal Legislation from 1796 to 1832

During the late 1780s only about a third of the 820,377 square miles of the United States was occupied. Western Pennsylvania was still a wilderness; Binghamton and Elmira in western New York were settled in 1787 and 1788. The Connecticut Reserve, which bordered Lake Erie's southern shore, was not ceded to the federal government until 1800. Nearly all of the few thousand inhabitants in the Northwest Territory lived in the Ohio Valley; Cincinnati, merely a garrison, was founded in 1780 and Marietta in 1788. The census of 1792 enumerated 292 counties in the United States over an area which by 1900 numbered 784 counties. Their outlines were generally not rectangular, and today Ohio's map of counties represents a transition zone between land divisions or irregular shape and those surveyed under the rectangular system. By the time Indiana was settled, counties of regular shape began to be the rule (Fig. 4-1).

Large land grants such as the Ohio Company Lands and the Miami purchase in the late 1780s led to congressional resistance against further grants and renewed opposition to "indiscriminate" (unsystematic) location of settlers in the absence of a land ordinance. A land act which retained the six-mile-square townships had been proposed by Hugh Williamson in 1792 but was not taken up by Congress at the time. Meanwhile, expeditions against the Indians slowly extended farther west, and adequate security for settlers was attained after General Anthony Wayne defeated the Miami in what is now northwestern Indiana. The area was ceded by the Indians in 1795 by the Treaty of Greenville. On May 18, 1796 Congress passed an act providing for the sale of lands in the territory northwest of the Ohio River and above the mouth of the Kentucky River—the Land Act of 1796.

53

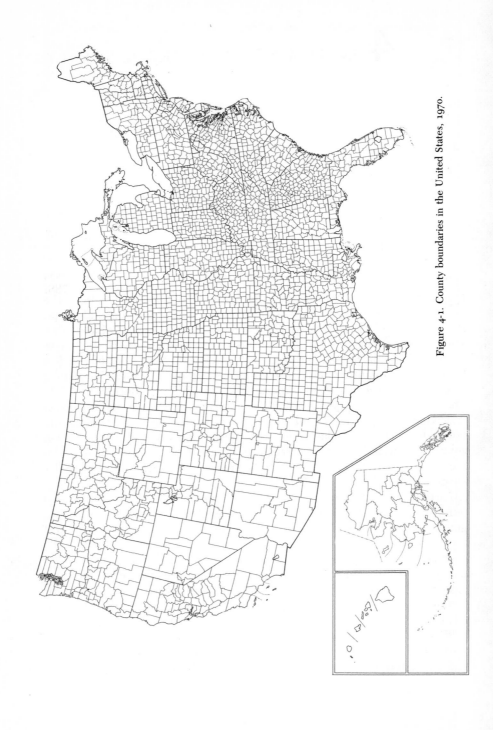

Figure 4-1. County boundaries in the United States, 1970.

The debates that led to the passing of this second land act reveal most of all concern over public revenue, but they also reveal distrust of speculators. Available sources contain no specific references to the Ordinance of 1785; its basic features, inasmuch as they assured safe title to individual settlers, appear to have been taken for granted by Congress. North-south-running lines were to be crossed at right angles, as Williamson had proposed in 1792, and townships of thirty-six square miles were to be subdivided into "sections" of 640 acres.*

The new act also changed the survey numbering system, beginning with the number one in the northeast section and proceeding west and east alternately through the township. This could be interpreted as a reflection of the westward movement of settlement and of the advance of surveyors from east to west. But in practical fieldwork, sections were not surveyed according to the numbering sequence, and the latter made no difference in the cultural landscape that was to emerge. There were occasional directives to auctioneers of government land that sections must be offered in numbered sequence, but even if the directives had been rigorously enforced (which they were not), undesirable parcels would have been bypassed. Furthermore, squatting, which was fully legalized by the Pre-emption Law of 1841, overrode any influence that the sequence in which sections were sold might have exerted.

The idea of alternation appears again: "Half of the said townships, taking them alternately, shall be subdivided into sections (640 acres) or as near as may be." The act stipulated that half of the townships, which were expected to be bought by men with capital, should be made available as quarter townships (nine square miles). In townships that were to be sold by section, trees were to be blazed at every mile along township lines, the trunks marked differently for township and section corners. Parallel section lines running north-south and east-west were to be surveyed every other mile; thus the sections of the subdivided townships could be identified through section marks represented by three corner-posts (Fig. 4-2). Gunter's chain was specified in the law as consisting of 4 perches (rods), 16½ feet each, and was to be adjusted to a standard kept for that purpose. This measuring distance of 66 feet was to have a lasting effect on the width of subdivisions, roads, and alleys in the United States.

The Act of 1796 repeated the rule of 1785 that all lines had to be run along true meridians, but as before did not touch on the problem of adjusting square tracts to the convergence of meridians. Nor did the first Surveyor General, Rufus Putnam, enforce the stipulation for noting variations of the magnetic needle.

*As a cadastral term, "section" became as American as *mir* (peasant commune) is Russian or *jori* is Japanese, and is rarely translated in non-English studies of the U.S. survey.

A Surveyor General was to engage by contracts "a sufficient number of skillful surveyors as his deputies," and, as in 1785, each surveyor was "to note in his field book the true situation of mines, salt licks, salt springs and mill seats" as well as "all watercourses over which the lines he runs shall pass; and also the quality of the land." The deputies were also to take charge of wages for chain carriers and markers and to oversee other surveying expenses. The contract system, which was similar to but less binding than that of 1785, continued unchanged until 1910, when professional government surveyors only were permitted to do the work formerly performed by private parties. While many deputy surveyors made a career of surveying and some rendered valuable service, others used their experience and knowledge of a territory to advantage as land agents and realtors. During the late nineteenth century, a surplus of applicants leaves no doubt that, in spite of the hardships involved, government surveying contracts were eagerly sought.[1]

A companion act in 1796 "regulating the grants of land appropriated for military services, and for the Society of the United Brethren for propogating the gospel among the Heathen" related to a tract northeast of the site of Columbus, Ohio, which was to be divided into townships five-miles square.[2] In involved language the act explained that corners were to be considered

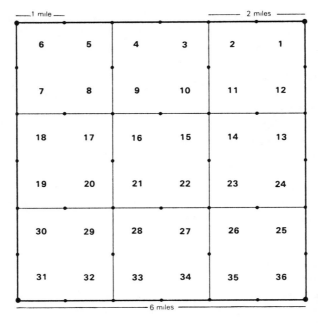

Figure 4-2. According to the Ordinance of 1796, sections were measured by lines two miles apart. Sections were designated by three posts, one mile apart, along these lines.

inviolate even if later surveys proved that they were not correctly set. If "the respective points of intersection of the lines ... shall not appear to correspond with the plat of survey which has been returned to the surveyor general they shall be considered ... the corners of the said townships." This meant that original errors of surveying were to be carefully measured but that they were not to be corrected, and that such errors should not lead to the changing of boundaries. This is the earliest expression of the inviolate nature of the American survey, a principle still in force.

After 1796 the practical details of implementing the survey were left to the Surveyors General. Congress, concerned with facilitating the advance of settlement, authorized further subdivisions and appropriated money for the westward extension of survey lines. These policies made it possible for individual buyers and settlers to acquire land directly from the government.

On May 10, 1800, an act to amend the act of 1796 established four land offices in Ohio, each under the direction of a Register (Registrar) of the Land Office to be appointed by the President. The 1800 legislation also specified that townships west of the Muskingum River, which in accordance with the Act of 1796 were being sold as quarter townships, were to be subdivided into half sections (320 acres). Corners were to be marked on the east-west running lines at every half mile and excesses or deficiencies of tracts incurred in measuring thirty-six square miles were to be placed at the northern and western lines of each township. Land was to be sold for two dollars an acre at public sales, with a down-payment of one-fourth of the total. Six dollars were to be charged for measuring a section, three dollars for a half section, and if the land was not paid for within a year, it was to be resold. The act also specified how payments were to be made and how patents were to be issued. The continuation of the north-south oriented system was safeguarded by the rule that all 320-acre tracts had to be on a north-south axis.

In 1804 Jared Mansfield, Putnam's successor as Surveyor General, ordered that a true principal meridian and a baseline be laid out as coordinates at an arbitrarily selected point in southern Indiana. From this point, townships were to be measured and counted; thus the first attempt was made to solve the problem of maintaining square townships in spite of converging meridians. It pointed to the possibility of running new straight east-west lines at certain intervals, along which lines running true north could be offset against township lines from the south. Such parallels came to be called correction lines (Fig. 4-3). In theory, a township to the south of the correction line is less than six miles wide and one to the north more than six miles wide, while in the middle, between two correction lines, there is one exactly six miles square. The problem was worked out pragmatically, and the process of its solution is traceable through manuals and instructions for surveyors, the first of which was the one issued about 1815. The *Manual of Instructions to Regulate Field operations of Deputy Surveyors*, issued by the

General Land Office in 1855, established the method that became standard: after every fourth township, or twenty-four miles, a new baseline is established from which meridians are shifted and run straight north.

Although important to surveyors, the excesses and deficiencies of tracts are rarely noticed in the field except by experts. Offsets through correction lines, however, can be seen from the air because of the sharp angles they produce on north-south running section roads. On the ground they make for awkward driving, even in the twentieth century. In hilly land this right-angled curiosity is less observable, and on good modern roads corners have often been replaced by a curve.

Between 1800 and 1804, land in Ohio east of the Muskingum River still could be bought by sections only; west of the river, by half sections. The purchase of smaller parcels was possible only from private landholders or from companies such as the Ohio Company. In 1803 a group of Ohio citizens

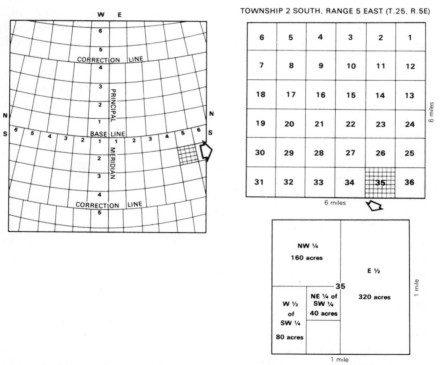

Figure 4-3. The U.S. Rectangular Survey System. After 1796, each township was numbered with reference to a baseline and principal meridian and subdivided into 36 sections, always numbered as shown. Tracts sold by the government decreased in size between 1796 and 1832 from 640 to 40 acres.

presented a petition to the House urging a reduction of the size of parcels for sale to one-sixth of a section. The petition, which was not granted, illustrates that the settlers perceived their land as square plats on paper, on which a square is easily subdivided into six equal parts. But a square mile divided by nine would give each farm the awkward size of 106⅔ acres.[3]

The same petitioners also asked Congress to abolish the existing credit system, to sell smaller tracts, to lower land prices, and to grant (free of charge) small tracts to actual settlers. Albert Gallatin, the Secretary of the Treasury, endorsed a small reduction in the size of tracts to be sold and the abolition of the credit system,[4] and also suggested a minimum price of $1.25 an acre for tracts of 640 and 320 acres and $1.50 an acre for tracts of 160 acres. But he ruled out free grants on the grounds that they would jeopardize revenue from land sales (900,000 acres had been sold between 1800 and 1803, for which $800,000 had been paid, but nearly $1,100,000 were still owed to the U.S. Treasury). The House committee endorsed practically all of Gallatin's proposals, but most of them were not accepted by Congress.

In 1804 Congress extended the power of the Surveyor General "over all the public lands of the United States to which Indian title has been or shall hereafter be extinguished, north of the river Ohio, and east of the river Mississippi." Thus, for the first time, a land act encompassed the whole of the Old Northwest. Land offices at Vincennes, Detroit, and Kaskaskia were to be established, and all persons who had made private land claims before 1783 were to have their claims verified. Details were spelled out regarding bookkeeping, the Surveyor General's reports to the Secretary of the Treasury, and the duties of the registers and receivers of money at the land offices. Indian boundaries were to be surveyed first.

The provision that reserved symmetrically placed sections for the government (Fig. 3-2) was still observed, its purpose still not specified. One could speculate, however, that the men who drafted the act were influenced by early plans for colonization, such as the idyllic Margravate of Azilia in Georgia, which featured four large wooded squares for public use. Later, Thoreau expressed a similar idea when he suggested for all towns a primitive forest of 500 or 1000 acres, one in which "a stick should never be cut for fuel." But at the beginning of the nineteenth century, romantic and communal ideas about the preservation of forests were far from the minds of most men, and in 1804 the provision for reserves was struck from the books. Lands reserved under the laws of 1785, 1796, and 1800 were to be sold as soon as possible after 1804. Yet some reserves were not disposed of until years later, as is illustrated by an 1830 report of the Committee on the Public Lands regarding sections 8, 11, 26, and 29 in the thirteenth township and seventh range in the Steubenville land district in Ohio. The petition by some residents that these sections be donated for assisting common schools in the vicinity was rejected on the grounds that the sixteenth section in each township was already designated for school purposes by federal law. The Commissioner of the General Land Office would be able to subdivide without further authorization the sections in question, and smaller tracts could be offered for sale.[5] Thus—one year before surveying began in the Upper Mississippi Hill Country—land reserved under the first two land laws still had not been disposed of in Ohio!

THE QUARTER SECTION

After nine lengthy paragraphs, the Act of 1804 launched one of rural America's most hallowed institutions, the *quarter section*. Section 10 reads as follows:

> And be it further enacted, that all the public lands of the United States, the sale of which is authorized by law, may, after they shall have been offered for sale to the highest bidder in quarter sections, as hereinafter directed, be purchased at the option of the purchaser, either in entire sections, in half sections, or in quarter sections; in which two last cases the sections shall be divided into quarter sections by lines running due east and west. And in every instance in which a subdivision of the lands of the United States, as surveyed in conformity with law, shall be necessary to ascertain the boundaries or true contents of the tract purchased, the same shall be done at the expense of the purchaser.

In sum, public lands, after being surveyed into townships, were from now on to be divided into sections, half sections, and quarter sections.

It is appropriate here to digress for a moment. Land tracts always have two aspects—size and form. A quarter section, after the half section had been oriented north-south, could also be measured by halving a half-section lengthwise. The possible consequences of repeating north-south subdivision staggers the imagination: 80-acre lots one mile in length and one-eighth mile in width could be created; halving this once more would yield a ratio of one to sixteen. By stipulating the north-south direction for 320-acre tracts in 1804, the option of east-west running tracts was ruled out, and the possibility of adjusting rectangular tracts to the lay of the land by alignment in at least two directions was eliminated. The reason that the long, narrow parcels never became a reality is that squares were most easily measured and defined. Yet consider the possibilities of the long lot: four rectangular farmsteads with 160 acres each in a square mile on average would be a quarter of a mile apart; eight homesites with 80 acres each facing the same road could initiate a row village, an arrangement quite suitable for irrigation farming. The implications for neighborliness and for services such as road maintenance and schools are obvious. Perhaps we might say that, through the quarter section, rectangularity was narrowed to "square-mindedness" in 1804. I shall never forget an interview with a distinguished American historian who could not be persuaded that a quarter section could exist in any form other than a simple square. However, as we shall see later, a quarter section of 160 acres could be purchased in four 40-acre pieces after 1832. They can be adjoined so as to result in several forms, of which the square is only one possibility.

In February 1805 an act concerning the mode of surveying the public lands was passed, deemed by an historian of the survey to be of great importance to the work of retracing surveyors.[6] It decreed that "each section or subdivision of one shall be considered as containing the exact quantity expressed in the returns of the surveyors." The essence of this rule is today expressed in the government *Manual of Instructions* (1947):

> Boundaries and subdivision of the public lands as surveyed under approved instructions by the duly appointed engineers, the physical evidence of which consists of monuments established on the ground and the record evidence of which consists of field notes and plats are unchangeable after the passing of the title by the United States. The physical evidence of the original township, section, quarter section and other monuments must stand as the true corners of the subdivisions which they were intended to present and will be given controlling preference over the recorded directions and length of line.[7]

In 1812 the General Land Office was established in the Department of the Treasury; it was transferred to the newly created Department of the Interior in 1849, and in 1946 was renamed the Bureau of Land Management. Land offices were opened in what is now Indiana, at Vincennes in 1804, at Jeffersonville in 1807, and at Brookville and Terre Haute in 1819. In Illinois, offices were opened at Shawneetown in 1812 and at Edwardsville in 1816. By 1820, eighteen land offices existed in the old Northwest Territory, a number of them serving merely for the investigation of claims, many of which dated from colonial times.

On April 24, 1820, Congress passed further legislation dealing with the sale of the public lands. The act provided that land could be offered at public sales, again for no less than $1.25 an acre, but in half quarter-sections (eighty acres). It further stipulated that "in every case of the division of a quarter section the line for the division thereof shall run north and south," with the corners and measurements ascertained in the manner described by the Act of 1805. The continuous progress toward making smaller parcels available to settlers is reflected in this act; its immediate effectiveness is shown in the early settlement of Rush County, Indiana, where surveying was completed in the summer of 1820 and land claimed as early as October of the same year.

One of the shortest of all land acts was passed in 1832—half a page long and supplementary to the several laws for the sale of public lands. It contained the provision that quarter quarter-sections were to be offered for sale and that fractional sections of less than 160 acres were to be subdivided into forty acres "as nearly as may be practicable." Through this act the "forty" became not only the basic, but also the most frequent cadastral component in the landscape of the Upper Middle West (Fig. 4-4). As a formalizing element for

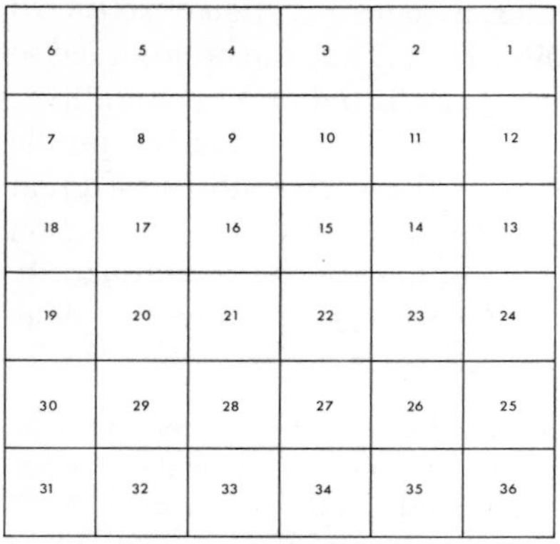

Numbering system of sections after 1796.

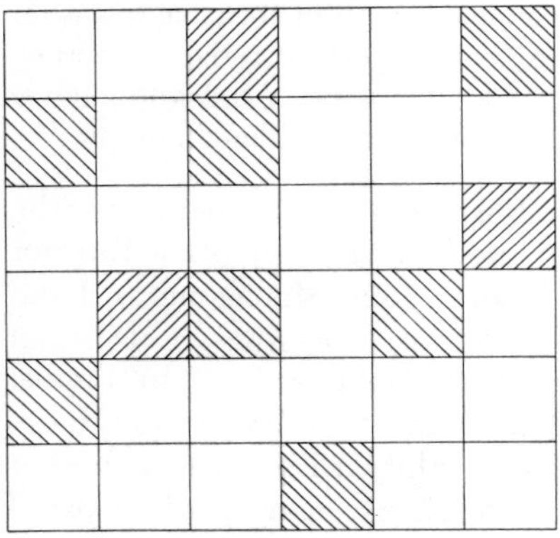

In 1796, sections (640 acres) were designated by three posts erected along exterior township and section lines, run every other mile only.

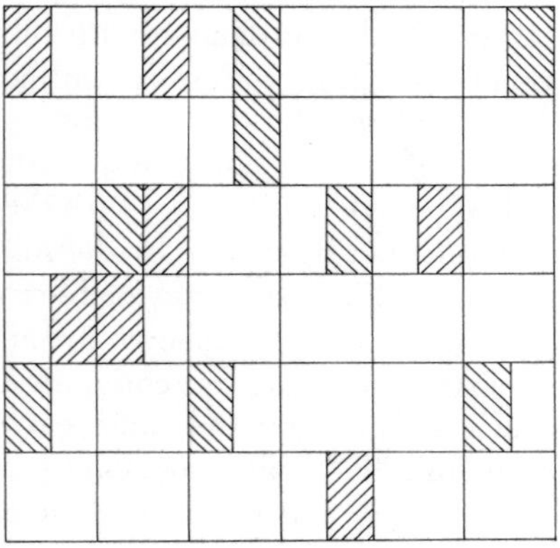

In 1800, half sections (320 acres, oriented north-south) were designated by half-section posts along east-west section lines only.

Figure 4-4. Decreasing size of land parcels obtainable directly from the U.S. Government, 1796-1832.

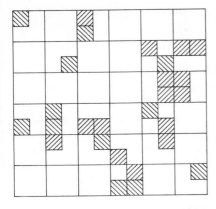

In 1804, quarter sections were designated by posts erected every half mile along section lines.

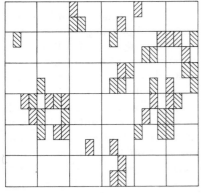

In 1820, half-quarter sections (80 acres and oriented north-south) were determined by the point equidistant from section- and half-section posts on east-west section lines.

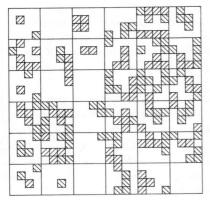

In 1832 the quarter-quarter sections (40 acres) were determined by equidistant points between half-section posts on north-south and east-west section lines. Cross-hatching indicates that many tracts of more than 40 acres were described by adding 40-acre parcels.

the landscape it deserves as much attention as the acts that are next described.

The Pre-emption and Homestead Acts

Two milestones in the history of American land legislation were the Pre-emption Act of 1841 and the Homestead Act of 1862. The first permitted, indeed encouraged, settlers and many who were not, to "squat" on public land and thereby to gain the right to purchase up to 160 acres (a quarter section) at the minimum price of $1.25 an acre. No person was entitled to more than one pre-emptive right by virtue of this act. When two or more claimants settled on the same quarter section, the one who had come first had the right of pre-emption; this and other disputes were to be settled by the register and receiver of the district in which the land was situated. The act ended the conservative policy of 1785,[8] which stipulated that land was not legally free for selection until it was surveyed. Squatting, however, had been going on since colonial times, and had become a pioneer institution. In fact, settlement in advance of the survey, or on surveyed land not yet offered for sale, took place so often in the early 1800s that a number of temporary pre-emption acts for limited areas were passed before 1841.

Pre-emption exacerbated the problem of dispersion of claims since it enabled land speculators to buy the best (or what they thought was the best) land at government prices. Thus less-desirable parcels often remained unsold, and prospective settlers, many of whom were unable to buy land from a private owner at three to five times the government price, were forced to go further afield. This led to the Graduation Act of 1854, whereby land that had been on the market for ten years was to be sold at a dollar an acre, for fifteen years at 75 cents an acre, for twenty years at 50 cents an acre, for twenty-five years at 25 cents an acre, and for thirty or more years at 12½ cents an acre.[9] The simplicity of the survey system doubtlessly aided the easy transfer of standardized parcels and thus supported speculation as well as the aggregation of less-desirable lands.

The Pre-emption Act was intended to facilitate legal assurance for squatter-farmers who surged westward in advance of the survey. It was not meant originally to assist the earliest frontiersmen of the nineteenth century in the Upper Mississippi Hill Country, who were not farmers or land speculators. At first they occupied small sites in the lead-mining region of Illinois, Wisconsin, and Iowa; or isolated spots, usually along rivers, as individual trappers and traders; or sites suited to sawmills, particularly in the Chippewa and Black River valleys.

After the Black Hawk War and the government's purchase of Black Hawk's land in 1832, settlers and land seekers fanning out from the Dubuque area sought agricultural land instead of mining claims. According to a rough estimate, more than 10,000 squatters had occupied land by 1836 in eastern Iowa, and more than 100 extralegal claim clubs, or squatter's organizations—formed to protect members against "claim jumpers"—are said to have existed in territorial Iowa. Not all members in such clubs, however, were bona-fide settlers.[10]

Among the best records of a claim association's activities are those of Johnson County, Iowa, where Iowa City, the territorial capital, was located. By 1839 two townships had been fully surveyed and exterior township lines completed for the rest of the county. The claim association had its own laws and a six-page constitution—signed by, among others, the governor of the territory. No member could claim more than 480 acres, which could be in three parcels but also "lye in a body," and the rules set up for claimants required them to blaze their own claims and to enter them in the association records.

All claim associations made their own township plats, on which they entered or crossed out claims. It was simple to subdivide the square plat into thirty-six sections and to designate the desired parcel in an approximate location of the tract paced off in the field. To find true north on the land was also easy; the settlers simply set up a vertical pole (the equivalent of the Roman gnomon), insured its verticality with a plumb line, and then observed the pole's shadow. One Iowa squatter summed it up:

> The absence of section lines rendered it necessary to take the sun at noon as a guide by which to run these claim lines. So many steps each way counted three hundred and twenty acres, more or less, the legal area of a claim. It may be readily supposed that these lines were far from correct, but they answered all the necessary claim purposes. . . . If a surveyed line should happen to run between adjoining claims, cutting off more or less of one or the other, the fraction was to be added to whichever lot required equalizing, yet without robbing the one from which it was taken.[11]

Claim associations have been idealized as a frontier triumph and a fulfillment of Jeffersonian democracy. Often, however, they were formed for purposes other than to assure that a poor land seeker obtained the land that he had improved. Some associations continued to operate after the Pre-emption law was in effect, protecting those who intended to resell; that is, the speculating claim traders and not the claim seekers. The claims corroborated by government records as to description by section and subdivision are comparatively few. But there are enough cases of claimants who acquired part of their original claim (or an adjoining claim) with the aid of an association to support the statement of the Iowa squatter who noted that he did not expect his field lines to be correct but knew that his pacing "would answer the purpose"—the purpose being that the building of a shack and the plowing of some land would assure him at least part of the intended claim.

Improved land could, of course, easily lie in a different quarter section than the one in which a dwelling had been erected. After purchasing land, some squatters decided to run the lines "so as to render their farms the most convenient to each." Their motive, described in 1838 by the *Iowa News* (August 18) as "the kind and generous spirit for which the squatters are characteristic," should perhaps be accepted with reservation.

Claim associations also existed in Minnesota and Wisconsin; from the latter a rather unlikely incident is reported. In 1834 a Swiss immigrant bought a claim near Gratiot's Grove on the Pecatonica River from a "regular squatter." After the survey, however, the new owner found that he had settled on the corner of four sections. So, when the land was offered for sale, he had the chance of selecting whatever section he desired. If such an ambiguity could be settled, there can be no doubt that squatting, legalized by the Pre-emption Act, was facilitated by the subdivision system of the survey, which made tracts an easily identifiable commodity.

The exaggerated claims made for the Homestead Act (1862) harmonize with its title: "An act to secure homesteads to actual settlers on the public domain."[12] Yet the Homestead Act made the quarter section—160 acres—an American institution. The act, passed during the Civil War following years of petitioning, had become associated during the debates of the 1850s with free distribution of land to settlers, and its defenders saw in it a potential safeguard against land speculation, land monopolies, and the development of tenancy, which was repulsive to Americans of that period. The results disappointed the hopes, and, to cite one statistic, fewer acres were passed on to settlers under the Homestead Act than were sold by the railroads for four dollars an acre.[13]

The Homestead Act was too late to affect settlement in Upper Mississippi Hill Country, where most of the better land had already been taken before the Civil War. In fact, the southern part of the area had attained a population density of eighteen persons per square mile in 1860, and by 1870 the entire area had the same density.[14] One hundred and sixty acres was more than was needed for a family farm in the mixed prairie and forest region in 1862. In forested parts of the Upper Middle West, in fact, that amount may well have been too much considering the average rate of clearing woodland (about five acres per year) before the use of dynamite. Thus, clearing eighty acres could be a task that would occupy a man from his twenty-first year (the legal age at which he could acquire a farm under the Homestead Act) to almost his fortieth year. But settlers, beginning in Massachusetts in the seventeenth century, had always been in the habit of claiming more land than they could effectively develop in a lifetime.[15]

The Forty—Modular Unit of Survey

In Europe the influence of the legal and managerial history of individual land tracts on the appearance of the landscape has long been recognized. In the

United States the grid used to subdivide the land of the Upper Mississippi Hill Country created land parcels of forty acres (the "forty," or one-sixteenth of a section) with histories of their own, often from the first day of entry. There is increasing evidence that settlers preferred the smallest possible tract in establishing a farm, and that those who owned a quarter section (160 acres) frequently acquired the land in parcels of forty acres each. Today the acreages of farms (usually divisible by 40) continues to be influenced by the forty, the most popular land parcel for later additions.[16]

The following examples substantiate how forty acres became the modular unit in the Upper Middle West after the Act of 1832: (1) In four townships in Hancock and Hardin counties in Ohio (surveyed in 1820, when eighty acres were the minimum size of a tract that could be purchased from the government), it was found that the most commonly occurring property shape and size combination was an 80-acre plot. But by 1955 only one per cent of the same area was in tracts larger than forty acres.[17] (2) In Springfield and Edwardsville townships in Sangamon and Madison counties in Illinois, three sections were partially taken up by 80-acre tracts between 1825 and 1830. But between 1832 and 1835 their occupation was completed by 40-acre claims.[18] (3) In southwestern Wisconsin a historian of the lead-mining region found that the average speculator distributed his purchases widely, buying, for example, 160-, 80-, and 40-acre tracts in different sections.[19] (4) And in Hamilton County, Iowa, separate land transactions by owner-operators were traced after 1852. They purchased or sold 514 parcels; 53 per cent of these were in 40-acre lots or less and only 9 per cent in quarter sections.[20]

In the dissected parts of the Hill Country, simple squares for quarter sections were rare from the beginning, for example, in the Whitewater River area in southeastern Minnesota, where tracts entered in 1855 reveal the usual scattering of claims, most of the quarter sections were composed of adjacent forties and were not square. Several 120- and 80-acre entries were also described by multiples of 40-acre tracts. Claims of more than forty acres often straddled section lines and those of square quarter-sections.[21] The rule decreed that land must be "lying in a body in conformity to the legal subdivisions." "Lying in a body" means that the sides of two squares must be adjacent to each other; for a quarter section to be contiguous, it would not suffice to have the corners of the 40-acre squares touch at a point.

Using plane geometry, four squares, one side of each of which must adjoin another, can be arranged to take five different forms. Nineteen different possibilities exist in geographical reality (taking into account directional aspects), and in the Whitewater area, all nineteen variations were put on the map when land entries were made, the composite forms for tracts larger than forty acres contributing to the scattering of settlement from the beginning. Unclaimed adjacent land could be bought by farmers who wanted to round off—by squares—their holding. Occasionally "leftover" forties were intentionally saved by German and Norwegian settlers for their countrymen (or by members of claim associations so that their neighbors might be of their own choosing); inevitably such settlements became more cohesive.[22]

Railroad agents charged with selecting land under the various railroad grants found that it was not always possible to limit themselves to alternate sections on either side of the roadbed within the six-mile limit. The reason for this was that squatters and early buyers had often taken up land in areas that would later be designated as "alternate sections," forcing the agents to patch together—often in 40- and 80-acre tracts—a parcel of land amounting to a full section. Two maps based on land transfers from the state of Minnesota to the Southern Minnesota Railroad Company illustrate the kind of ownership patterns that came about under the railroad grants—patterns that

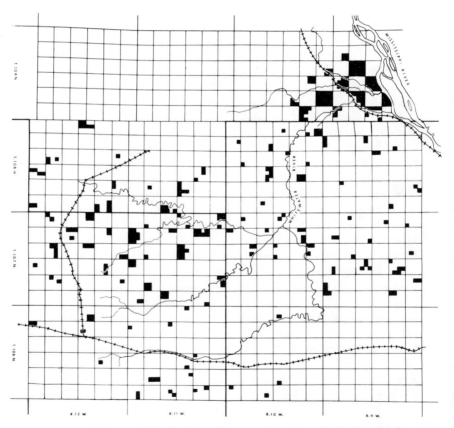

Figure 4-5a. Lands conveyed by deeds to Winona and St. Peter Railroad in southeastern Minnesota, 1864-67. (*Minnesota Register of Deeds*, 1876)

differ considerably from the checkerboard diagrams often used as illustrations (Fig. 4-5).

In the hill country of southeastern Minnesota, which was settled in the 1850s, railroad lands were scattered and often in forties. Farther west, however, the railroad agents came early enough to claim whole sections; the Burlington and Missouri River Railroad, for example, obtained for the most part full sections under its grant. The company's own surveyors measured in about one month 453 forties and eighteen 120-acre tracts. Bernard Henn, of Fairfield, Iowa, an experienced land agent himself, gave to his surveyors the following instructions:

> Examine minutely each 40 acre tract described in the list—taking them in numerical order as respects, Townships, Ranges and Sections, making note in

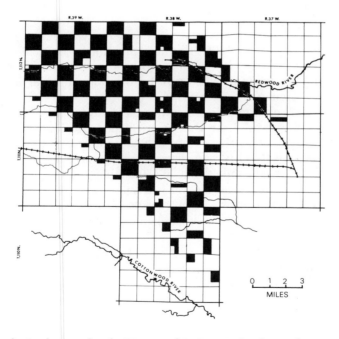

Figure 4-5b. Lands granted to the Winona and St. Peter Railroad in southwestern Minnesota based on a deed for 252,356 acres dated February 26, 1872. The six-mile limit is recognized by the full section parallel to the railroad. Additional small tracts were selected in the next tier to compensate for tracts occupied by settlers before the grant.

your blank book of each 40 separately, giving the quantity each of prairie and timber—the quality and component parts of the soil—the slope of surface—the growth of vegetation—the average diameter and height of timber—the kinds of trees.—Note all the streams, sloughs, bayous, ponds, lakes & springs of pure and mineral water—giving their flow and duration. Note all Rocks, ledges and quarries of Limestone, Sandstone, granite, marble Slate, &c. Note all evidences of coal, gypsom, iron ore, lead, water-lime, grindstone, rock, zinc, copper, and other mineral deposites—Take specimens of all minerals and of all important quarries of building rock and label each specimen with the Description of the tract of land on which it is found, thus: "Found on N.W.¼ of S.E.¼ sect. 15, T. 75, R. 16 W." Note the quantity and thickness of any mineral or stone deposite. Mark on the map in your blank book the locality of all streams, bluffs, prairie depressions and topographical data, and write your notes on the opposite page as fast as you examine each 40 acre tract.

He emphasized the importance of the forty:

Make your examinations as thorough & your reports as full as if on each 40 you were writing to your ladylove & describing the Paradise where you hoped to pass with her a blissful middleage![23]

Land sales by the Burlington and Missouri were overwhelmingly in 40-acre tracts between 1863 and 1866. Further, the Northern Pacific Railroad announced in 1871 that persons who used a land-exploration ticket to inspect land in Minnesota would receive credit for the amount of the fare if they purchased a minimum of forty acres.[24]

Mortgages were often taken out in forties, and farmers talked of "swapping forties." They re-surveyed the land by pacing straight lines as surveyors paced them, counting alternate steps only and never counting above the number required by the forty, or quarter mile. One surveyor noted: "On the basis of 1000 steps to the mile the 40 of 250 double paces is the examiner's unit of distance as much as the yard or metre are of their respective systems."[25] Tenant farming was often restricted to units of forty acres, which were separately managed; large holdings in central Illinois, for instance, often included scattered forties.[26]

The popular expectation that larger farms would develop from an initial 40-acre tract is illustrated by a map advertising land for sale by two railroads along the northern margin of the Hill Country (Fig. 4-6). The map shows that two full sections were sold—certainly by smaller units—and many 40- and 80-acre tracts. The text accompanying the ad reads: "Have you $100 cash as a first payment? You can then select 40 acres of land, 1 to 3 miles from station and covered with the finest hardwood timber in the Northwest, prices $8.00 to $12.00 an acre, or $320 to $480 for the Forty."

In the vicinity of urban places the development of the forty as a modular

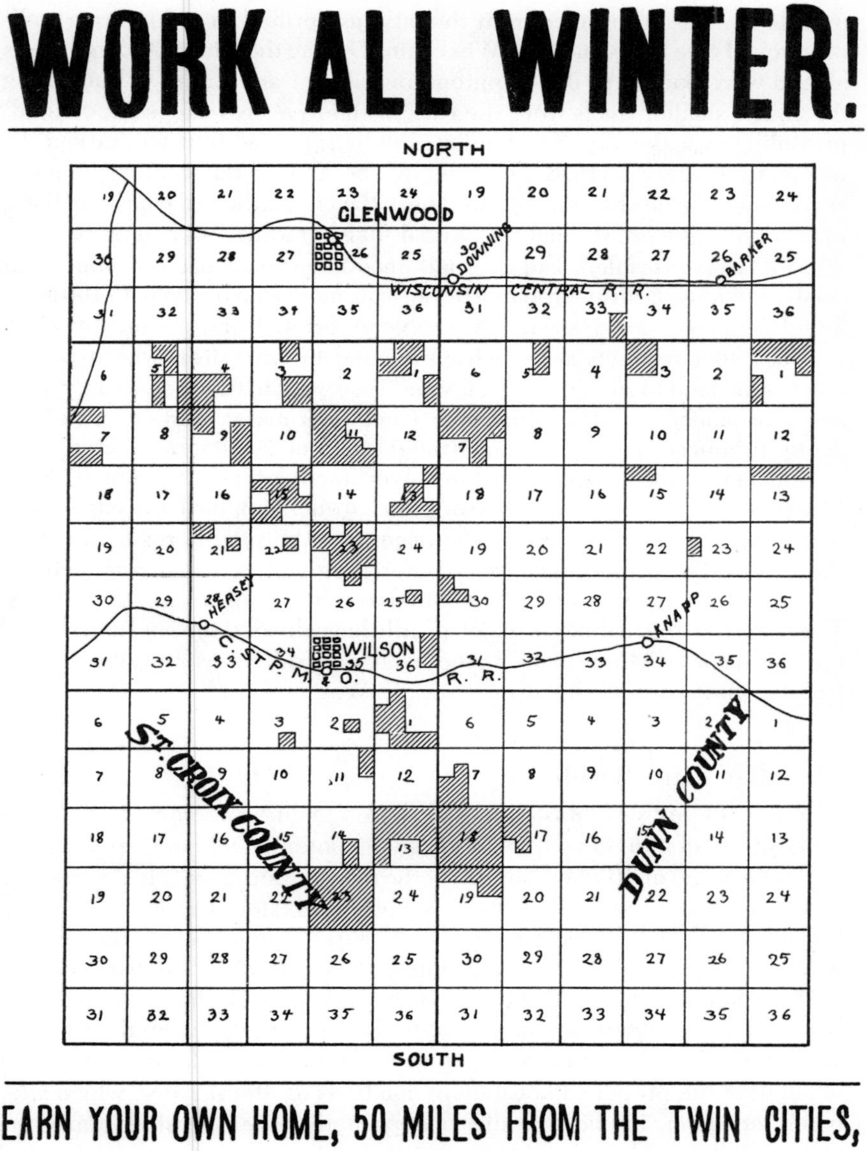

WORK ALL WINTER!

EARN YOUR OWN HOME, 50 MILES FROM THE TWIN CITIES,

Figure 4-6. Railroad advertisement from the 1860s offering timbered land for sale east of the St. Croix River. Shaded areas indicate land already sold or occupied earlier.

unit depended on distance from the city, as verified in at least one well-researched case near Madison, Wisconsin. During the late 1830s large tracts of land were bought in Bloomington Township (Dane County), but during the 1840s smaller tracts were the rule, with forty acres, some subdivided, prevailing near the city. Speculation, subdivision, and transfer marked the whole study period (1836-99), and, by the end of the century, quarter sections and forties had disappeared near the city, although many small lots in subdivisions were still not residential. Farther away, 80- and particularly 40-acre farms prevailed, and over-all, once-large tracts had developed into small individual farms—probably because farmers who began with 160 acres found they needed less land and were able to part with one or more forties.[27]

Today 40-acre tracts are much in demand by urbanites, who may rent most of the land to a neighboring farmer, reserving to themselves only a few acres for family use. The Minnesota Land Information System, which recently produced a computer-constructed map of the state, selected as its basic data unit the 40-acre parcel, or government lot, and explained: "Most blocks of land, whether in private or public ownership, have the edges of 40-acre parcels as boundary lines. The majority of Minnesota roads run along these lines. The parcel edges are reflected in agricultural areas as field lines, in forested areas as timber cutting boundaries; in urban areas as city streets. They describe the manner in which people have divided the land and shaped the landscape of Minnesota."[28] And what was true for Minnesota was also true for most parts of the Upper Middle West.

Meridians and Baselines

The U.S. survey system is eminently suited to guaranteeing unambiguous descriptions of individual tracts and has the potential for completely covering any area, no matter how large. Yet the distribution of principal meridians and baselines in the United States reflects no system but is the result of historical and geographical forces, such as settlement before the survey, westward migration along certain routes, and the cession of Indian lands. In 1855 the Surveyor General at Dubuque remarked that Indian cessions "have been obtained without any reference to the accommodation of the surveys, and have been so limited in area and so various and irregular in figure as not to admit of the proper establishment of a basis for the surveys, which after much reflection, I believe would most properly have consisted in marking given parallels without reference to civil divisions, and at stated and equal distances, establishing true meridians."[29]

After Ohio, in which various cadastral systems were used, Indiana was the first state in which all land was surveyed by reference to only one meridian and one baseline. Subtle variations in field and farm layout resulted from the Clark grant (which bordered the Ohio River around Clarksville), from the

French claims around Vincennes, and from former Indian land in the Wabash valley. To this day, fields in these areas do not fit the grid of the survey, and irregularities are noticeable from the air.[30] Private claims dating back to French, British, and Spanish sovereignty interrupt the geometric uniformity elsewhere.

In Missouri, which was surveyed earlier than the Upper Mississippi Country, private claims of various origin preceded the government surveys and interrupted the township grid; for instance, in the peninsular lobe formed by the Missouri and Mississippi. In Louisiana, deputy surveyors despaired of carrying out the survey; landholders of French descent did not understand township lines and sections and persisted in using the riparian system. Extensive Spanish claims only made matters worse, and in 1811 Congress authorized deviations from the rectangular system for the state. Spanish landholdings in California also interrupted the uniform application of the survey.

The Mormon migration to Utah was one historical event that caused the survey to leapfrog: in 1855 the Salt Lake City Meridian was established, and this at a time when much land to the east had not yet been surveyed. The Mormons had arrived several years earlier (1847), and had designated at Salt Lake City the site for a temple. They ran true north and west lines and measured out a 40-acre square for the Temple block later reduced to ten acres as well as blocks of ten acres surrounding the square. Today a plaque in the Temple wall announces the initial point of the Mormons' meridian: 11° 54′ 00″ longitude west of Greenwich and 40° 35′ 04″ latitude north. If there is one place in the United States that brings to mind the religious symbolism of the center in Roman centuriation, it is this crosspoint at the corner of the hallowed square. Eight years later, David H. Burr, the first Surveyor General for Utah, found an error of only fifty feet when he established the official Salt Lake City Meridian with more refined instruments. Mormon settlers fitted their own system of rectangular fields and villages into the U.S. survey system quite easily.[31]

Jared Mansfield, who became Surveyor General in 1803, set precedent for later decisions when he determined astronomically a new initial point from which to lay out the Second Principal Meridian—thus making it possible to advance the survey farther west without completely surveying all the land between two principal meridians. Such arbitrary selection of an initial point and difficulty in obtaining congressional appropriations for the surveying of large areas led to variations in the length of meridians and the intervals at which they were established. The Second Principal Meridian was run from the confluence of the Little Blue River with the Ohio (86° 51′ W) to the northern boundary of Indiana and governs surveys in Indiana and eastern Illinois. The Third Principal Meridian was run north from the mouth of the Ohio River. Since the peninsula between the Illinois and Mississippi had been reserved as military bounty land for soldiers of the War of 1812, the survey of this area could not be delayed, and the Fourth Principal Meridian was laid out. Beginning at the mouth of the Illinois River at latitude 30° 58' 12" N and running along longitude 90° 29' 56" W, the Fourth Principal Meridian extends as far as Lake Superior and governs the surveys in Wisconsin and the part of Minnesota east of the Mississippi. In 1838 the *Traveler's Directory for Illinois* described its course as follows:

> The fourth principal meridian commences on the right bank, and at the mouth of the Illinois river, but immediately crosses to the east shore, and passes up on that side, (and at one place nearly fourteen miles distant,) to a point in the channel of the river, seventy-two miles from its mouth. Here its base line commences and extends across the peninsula to the Mississippi, a short distance above Quincy. The fourth principal meridian is continued northward through the military tract, and across Rock river, to a curve in the Mississippi at the upper rapids, in township eighteen northward about twelve or fifteen miles above Rock Island. It here crosses and passes up the west side of the Mississippi river fifty-three miles, and recrosses into Illinois, and passes through the town of Galena to the northern boundary of the State. It is thence continued to the Wisconsin river and made the principal meridian for the surveys of the territory, while the northern boundary line of the State is constituted its base line for that region.[32]

The well-meaning author of the *Directory* explained the numbering systems of township, ranges, and sections and added that he had been "thus particular in this account of the survey of public lands, to exhibit the simplicity of the system, that to strangers, unacquainted with the method of numbering the sections and the various subdivisions, appears perplexing and confused." Indeed, strangers must have found the meridian perplexing after all, and probably would have agreed with the Commissioner of the General Land Office, who wrote in 1815 that it was "indeed a more difficult task than imagined to survey with the correctness which the laws of the United States contemplated."[33]

In 1815 the same Commissioner was charged with laying out the Fifth Principal Meridian at longitude 90° 58' 00" W from the baseline in Arkansas, a directive resulting in the most extensive numbering system in the survey as well as the largest single area referred to a single point. In Iowa and Minnesota all ranges and townships west of the Mississippi were referred to that meridian and baseline, and when the boundary between Canada and Minnesota was reached, 164 townships had been stacked on the baseline. Figure 4-7 shows the distribution of this and other meridians and baselines.

Surveying of the Hill Country in Illinois, Wisconsin, Iowa, and Minnesota began in 1831, 1832, 1836, and 1848, respectively. Procedures were generally the same over the area, with exterior townships measured first. In 1834 a directive was issued requiring surveyors to take random lines and to retrace

75

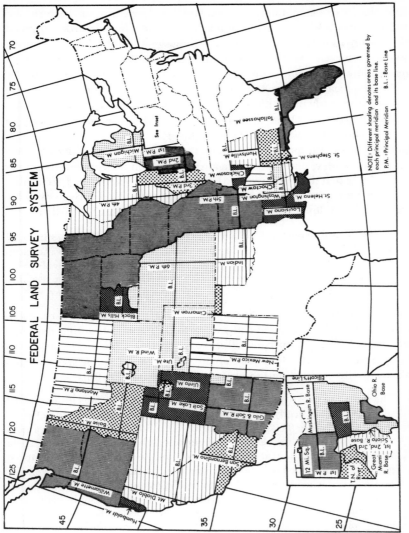

Figure 4-7. The Federal Land Survey System.

them when laying out townships. This was still the rule when William A. Burt, deputy surveyor in Iowa and inventor of the solar compass (more reliable than the magnetic compass), laid out townships in eastern and central Iowa east and west of the Fifth Principal Meridian. In order to speed up the survey of western Iowa, only "fallings"—lines obtained by merely following a compass without rechecking the random lines—were used. Along random lines, surveyors were expected to "close the corners" by adjusting the locations of section corner posts set earlier at every half mile along the exterior township lines. Figure 4-8, based on *General Instructions to Deputy Surveyors* (1834) illustrates how a surveyor and his party of flagmen, chainmen, and axemen proceeded.[34]

Among the most important of the Surveyor General's directives for surveying hilly country, one repeated again and again in instructions to deputy surveyors, was that distances were to be measured *horizontally*. This implies a bird's-eye view, not a survey laid out directly on the land surface, which is rarely completely level. In 1815 Surveyor General Tiffin had instructed:

> As the measurement by the chain is the principal source of error in surveying you will be careful to attend to your chainmen that they carry the chain horizontally, and to prevent their losing a tally rod you must be provided with a set of them pointed with iron or steel, and to allow no other to be used but the precise number which you shall have selected for the Purpose.[35]

In 1855 the *Instructions to the Surveyors General of Public Lands* repeated that township and subdivision lines were to be measured with a two-pole chain, 33 feet long, comprising 50 links, each link 7.92 inches long. On uniform, level ground a four-pole chain was permissible. A special paragraph dealt with "Levelling the chain and Plumbing the Pins:"

> The length of every line you run is to be ascertained by precise horizontal measurement, as nearly approximating to an air line as possible in practice on the earth's surface. This all important object can only be attained by a rigid adherence to the three following observances 1. Ever keeping the chain *stretched* to the utmost degree of tension on even ground. 2. On uneven ground, keeping the chain not only stretched as aforesaid, but horizontally leveled. And when ascending and descending steep ground, hills or mountains, the chain will have to be shortened to one-half its length, (and sometimes more) in order accurately to obtain the true horizontal measure. 3. The careful plumbing of the tally pins, so as to attain precisely the spot where they should be stuck. The more uneven the surface, the greater the caution needed to set the pins.[36]

The government *Manual of Instructions* (1947) repeats that

> in Land surveying, the distance between two points or length of line, means the horizontal distance. On sloping ground the tape may be held horizontally,

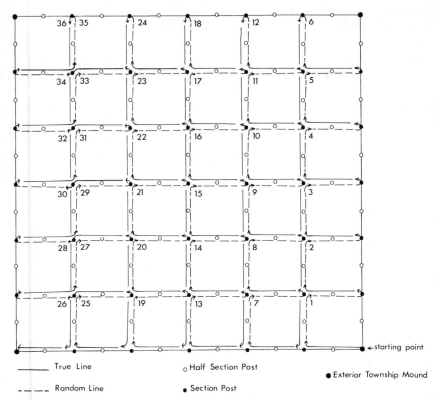

Figure 4-8. The route surveyors followed when subdividing a township into sections proceeded from the southeast corner straight north, returning to the southern township line and repeating the south-to-north route for the first four tiers. The last two columns, beginning with 25, were measured by going back and forth or east and west along the westernmost section line inside the township. The measuring sequence was different from the numbering system of sections; compare Figure 4-3. The procedure explains how excesses and deficiencies resulting from the subdivision of 36 square miles were moved to northern and western township lines.

or supported in that position by using a plummet at the end which is higher than the surface, for the projection of the tape length to the ground. . . . The law prescribes the chain as the unit of linear measure for the survey of the public lands, and all returns of measurements are to be made in true horizontal distances, in miles, chains, and links.

From its incipient stage, the survey delineated tracts for which measured acreages can be true only when they cover level land. The ground surface of sloping land comprises areas that are larger than the quantities given on township plats for squares and rectangles, the usual form of real estate in the Middle West.

By 1860 the Hill Country had been almost fully surveyed. The survey was nearly completed in Iowa, where new baselines (correction lines) were ten townships apart; the jog in the north-south lines (meridians), was considerable. An example appears in the latitude of the counties of Grundy, Black Hawk, Buchanan, and Dubuque and can be seen on any state road map. After 1855 the rules stipulated that correction lines were to be used more frequently; that is, after every twenty-four miles, or four townships apart. As an example, the sixth guide meridian (west of the Fourth Principal Meridian) jogs slightly after every fourth township.

SURVEYORS' PLATS

Beginning with the Ordinance of 1785, government rules required surveyors to take notes of geographical features such as salt springs, the occurrence of minerals, and mill sites. Through the years, as deputy surveyors insisted more and more that trees should be identified, swamp land outlined, types of undergrowth distinguished, bluffs, roads, and rapids located, and mineral occurrences recorded, surveyors' notes began to represent a first, if superficial, inventory of the land. After an expedition they delivered their notes—written in octavo-sized notebooks with quill pens and homemade ink—to the Surveyor General's office in St. Louis or Dubuque, where clerks and draftsmen neatly transcribed them. Maps and diagrams were transferred to official township plats, of which three copies were made: one for the regional office, one for the General Land Office in Washington, D.C., and one for the local land office where the surveyed land was to be offered for sale. [37]

While not all surveyors were well-qualified, and their survey notes—such as "first-, second-, or third-rate soil"—were usually based on superficial evaluations, the land inventory under the survey was systematic and standardized to a considerable degree. Inasmuch as the survey lines represent a random grid, along the lines of which the diameter and species of trees, for example, were listed at predetermined points, the inventory can be considered statistically sound. Marking trees at specified intervals along a traverse and describing the country's topography had been done since colonial times; for example in 1746 one Thomas Lewis, in surveying the southwestern boundary of Lord Fairfax's grant in Virginia, ran a traverse that made it possible to compare the distribution patterns of vegetation 200 years apart. [38]

In 1954 I found one forty that had never been sold. It remains public land, accessible only through fenced fields and woods in the Whitewater valley of southeastern Minnesota. The original surveyor noted in 1854 a small stand of

white pine, American elm, white oak, and sugar maple that still exists. He
also noted broken trees with flood marks; I found one tree with its bark
recently stripped off to about five feet above the ground, which indicates that
the land is still flooded from time to time. Dissected land along the Upper
Mississippi has many such hidden valleys that have remained almost undis-
turbed through the more than 100 years since a surveyor climbed the
hillsides.

Original township plats are usually easy to read, but the copies to which
many users added letters, numbers, lines, and shading for claims, are
difficult to decipher. The plats show bluff lines, creeks, rivers, roads, lakes,
and swamps. Lake and navigable waterways were "meandered," meaning
that their naturally irregular and curved shores were measured by a series of
angling lines with posts marked "MC" for meandered corners. Surveyors
were also asked to indicate the sites of Indian villages and mounds, ar-
cheological sites, wood clearings, and plowed fields, as well as houses.

Unless they worked in thick forests, many surveyors looked farther afield
than along the lines, often preparing useful short descriptions of townships
after measuring their sections. For example, in May 1854 the surveyor in
Winona County summarized Norton Township (T. 107 N., R. 9 W.) and
Mount Vernon Township (T. 108 N., R. 9 W.) of the Fifth Principal Meridian
as follows:

> Of superb soil the whole township is an elevated plain intersected with deep
> and precipitous ravines which drain all the water from the upper level of the
> country therefore all the water issues in springs low down in these ravines and
> forms beautiful clear brooks. The water is inconvenient for farming purposes.
> All the springs in this township empty through the Rollingstone [River]. The
> timber excepting a little on the main fork of the Rollingstone is very small and
> poor not enough for farming purposes. Sandstone is the prevailing rock
> underlying the township.

> This township like the one immediately south of it is very fertile, has a rich
> alluvial soil but is almost entirely without timber. The wood is covered with
> small scattered oak which will furnish timber whether for building houses or
> fuel. There is not a supply of water. Trout Creek runs through the NW portion
> of it and a small spring branch is in the SE corner. The Mississippi bluff furnish
> two small spring branches. All the water in this township is deepdown in the
> ravines almost inaccessible from the highland. On the whole this township is
> far from valuable for farming.

The general description of the upland prairie in neighboring Olmsted
County was simpler, for instance, of T. 106 N., R. 111 W.:

> This township is mostly rolling 1st rate prairie. Where timber is found it is
> mostly of 2nd or 3rd rate quality. Water cold and pure but rather scarce. The

surface rolling and generally dry except in the marshes which *of course* are *wet*.

Occasionally the old notes lead to interesting puzzles, such as the mention in 1854 of floodmarks on trees three feet above ground—in an area which, according to an old-timer, never had floods in the good old days. The notes also reflect the vocabulary of the frontier. What Indian agent Henry Schoolcraft called oak groves in this area were more commonly called "oak openings," and woods were usually referred to as "timber," ranging from good to maturing. "Rolling prairie," "smooth and gently rolling soil," and "rolling and level land" were used for what is often called undulating prairie in literature. In fact, "Undine Region" was the imaginative name that geographer Joseph Nicolet gave to the prairie in Minnesota when he mapped and described the Iowa Territory for the War Department in 1836.[39]

Surveyors' observations of the original vegetation along the lines of the township grid were integrated by twentieth-century scholars to show the distribution pattern of predominant species in Minnesota, Wisconsin, and some other parts of the country.[40] These composite maps, of smaller scale than township plats, resulted in curved lines similar to those on land-use capability and soil maps and reflect the natural, unsystematic extent of woodland and prairie very well.

Surveyors' plats were also the source for county atlases, which were usually prepared with the help of former surveyors. They copied the plats, drawing

Figure 4-9. Section road drawn in one-point perspective, a technique typical of state atlases. (A. T. Andreas, *Illustrated Historical Atlas of the State of Minnesota, 1874*)

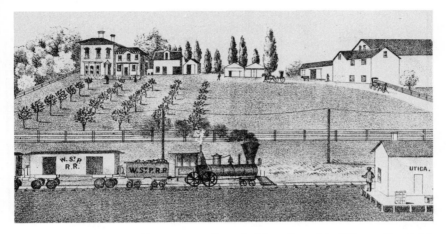

Figure 4-10. Above, the residence of B. Ellsworth (Utica Township, Winona County) in 1875. The farmhouse faces the section line and the railroad parallels the territorial road (not shown). Below, the same residence in 1973.

in recent additions such as roads, townsites, cemeteries, and woodlots, and adding the names of property owners to all tracts. In time, these atlases, which were sold by subscription, became a rural Who's Who. Agents obtained biographies and pictures of their subscribers along with lists of livestock and draftsmen then prepared idealized renditions of residences, often adding such touches as ladies with parasols strolling in symmetrically laid out gardens and livestock grazing nearby. Before the turn of the century every county in the Upper Mississippi Country had an atlas, and in some counties more than one edition appeared.[41]

Surveyors' plats were also updated and used for state atlases. A. T. Andreas, a publisher of atlases in Chicago, brought out *The Illustrated Historical Atlas of the State of Minnesota* in 1874 and *The Illustrated Historical Atlas of the State of Iowa* in 1875; *The State Atlas of Wisconsin* appeared in 1878. Illustrations in these volumes reflect the hold of rectangularity on the minds of the draftsmen—roads are usually straight, fields are square and neatly fenced, and orchards, barnyards, and gardens are extremely orderly. Views are drawn in one-point perspective, and the additions of many details substitute for composition (Fig. 4-9). But the likeness of the houses is accurate, and if they have survived the century, one can recognize them along the road today (Fig. 4-10). All of the volumes are large and richly illustrated, with some views of cities in color and both they and the county atlases have become collectors' items today.

5 PRE-SURVEY OCCUPANCE OF THE HILL COUNTRY

Trails and Roads

Surveyors, whenever possible, used earlier trails and roads to move their equipment into the areas to be surveyed. In hilly areas the Indians had cut trails to the major trading posts; these routes followed rivers into tributary valleys and climbed over local passes to the next valley. On the upland the trails led across broad ridges and almost level open prairie, bending around every small obstacle. They were rarely straight, but usually they were easy to recognize, imprinted as they were by travois—loads fastened between two shafts harnessed either to dog teams or a horse.* Around the Mississippi-St. Croix river junction, the many trails of the Sioux converged. In 1805 Zebulon Pike secured the region for the United States, but the Sioux were still permitted "to pass, repass, hunt and make other uses" in the area; thus their trails remained intact.[2]

In the same year Lieutenant Pike estimated that 370 persons lived at Prairie du Chien. They had developed many short trails into the hinterland, and trails also fanned out from other landing sites. Yet the Indians knew the best ascents to the upland on both sides of the Mississippi, and pioneer histories often report that the land seekers who arrived before the land was surveyed followed Indian trails deep into the lands of Chippewa, Sioux, and Sauk in Wisconsin, Minnesota, and Iowa.

The overland trail from Prairie La Crosse on the Mississippi to Traverse des Sioux near the present-day town of St. Peter on the Minnesota is a good example of a heavily traveled Indian route. In the early 1850s many land scouts and squatters—most of them from St. Louis or Dubuque—moved

---

*Peter Rindisbacher, a Swiss artist posthumously recognized as an important illustrator of the Indian frontier, realistically portrayed this mode of transport on his paintings.[1]

across this trail, which is still called "the old territorial road" by descendants of pioneer settlers in Winona County. Meandering through the Mississippi flats on the west bank of the river opposite Prairie La Crosse, the trail climbed the divide between the Root River and Pine Creek and, after a short distance on the upland, joined a road from Wabasha Prairie. It entered Winona County at the southeastern corner (section 36) of Pleasant Hill Township and continued through the settlement of Ridgeway, extending into sections 9 and 8 of the same township. The road continued on the divide between tributaries of the Root River toward the south, and Garvin Creek, Rollingstone Creek, and the forks of the Whitewater River toward the north. A scouting party from Wabasha Prairie investigating this mixed prairie and forest region in 1852 still called the road a "trace," but a year later the stretch of the road along the Mississippi north from Winona to Minnesota City was improved and in 1854 became part of the U.S. mail route to Traverse des Sioux. Mail was also carried via Minnesota City to the new settlers on the upland in the region of St. Charles, from which, according to local history, roads led in all directions.[3]

Claim seekers struck out from the territorial road on their own trails to the "timber" around the headwaters of streams and to choice locations on the prairie, preferably within hauling distance of wood. In the river valleys settlers beat individual paths to reach the main road. Such trails and paths, which served personal needs, preceded surveyors' lines and, like the Indian trails, were rarely straight.

The surveyors frequently marked on their plats earlier wagon roads that crossed township and section lines. One, between Faribault and Red Wing in Minnesota, was an extension of an earlier fur trade trail that ran between Fort Snelling and Dubuque. In Wisconsin, wagon roads connected the mills along the Red Cedar, the Chippewa, and the Black rivers. One such road, which more or less followed the direction of the meandering Eau Claire River, led to a logger's claim on the river, although the road also served local needs.

Regional roads were supported by territorial governments and were often developed before the land was officially surveyed.[4] Immediately after the Sioux Treaty of 1852 the territorial legislature of Minnesota authorized a road from Read's Landing on the Mississippi westward to the bend of the Minnesota River, the present location of Mankato. And, at about the same time, a road running south from the St. Paul area and along the west bank of the Mississippi was extended to the settlements south of Lake Pepin; because that body of water was regularly frozen in winter a year-round route was needed between the fast-growing settlements of St. Anthony Falls and St. Paul and landings in southeastern Minnesota. The landing site with the greatest promise for the future was Winona. Winona Township (T. 107 N., R. 7 W. of the Fifth Principal Meridian) was surveyed in 1854, the surveyor noting that Winona had an excellent landing and good roads leading to the back country. Modern regional highways follow some of the pre-survey roads—for example, those along the east west branches of Burns Creek. These roads join as Highway 6, which continues to Chatfield on the Root River farther west.

In Wisconsin one of the regional roads became known as the "Military Road." During the Black Hawk War, a secure route from the lead-mining region to Lake Michigan was needed, and in 1832 Congress appropriated $50,000 for the survey of the road that connected Fort Howard on Lake Michigan to Fort Crawford at Prairie du Chien. The 234-mile route ran southwest from Green Bay to Portage and Fort Winnebago, turned south to Poynette and the northern shore of Lake Mendota, and then bent west to follow the divide between the Wisconsin and Rock rivers (the "Military Ridge"), passing through Dodgeville and Monfort (both lead-mining towns dating from the 1820s) to Fennimore and Patch Grove, where it bent back across the Wisconsin to Prairie du Chien. The commandants of the three forts were responsible for construction of the road, which was begun in 1835 and completed in 1837.[5] Described in the 1840s as "very high and commanding a fine view,"[6] on road maps today it is designated as a "scenic route."

The Military Road had many more ascents, inclines, and curves than modern Highway 18, which follows it closely. But it was important for the shipping of lead until railroads began to reach the lead-mining region in the mid-1850s. Before the road was built, lead from southwestern Wisconsin was shipped to Milwaukee via New Orleans, New York, the Erie Canal (where shipments of Wisconsin lead were granted special rates), and the Great Lakes back to Wisconsin's shore on Lake Michigan.

For an example of the persistence of roads marked by the surveyors on their maps let us follow the journey of a man from Braintree, Vermont, who according to his diary was determined to reach River Falls on the Kinnickinnic River at the northernmost edge of the Hill Country.[7] Leaving Vermont in late fall 1855, he traveled by railroad to Chicago and continued by wagon to Galena. In February 1856 he and a party of other travelers arrived at Prairie du Chien and proceeded to Viroqua, a small village in the "timber" on a ridge, where they were delayed for a few days by a snowstorm. Continuing on the height that divides the Kickapoo River from Raccoon Creek and the La Crosse River, they descended to the flats of the La Crosse and the settlement of Sparta, where they transferred to sleds for the journey to Black River Falls. The route continued around the ravines of the headwaters of the Trempealeau River to "Beef River Station" on the Buffalo River, to Eau Claire, and to Wilson's Mills on the Red Cedar River. The Vermonter reached River Falls on the Kinnickinnic in March. His route may be followed on the surveyors' plats, which are marked with notations such as "Road from Prairie du Chien to Lake Superior" or "Wagon Road to Black

River Falls." The course of this route, which is followed for roundly 220 miles between Prairie du Chien and River Falls by modern roads and in part by an interstate highway, was dictated most of all by topography. Complaints that a stage traveler in the 1850s expressed about the "perilous succession of ups and downs" did not refer to steep ascents and inclines, which are a feature of straight roads in the Hill Country today, but to the jolts caused by wagon wheels hitting the not-infrequent stumps in the road.[8]

Some stagecoach routes could be followed by the railroads. Railroads require a nearly "water-level route" as the Burlington Railroad calls its line from Chicago to St. Paul, which follows the Mississippi floodplain from Savanna, Illinois, to the Twin Cities. Laying tracks on alluvial plains and broad ridges was not difficult, and the major lines used these easy thoroughfares. The Milwaukee & Mississippi Railroad from Madison to Prairie du Chien, completed in 1854, followed the Wisconsin River Valley. The Northwestern Railroad out of Madison followed the Military Ridge west of Mount Horeb. The Milwaukee and St. Paul Railroad, completed in 1867, skirted the northern edge of the Hill Country, connecting towns which originated near the sites of early sawmills, such as Eau Claire and Menomonie. But pulling trains from the river bottoms to the upland involved rock cuts, sharp turns around hills, and bridges over swales and ravines. Many roadbeds were laid on narrow, band-like terraces cut from the hillsides and on embankments across valleys, and wooden trestle bridges were frequent. Few of these bridges remain today, most of them having been dismantled after branch lines were discontinued. Cast-iron bridges, patented in 1876, were rare, although one spans the Upper Iowa River near Bluffton, Iowa.

Crossing the Mississippi presented another problem during the westward movement of settlers and the eastward movement of wheat, the first major cash crop west of the Mississippi. Ferries worked around the clock between Prairie du Chien and McGregor on the Iowa side of the river transporting railroad cars—one at a time—across the water, a time-consuming and risky procedure. In 1874, however, the ingenious construction of the wooden pontoon bridge, the largest of its kind, eliminated the awkward loading and unloading of cars and permitted trains to cross the river without impeding navigation.

Motor transport increasingly replaced railroads in the twentieth century. The Great River Road follows the earliest transportation route in the Upper Mississippi Country, and in several stretches runs parallel to or directly over earlier roads. Interstate Highway 94 follows the Vermonter's route of 1856 between Black River Falls and Menomonie, and Interstate 90 runs through the alluvial flats of the La Crosse River between Sparta and La Crosse. On the opposite side of the Mississippi out of La Crescent the interstate highway is projected to continue over the ridge separating the Root River and the

Whitewater River watersheds. These examples must suffice to illustrate the enduring relationship between roads and topography. It makes the study of their antecedents, the trails and roads in the surveyors' notes, meaningful in historical geography. Of possibly greater historical interest are the settlements which preceded the survey, particularly those in the lead-mining region.

Lead Mining and Lumbering

In the southern part of Upper Mississippi Country the Indians mined and traded lead with the French throughout the eighteenth century. Around 1811 they were mining north of the Galena River in northwestern Illinois, according to a report submitted to the Secretary of War by the federal Indian agent at Prairie du Chien.[9] The lead was shipped downstream to St. Louis and upstream to Prairie du Chien; from that point it was taken via the Wisconsin and Fox rivers to Lake Michigan to be shipped east.

THE LEAD-MINING REGION

The land west of the Mississippi was still under Spanish sovereignty in 1788, when Julien Dubuque first began to extract lead from diggings known as the "Mines of Spain" near present-day Dubuque. From 1788 to 1810 Dubuque resided on his estate, which according to the surveyor's plat,[10] stretched for three miles away from the river and for about six miles along its shore. The section lines of the survey met the rectangular boundaries of his claim at a 48° angle, which was reflected in the orientation of the original city limits on the survey plat. Property or field lines cannot be traced today; a monument of Julien Dubuque overlooking the Mississippi south of the city in Julien Township, Dubuque County, is the only physical reminder of the large grant.

The area continued to attract miners, including a group of squatters who, immediately after they arrived in 1832, formed a claim association and drew up a "Miner's Compact." They were driven from their claims during the Black Hawk War (1832) but soon returned, and by September 1834, 1000 government mining permits [11] had been issued in the area.* Dubuque was a "straggling, unkempt village" around 1832; its main street now angles slightly along the foot of the bluff, where rock cavities in the heart of the city are said to date from the early years of mining.[13]

East of the Mississippi, miners and traders had come into the Galena area in the early 1820s, and by 1829 the area of lead-bearing strata was generally

---

*The leasing of mineral lands began in 1807 with an act for the sale of certain lands now in Ohio and Indiana, and was affirmed by an act of 1816, whereby a tract of land containing a lead mine or a salt spring could be worked by special permit from the government only.[12]

known; it extended into present-day Grant, Iowa, and Lafayette counties in southwestern Wisconsin. The first mines were at Hazel Green, originally called Hardscrabble, and at New Diggings north of the Fever River (the Galena River). Lead was found next a short distance to the south near the Apple River in Jo Daviess County, Illinois. But the richest ores were discovered between 1824 and 1829 in Wisconsin in the vicinities of Mineral Point, Shullsburg, Dodgeville, and Platteville—all villages with lots and streets staked out provisionally before 1830. The number of diggings increased in the 1830s, but the area of exploitation did not extend further north than southwestern Wisconsin. All trading and mining activities focused on Galena, the name of which means lead sulphide (Fig. 5-1).

Galena faced south and depended on the Mississippi for its development. There was no good road to the east and to Lake Michigan, and only a trail southeast to Peoria. Today it is difficult to visualize the narrow and silted streambed at Galena as the former Fever River, which was 340 feet wide and three to four feet deeper than the main channel of the Mississippi. Still, the town was once the head of navigation on the Fever River and the gateway for immigrants, who poured in mainly from Kentucky and Missouri bringing with them a southern influence to the style of Galena's early houses.

The first boatload of Galena ore, which the Indians mined just north of the present-day town, reached St. Louis in 1816. The junction of the Fever River with the Mississippi three miles below Galena, called Portage, attracted Indians and settlers until a channel was dredged and passage extended to Galena, then known as La Pointe and Fever River diggings. In 1823 the steamboat *Virginia*, on her way from St. Louis to Fort Snelling—the forerunner of the "Fashionable Tour" mentioned earlier—landed at Galena. Thereafter immigrants, particularly prospectors, came on every boat, mostly keelboats and flatboats. Some came overland in wagons in which they lived during the summer. Many of the Southerners returned to their homes during the first winters, a habit that reminded contemporaries of the fish that migrated seasonally up and down the Mississippi, gaining Illinois the nickname "Sucker-State."

By 1826 Galena had a post office, and in the same year the government superintendent of the lead mines came from St. Louis to lay out streets and lots for a town. In 1827 the government lead-mining agency was moved from St. Louis to Galena in order to better supervise the issuing of permits and the collecting of taxes on mined lead, and Jo Daviess County, comprising a large area between the Mississippi and the Rock River, was organized with Galena as its county seat. A number of settlers from Lord Selkirk's settlement on the Red River, most of them farmers, came in 1829 and began to till the hills near the burrowings of the miners; they could hear the "rumble of the blasts deep in the earth" beneath their furrows. [14]

The early street pattern still persists, and to this day Galena has no

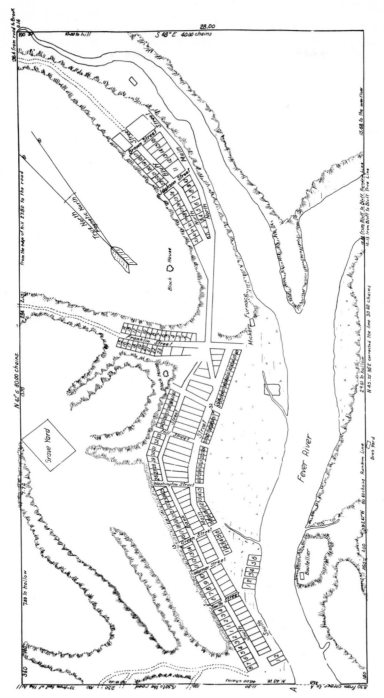

Figure 5-1. Map of Galena about 1828. (State Historical Society of Wisconsin)

rectangular grid pattern. The main thoroughfare changes names three times, starting at the waterfront as Water Street and becoming Main Street and then Broadway as it follows the curve of the steep valley side. Prospect Street and High Street are reached by steep stairways in the heart of the city. Spring, Hill, and Diagonal streets climb the hill and serve motor vehicles today. Along Main Street, warehouses—many of them granaries—form what is called "The Wall," a continuous facade of buildings built directly against the hillside, so that a building three stories high on Main Street may be but one story on the upper street (Bench Street). It was to the latter street that lead was brought by oxcart. There it was unloaded and lowered to Main Street and the waterfront, where boats waited to take on the cargo.

In 1835 the city limits were extended over the bluffs, and in 1841 Galena was incorporated. Wealthy families live on "The Hill," in mansions which remain the best examples of Victorian architecture in the Middle West today and make Galena a "Quality Hill" town* par excellence. The town's layout with its curving main street gives Galena an Old World appearance and a sense of place that is different from a grid-pattern town.

In the lead-mining region of northwestern Illinois, government leases required that two or three men work together; each was entitled to a tract of ten acres laid out rectangularly in cardinal directions. In 1822 the government began to lease land in Wisconsin as well, stipulating that miners had to deliver the lead to government-licensed smelters at Galena, which collected one-tenth of the value of the delivered product. Estimates of the acreage of lead-bearing land that the government had reserved by 1834 vary from 14,500 to 250,000 acres.* Chandler's "Map of the United States Lead Mines on the Upper Mississippi River" (1829) shows diggings, roads, houses, farms and villages (Fig. 5-2); the latter were clusters of mines and houses rather than compact settlements. Among the centers that the surveyors acknowledged as towns was Mineral Point, Wisconsin. The settlement started in 1827 as a cluster of cabins around Jerusalem Spring, from which Jerusalem Street (now Fountain Street) led to a second cluster of crude huts at the bottom of a ravine with a brook "five links wide." The miners' pits were along High Street, which paralleled Fountain Street and other unusually narrow and steeply sloping paths. Shakerag Street, widely known for its well-preserved Cornish houses, follows the ravine in northeasterly direction.

---

*The term "Quality Hill" describes, in the Upper Midwest, the site of the finest residences on a hill or bluff overlooking a town. In Galena, Prospect Street, the most prestigious address in town, was a promenade reached by stairways from Main Street and by one diagonal street, Spring Street, so that carriages could drive up in front of the mansions.
*On the basis of surveyors' plats, 14,500 acres were reserved; the Mineral Point Land Office reported totals ranging from 67,000 to 102,000 acres. One land speculator, Moses Strong, reported 250,000 acres (1834).

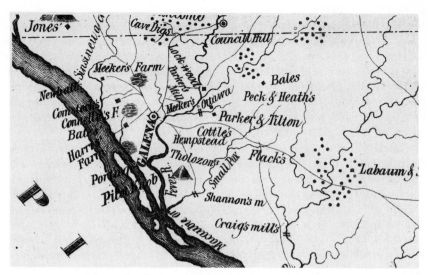

Figure 5-2. Section from Chandler's Map (1829) of lead mines in the Galena area also showing farms, taverns, roads, and other pre-survey features of occupance. (*State Historical Society of Wisconsin*)

The government surveyors who began work in the township in 1832 found "a few scattering trees of white and burr oak" in section 31, the site of Mineral Point, but in 1834, when a land office was opened in the town, a traveler reported that the town's "hills were stripped of their trees"; windlasses, mineral holes, dirt piles, and rocks greeted him on all sides. In 1836 the town was found unsuitable as the site for a territorial capital, partly because of a lack of timber in its vicinity. [15] A hilly location and unusual street pattern contribute to the charm of Mineral Point, which is conscious of its history and preservation minded. A bird's-eye view dated 1872 shows the streets in the core of the town dipping toward the southeast, and High Street crossing diagonally an addition of three by four blocks with a central square (Fig. 5-3).

Dodgeville and Shullsburg also have irregular block patterns dating from pre-survey years. Potosi, an important river town until 1847, when the Great Slough connecting the town with the Mississippi filled in, dates from the discovery of a rich lead vein in 1829 and is strung out for nearly three miles in a narrow valley that permits but one street. No surveyors' lines could overcome the influence of topography. Nor were surveyors in time to get the land ready for sale to farmers, whose products were badly needed.

Because food was short in the lead-mining region, the government encouraged farming before the land was surveyed, and much mineral land was settled by farmers. Most of the diggings were in hilly land with some timber, but the lead veins extended into the prairie, where timber was scarce. Wooded land was highly prized by miners as well as farmers. The interspersal of mining activities, agricultural clearings, and beginning towns gave the area a settlement pattern that was "neither completely dispersed nor agglomerated in character."[16] The population of the tri-state (Iowa, Illinois, and Wisconsin) lead-mining region, including Galena and Dubuque, was estimated at 100 persons in 1824 and at 10,000 in 1828. Townships were surveyed in 1832-33; subdivisions later.

The details of the pre-survey settlement entered by the surveyors on the township plats make the plats difficult to decipher. Let us compare a small section of one of these maps in the core of the mining area with the corresponding notes. We follow the surveyor for two half-miles around a section corner, which will determine one quarter-section in congressional Township 28 N., R. 4 W. of the Fourth Principal Meridian—West Galena Township (Fig. 5-4). The township borders the Mississippi and is easily located on Chandler's map (Fig. 5-2). On the plat, the road from Dubuque to Galena is noted in section 2 at the upper right-hand margin. The Fever

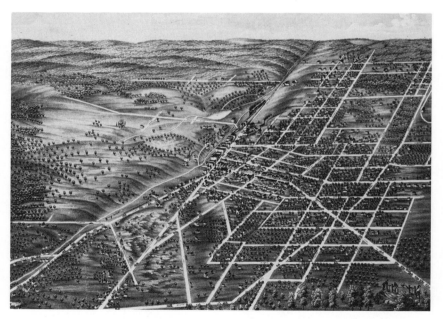

Figure 5-3. Mineral Point, Wisconsin (1873). The view is toward the south showing the diagonal direction of the first streets and narrow, long blocks dipping into the valley. The straightness of valley followed by the railroad is exaggerated. Roads in the distance and the rectangular addition to the northwest (lower left) follow survey lines. (*State Historical Society of Wisconsin*)

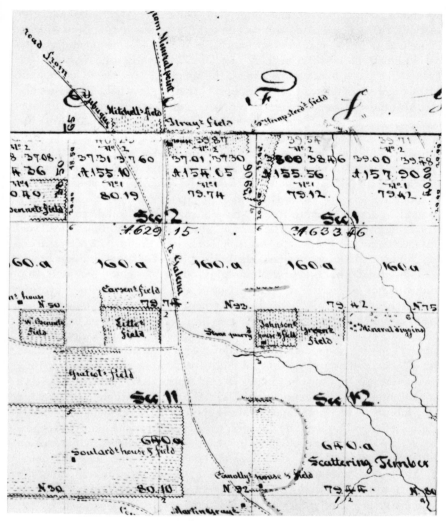

Figure 5-4. Northeastern corner of West Galena Township plat. Conolly's field and house are in southwest quarter of section 12 (lower right); Johnson's house and field are in the northwest quarter. The Dubuque-Galena road enters from the northwest.

(Galena) River is shown in the southeast corner of section 36, and Comstock's house in the southwest corner of section 14 appears on Chandler's map as Comstock's "place."

We continue with the surveyor from south to north, measuring the section line between sections 12 and 11. The survey of one quarter-section begins at

40 chains; that is, at the half-mile point along the western boundary of
section 12. The notes read: "Set post for quarter section corner from which a
white Oak 14 inches in diameter bears N 5½ W 271 links distant and a white
oak 12 inches in diameter bears N 21½ W 277 links distant." Sixty-six feet
farther to the north (one more chain), the surveyor has noted: "left field of
Mr. Conelly & enter scatterring timber." Mr. Conelly's field and house are
shown at the southwest corner of section 12, and a curved line indicates the
eastern boundary of his field. Twenty chains farther along (61 chains from the
southeast corner of section 12), the notes read: "Spring branch 3 links wide
runs East," and at 62.50 chains, "Road leading East & NW leaving timber."
One line for the spring branch runs diagonally across section 12 and another
indicates the road that joins a main road from Dubuque to Galena. After 63
chains the surveyor entered the "field of Mr. Johnson of 25 acres lying
principally about 350 links East." Mr. Johnson's house is indicated and the
square field is shaded. At 73 chains a "Stone Quarry 100 links west" was
observed, and the words "stone quarry" appear on the map directly west of
Mr. Johnson's field. At 80 chains the mile on the west side of section 12 was
completed and the surveyor wrote: "deposited 3 stones in the ground the top
one 3 inches below the natural surface of the earth. The other two immediately and successively below it. The upper stone 8 inches long 4 inches
broad & 3 inches thick. The middle one 7 inches long and 4 inches square.
The lower one 7 inches long and 3 inches square." Over this he "raised a
mound and set a post for corner to sections No. 11, 12, 1 and 2." The land, he
noted, was "rolling soil good fit for cultivation Timber small black & Burr
Oak, undergrowth Oaks and Hazle." Then he turned east and struck out on a
random line between sections 1 and 12.* The notes continue: "Left field of
Mr. Johnson" to "enter field of Mr. Green of 30 acres lying principally
south." Mr. Green's field, nearly square, is also slightly shaded. At 40 chains
he "set a post for temporary ¼ section corner." At 50 chains farther east he
noted "diggins North and South" and at 57 chains, "Extensive Lead Mineral
Diggins." After checking the section post on the exterior township line, the
surveyor returned and adjusted the temporary quarter-section post between
sections 12 and 1 and returned to the post at the corner of sections 12, 1, 2,
and 13. The reader's patience will not be tried further at this point. The plat
was approved in St. Louis in November 1840 by the Surveyor General for
the public lands in Illinois and Wisconsin.

Section measurements were still made with the magnetic needle and the
presence of minerals caused violent fluctuations, according to a report issued
by the Surveyor General of Dubuque in 1848. On the West Galena Township plat, a variation of 9 degrees and 15 minutes was registered. But for

*The notebook reads "after 100.00 chains," a mistake probably made by the copy clerk in the
surveyor general's office in St. Louis. The correct reading is 10.00 chains.

miners and land seekers the difficulty in surveying a straight north-south line in the lead region was likely less important than the confusion resulting from conflicting leases and claims during the period from 1821 to 1846.

In Grant, Iowa, and Lafayette, the three southwestern counties of Wisconsin, surveyors found approximately sixty-five parcels of cultivated land between 1832 and 1835. Nine of the clearings were of considerable size; 60 per cent were on the prairie close to timber. The sequence in which land, after it was surveyed, was taken up for agricultural purposes showed that timbered lands were preferred, particularly by speculators.[17]

Speculative buying of mineral land reached a peak in 1836; thereafter land was increasingly bought for farms. In Green Bay the *Wisconsin Democrat* commented that the "services of the prospector were likely to lose greatly in the process of percolating through several strata of owners before reaching the farmer." And the register of the Land Office at Mineral Point reported that "miners had expended much labor to find spots worthwhile for staking off their permitted ten-acre lots bounded by lines running due east, west, south and north" and that "the lots claimed [by would-be farmers] would probably embrace about three thousand acres." These parcels were the sole dependence of many families.[18] On the other hand, 44,117 fraudulent entries were reported in the three lead-mining counties of Wisconsin by 1842. Much of the reserved land, which according to surveyors plats amounted to 14,590 acres, was timberland adjacent to the smelters.

In 1846, Congress passed a law for the sale of Wisconsin's lead-mine lands, which previously had been reserved from sale. Township maps showing sections and fractions of sections thus released were ready at Mineral Point for public sale by 1847. The minimum size a miner could acquire was now 40 acres. Yet some had been leasing claims of ten acres or less for more than twenty years, and the historian of Mineral Point describes their reaction as follows:

> The miners realized that the purchaser of the smallest legal subdivision, forty acres, would almost certainly purchase the claim of someone else. In order to solve the problem, the claimants organized themselves into mining claim associations. Whenever there was more than one claim in any legal subdivision, the miners put up their proportionate share at $2.50 per acre; some one person was selected to buy the entire forty acres, thereafter to make individual deeds conforming to the respective claims. The association also made arrangements to arbitrate disputes within each group.[19]

The auction was held at the land office on High Street and the few speculators who appeared were discouraged. The claim association saved the day with the assistance of the forty as a module of the survey; larger subdivisions of 80 or 160 acres when miners wanted as few as five acres would have been more difficult to pro-rate among claim association members.

An example of the disappearance of pre-survey claimants was the sale to separate parties of section 12 in West Galena Township in April 1847. One party bought 280 acres, described as five "forties" and one 80-acre tract. Two parties bought "quarter sections," each described as two 80-acre pieces, and three names appeared as one party for one 40-acre tract (Fig. 5-5). Neither the aforementioned Mr. Green nor Mr. Johnson (see p. 94) made entries in section 12, where the surveyor had observed their fields; Mr. Conolly was listed as a claimant of the SW ¼ of section 12 on January 29, 1842. But the same 160 acres were offered once more for public sale in 1847.

The land that was leased, surveyed, and finally sold was deeply affected by destructive occupance. Its disorderly appearance often shocked visitors. A journalist on the Fashionable Tour described the scene at Galena as follows:

> There is scarcely any timber, for useful purposes, about Galena; the wood for the furnaces is brought from some distance, on the Mississippi. We rode along, over lightly shrubbed hills, until the slopes presented simply a surface of short grass; everything assumed a more barren appearance, and now the eye was attracted by what seemed to be an incalculable number of new-made graves! Commencing near the bottom the mounds of fresh turned earth neighbor each other, even to the top of every hill;—these were "the diggings." Anon, figures were seen at work, seldom more than two together, hoisting, by means of a crank and roller, large buckets of red earth from what seemed the mouths of unfinished wells, while others, soiled by clay and shouldering pick or shovel, took their way to and from all sorts of odd-looking little huts—log, plank, and even turf—which appeared to stow themselves away in the hollows.[20]

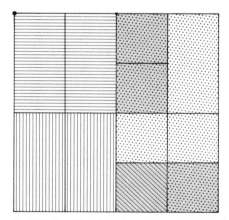

Figure 5-5. Section 12, T. 28 N., R. 1 W. of the Fourth Principal Meridian, sold in 1847 at the land office in Dixon, Illinois. Shaded forties, formerly mine leases, sold for $2.50 an acre; all other tracts for $1.25 an acre. Stippled area indicates the 280-acre tract.

The flat-topped cones of dirt which were piled up next to the diggings can still be seen in farmers' fields, particularly north of Galena from the county road east of Hazel Green to New Diggings and from Highway 11 north of Hazel Green.

The land to be sold from Mineral Point extended north and west beyond the Wisconsin and Fox rivers.[21] But the surveys of the 1830s and early 1840s stopped south and east of these rivers, and the more sharply dissected part of Upper Mississippi Hill Country (part of the Chippewa Land District) was not surveyed until the late 1840s and early 1850s.

In 1847 Congress authorized a geological survey of the Chippewa Land District in Wisconsin and Iowa, which was carried out by David Dale Owen, a distinguished government geologist. Between the Upper Iowa River and Lake Pepin, Owen found that the land, although broken, still offered good pasturage. He praised the "thick and high growth of prairie grass with, perhaps, a faint outline of timber cutting the distant Horizon near the Volga and Turkey River." He proceeded up the Mississippi, which he compared to the Rhine, and explained that bare rock exposures on the southern and western sides of the bluffs were "caused possibly by the more rapid decay through alternate freezing and thawing on the sunny side which prevents trees from developing into maturity." Owen concluded his description with a few statistics on lumber manufacturing in the area, counting 24 mills running 45 saws on the Wisconsin River; 13 mills and 16 saws on the Black River; 5 mills and 7 saws on the Chippewa and tributaries; and 5 mills and 12 saws on the St. Croix. He estimated that "five thousand acres of land must annually be denuded of its timber to produce the lumber sent into the market from the Chippewa land district."[22] Owen's report reached Washington, D.C. at a time when few tracts in the Chippewa Land District were surveyed or ready for sale.

LUMBERING

The pre-survey occupance pattern of the Hill Country north of the Wisconsin River was very different from that of the lead region. Incipient settlements were river oriented and in isolated spots; cabins and small clearings formed clusters around mills, landing sites, or trading posts, the latter often dating from the fur-trading era. Gullies and ravines in the region were called *coulees* by the French, a term that has survived in individual place names such as Morgan Coulee, Stone Coulee, and Bearpen Coulee around the Rush River, or Fisher Coulee near La Crosse. In local parlance "coulee" is common for any gulch or small valley, and geographers refer to "Coulee Country." Upper Coulee Country has fairly broad ridges and sloping hills in its northern part between the St. Croix River and the tributaries of the lower Chippewa River, such as the Red Cedar. Its southern part is sharply dissected into ridges and steep valleys and has little level summit land suitable for farming, particularly in Buffalo and Trempealeau counties. Lower Coulee Country, between the La Crosse and Wisconsin rivers, has generally wider main valleys, broader ridges, and more gently sloping surfaces. Still, small tributary creeks of shorter rivers such as those of the scenic Kickapoo River often rise close together and drain the opposite sides of upland ridges, scalloping their flanks into spurs.[23] In Lower Coulee Country, where exterior township lines were completed by 1845 (Fig. 5-6), there were a few stretches of prairie and mixed deciduous forests; oak openings particularly prevailed. The large Wisconsin pineries of the lumber barons lay mainly to the north of the Driftless Area, but there were some stands of white pine in the mixed forest of Upper Coulee Country. Surveyors found logging, sawmills, and associated activities along the Black River, the lower Chippewa, and the Red Cedar; at some spots along the Eau Claire; and around the Falls of the St. Croix and the junction of the Apple River with the St. Croix. Early lumbering beyond the Hill Country went on as far north as the village of Big Bull Falls (Wausau) on the Wisconsin River.

In 1828, emissaries from Fort Crawford at Prairie du Chien came to the Chippewa region and exchanged blankets and other articles of trade with the Indians for permission to cut pine along the Red Cedar River. But the first raft of logs, which was to be floated down the Chippewa and the Mississippi to Fort Crawford, broke up and the officers in its charge had to return overland to the fort. It remained to a Frenchman, after whom Brunet Island State Park north of Chippewa Falls is named, to float a raft successfully downstream and to pilot up a steamboat on the Chippewa. He also built the first dam and mill at the site of Cornell near Brunet Island.[24] The importance of the large Chippewa drainage basin, which contained about one-sixth of all the pine timber in the United States west of the Appalachians, was well-appreciated by the government. Virgin timber was the special concern of the departments of War and Navy, and in 1817 the Secretary of the Navy was authorized to select preservation tracts of live oak and red cedar. In 1831 Congress made it a felony to cut or remove timber from public land without due permission from the government.[25] After 1830 the Secretary of War began to issue licenses for logging on land not yet ceded by the Indians, but he had no statutory power to do so. With or without permission, loggers worked in convenient spots in the Red Cedar, Chippewa, and Black River valleys and beyond the Hill Country on Indian lands.

Saw timber was in short supply in the Upper Middle West; even the panic of 1837 did not diminish the demand for lumber, which was steadily increasing in the lead-mining region and along the Upper Mississippi. (Regions which had supplied timber earlier (the East and Missouri) were no longer able to supply the demands of settlers in the Middle West.) In fact, wood was so scarce in the lead-mining area that in 1836 the lumber for the temporary

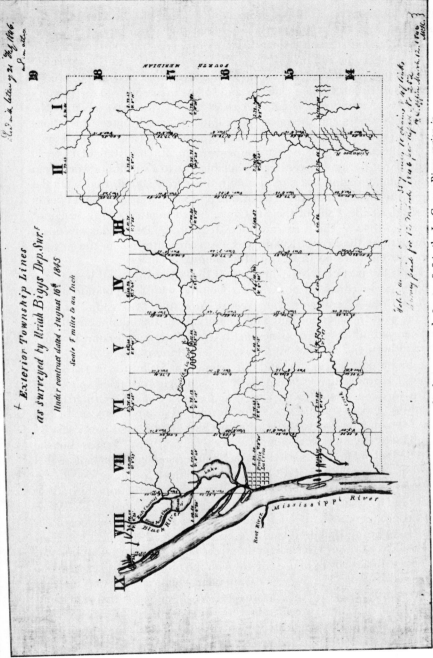

Figure 5-6. Exterior township lines surveyed 1845 to 1846 in the La Crosse River region in Wisconsin. The block design (center left) indicates the town of Prairie La Crosse. (*National Archives*)

capital at Belmont was shipped from Pennsylvania via the Ohio and the Mississippi. And the same source notes that the house of a Meadsville, Pennsylvania, minister was dismantled and the boards transported to Prairie du Chien, where he rebuilt his home.[26]

In 1837 the Winnebago, Sioux, and Chippewa were persuaded to cede their lands in Upper Coulee Country and so lost their rights to the region's pine forests. Around the same time, Easterners with experience in the lumbering business and the necessary capital to launch bigger operations began to replace Frenchmen and half-breeds, who had engaged only haphazardly in logging. The first camps were small, consisting of 15 to 20 men, but labor became increasingly available due to a surplus of workers in the lead-mining region and diminishing returns from the fur trade. On the St. Croix the first sawmill was in operation by 1839 at Marine, about twenty miles south of the Falls of the St. Croix; board manufacturing began at Stillwater in 1843.[27] The early sawmill of 1828 on the Red Cedar was taken over in 1846 by the firm of Knapp and Associates after whom the town of Knapp, eleven miles northwest of Menomonie, is named.

In 1840, the part of Wisconsin north of the Mississippi and west of the Wisconsin River consisted of St. Croix County, with a population of 808; Crawford County, covering the expanse from the Mississippi to Lake Superior, with 1502 people; and Sauk County, with 102 inhabitants. In the same year, post offices were opened in St. Croix Falls and in Point Douglas at the southern end of Lake St. Croix on the Minnesota side. By 1843 La Crosse had a post office, too, and one opened in Stillwater in 1846. The number of sawmills increased rapidly.[28] Small loggers occupied spots from which it was convenient to float logs, and clusters of cabins, fields, and blacksmiths' and wagon-makers' shops developed around early mill sites, such as Menomonie, Eau Claire, Chippewa Falls, and Black River Falls. By the mid-1840s logging was no longer restricted to authorized areas, but the mounting demand for lumber led to much timber-stealing from land in the' public domain. In addition, it was increasingly difficult to supply food for the growing crews in the camps; provisions had to be brought in from the outside by boats and by wagon over tortuous roads, many of them only trails. More local food production was needed and squatter farmers were welcomed.[29] Squatters' rights on timbered land were acknowledged specifically in 1845 when the U.S. Attorney General rendered the opinion that pre-emptors had the privilege to destroy or to use any trees on the tracts they had claimed for clearing and fencing. The Surveyor General at Dubuque was pressured to hasten the surveys north of the La Crosse River after 1845 so that land could be offered for sale, and exterior township lines were laid out in the Hill Country during the following three years as far west as the St. Croix River. One surveyor's note read as follows:

83:60 Set post at corner to Townships 23 & 24 North between Ranges 8 & 9
West of the 4th Meridian Wisconsin in mound of earth and sod pit 10
links north and south.

The location of the original post has been identified by the county surveyor
and re-established by a modern marker and post placed by the overgrown
roadbed of an early stagecoach route from Whitehall to Eau Claire. The spot,
on the rise of a hill, offers an excellent view of the line between Townships 24
and 23 N., range 8 W. of the Fourth Principal Meridian. It is a straight
east-west running line, marked by a fence which crosses a creek and sepa-
rates fields and pastures (Fig. 5-7).

Along the western exterior line of T. 24 N., R. 9 W. of the Fourth Principal
Meridian (Albion Township) at the northwest corner of Trempealeau
County, the straight road is now the boundary between Trempealeau and
Buffalo counties. The setting of that section post in 1848 was described as
follows:

40:00 Set post at ¼ section corner.
Bur Oak 8″ bearing south 85° west
1.26 [chain] distant
Bur Oak 7″ bearing south 75° east
.83 distant

The oaks mentioned are beautiful and healthy trees, about 130 years old
(Fig. 5-8). A third very old "bearing" tree dating from the later survey stands
at the northeast corner of a north-south section road crossed by County Road
Y. The note of September 6, 1852 reads:

80:00 Set post corner to Sections 7,68, 17 and 18
Bur Oak 11″ S. 56° E. 154 links
Bur Oak 5″ N. 53° W. 181 links

The Albion oak is probably 132 years old and stands on the lawn of a
farmhouse at the section corner. Documentable bearing trees such as these
are extremely rare, and their protection must be left to the goodwill of the
owners of the property on which they stand.

It took only one week to subdivide Albion Township in 1852—a feat that
could have been achieved in this hilly and difficult terrain only if no random
lines were taken. Certainly the surveyors proceeded in haste, recording no
mill-sites, shanties, or other signs of pre-survey claims. The township is
traversed by the Beef River (known in Buffalo County as the Buffalo River),
which had no rapids for millsites and no significant stands of timber. In
contrast, the township plats which cover the course of the Black River as far
as its junction with the tributary Poplar River have many notations.

Figure 5-7. Exterior township line, surveyed August 9, 1848, between townships 24 and 23 N., R. 8 W. of the Fourth Principal Meridian. To the North (left) is Unity Township, to the south (right) Hale Township.

Figure 5-8. Bearing trees along an exterior township line. Seven and eight inches in diameter in 1848, the trees are about 130 years old. The road at the left divides Trempealeau and Buffalo counties.

In T. 22 N., R. 3 W., which the Black River traverses from section 2 in the northeast to section 31 in the southwest, inscriptions note "Baker's house and saw mill" in section 20; "a mill with a four feet fall" in section 16; and a "wagon road to Fall of Black River," and patches of pine swamps, pine woods, pine plains, tamarac, and windfall—the last possibly the result of an earlier tornado—are outlined.

Along the Chippewa River, mills, houses, gardens, carpenter shops, and blacksmith shops were entered as far as township 30 to the north. There the surveyors offset the north-south township lines by a correction line. The precision with which forties were measured along the northern and western township lines, toward which the irregularities were moved, is illustrated by the broken sizes for forties, such as 35.15, 44.50, or 37.75 acres. The desire to inform prospective farmers about the surveyed land is reflected in notations such as "sheep pasture," "wheat," "hay," "good bottom Land," "prairie," "wet marsh." In summary, with the greatest possible speed the heart of the dissected country was inventoried for the expected influx of agricultural settlers and for sale to lumbermen.

Composite general maps do not reflect the piecemeal sequence of surveying as it was dictated by practical erations. For example, in 1848 land was surveyed along and even north of the Black River, and a broad band of townships was measured from the St. Croix, where two rows of congressional townships were extended east in order to reach the Menomonie mills on the Red Cedar. But the Chippewa River drainage basin still did not have, according to Owen's report of 1848, the "lineal survey." Without it "nothing could be done in the way of minute examination with reference to sections and quarter sections."[30]

Because some areas were designated as having priority for subdivisions, adjacent congressional townships came to be subdivided two or more years apart. A somewhat extreme case was the subdivision in 1840 of the mill site region at Wisconsin Rapids, which extended into three townships, the rest of which were surveyed in 1851 and 1852 (T. 21 N., Ranges 5, 6, and 7 east of the Fourth Principal Meridian). The variations of the needle introduced another irregularity—one of measurement—and made it difficult to close and match the lines of townships after they had been separately laid out. Such irregularities were of little concern to claimants who secured their tracts with the help of individual township plats.

A third type of pre-survey occupance took place at landings and at some towns that were laid out before the opening of land offices and the announcements of public land sales.

Landings and Townsites

Fur trading posts were the first settlements in the Upper Middle West with the potential of developing into nucleated settlements. The earliest and most important post along the Upper Mississippi (and the second oldest settlement in Wisconsin) was Prairie du Chien. First the French and then the British maintained a fort there, and by 1800 the village, mostly French, consisted of about ten or fifteen houses. In 1816, the Americans built a wooden stockade close to the river and by 1820 several Americans had claimed land in the area.[31]

The Borough of Prairie du Chien was incorporated in 1821 under the laws of the Michigan Territory, but it took several years to settle the land claims of the French villagers, whose long lots Colonel Izaac Lee had mapped in 1820. A few villagers, however, received deeds to their lots in 1823. This was possible because a rule requiring occupancy of claims made before 1796 was changed: claimants of lots needed to prove residence after 1812 only. A few other claimants, including those who had lost land to the site of the second Fort Crawford, which was erected on higher ground in 1829, had their titles confirmed in 1828.

A survey of the lots was undertaken by the government in 1821 and the French villagers received their titles during the 1820s. This was the first official land survey along the Upper Mississippi and immediately gave rise to land speculation. Some of the most desirable lots were purchased by Hercules Dousman, agent of John Jacob Astor's American Fur Company, who in 1843 built Villa Louis on the site of the first Fort Crawford. The two-story red-brick mansion was the most elegant residence along the Upper Mississippi during the mid-nineteenth century and is now a historical museum open to the public.

The shape of the French claims, of course, did not fit the rectangular grid of the survey (Fig. 5-9). Village streets paralleled the long-lot lines, running straight to the water's edge on the low bank between the slough (the Marais St. Feriole) and the Mississippi. The village was platted to consist of twenty-eight blocks—squares and rectangles of different sizes. Above the Marais was the river road, which followed the length of the slough, angling slightly at several points. Bluff Street crossed Main Street at right angles, not in a strictly east-west direction. Some blocks in the first addition above the Marais were not exactly rectangular, and none of the later additions had rectangular grids oriented north-south and east-west. The layout of Prairie du Chien can be characterized as a composite, river-oriented grid pattern.

The surveyors marked several small settlements and many landing sites between Dubuque, the gateway port for the Upper Mississippi, and Hast-

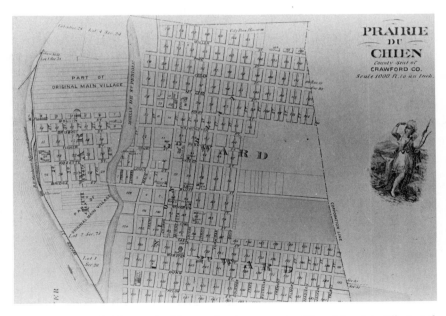

Figure 5-9. Prairie du Chien, 1881. Plat map showing remnants of French long lots. (*Illustrated Historical Atlas of Wisconsin,* 1881)

ings opposite the mouth of the St. Croix. The notations "McKnight's house and smelting furnace" (north of Dubuque) and "Bailey's ware house" (near Hastings) reflect the early primary activities of the two settlements. Some landings had attracted enough residents to give them the appearance of villages and to arouse their hopes of becoming river ports. Calling themselves "towns," such landings achieved the distinction of being noted on surveyors' maps, their names accompanied by a standardized symbol for a grid pattern, a shaded quadratic block design. Among such villages were Cassville and La Crosse in Wisconsin and Brownsville, Rising Sun, Winona, Mt. Vernon, Read's Landing, Lake City, Center Point, Red Wing, and Hastings in Minnesota.

La Crosse, once a Winnebago camping site where French traders occasionally stopped, was settled by two young New Yorkers who in 1841 landed on Barron's Island in the Mississippi. They then moved across the channel, settling at the mouth of the La Crosse River, where they set up a small logging operation. The excellent site combined a natural harbor with a nearly treeless prairie, which offered room for growth and had potentially good connections with the hinterland. A first plat was drawn in 1842. A few years later the first logs were floated down the Black River to be sorted and rafted at La Crosse and sent on to St. Louis. But by 1848 when the land was put up for sale at Mineral Point, there were few houses in the settlement, and only five men had verified claims for the prairie of La Crosse. The official town plat, recordéd in 1851, represented no particular change from the first plat of 1842. Front Street, surveyed above the original shoreline in northeast-southwest direction, was paralleled by Second, Third, and Fourth streets and crossed Main, State, and Vine streets at right angles. Additions made between 1852 and 1855 were along cardinal directions and parallel to the lines of survey subdivisions.

The original location of the town was in government lot 3, a fractional forty in the southeast quarter of section 31, T. 16 N., R. 7 W. On the map of exterior township lines (Fig. 5-6) the surveyors used a relief-like grid-pattern symbol. The upright position of this symbol does not reflect the pre-survey layout of the first settlement, and the symbol also covers too large an area; one fractional block in the upper-left hand corner would be enough to indicate the size of the town the surveyors found.[32] A second example of the surveyors' merely schematic use of the block-relief pattern may be seen on the plat of Winona, T. 107 N., R. 7 W. of the Fifth Principal Meridian (Fig. 5-10).

The site of Winona on the low-lying Wabasha Prairie was selected as a landing by the captain of the river packet *Nominee* in 1851. He speculated correctly that a major river port approximately midway between Dubuque and St. Paul would thrive on this unusually broad expanse of flat terrain—in spite of the risk of flooding. A lumber dealer from La Crosse also was

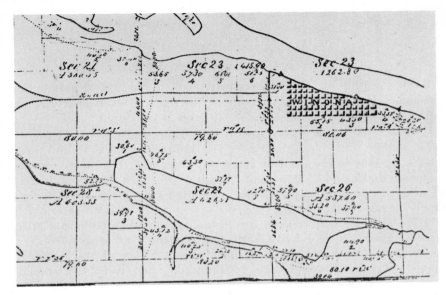

Figure 5-10. Winona City in block design on surveyor's township plat, 1855. The shoreline of the river is meandered (as is Lake Winona) in sections 28, 27, and 26.

interested in founding a town on the Wabasha Prairie, and both men staked out plots, for which each paid the Sioux a barrel of flour. The large influx of land seekers into southeastern Minnesota in 1852 encouraged the captain to hire a surveyor to plat a town; four blocks along the river front were reserved for a public levee, the site of Levee Park today. In 1853 a government surveyor measured the section line between sections 22 and 23 in Winona Township, walking north, and noted:

    Chains
    23.38 Road from Winona bears west
    39.50 Intersect Right Bank of Mississippi river and set post for mound for
           meander corner
           Surface level prairie   Soil gravely
                                    2nd rate

He then turned east to "meander" (measure by short straight lines the curving river shore) and wrote:

    Courses Chains
    S 68 E   34.40
    S 66 E   4.70   on this fraction [of a section] is situated

S 77 E   27.20   the town of Winona
S 74 E   5.30
S 79 E   6.70   To post on Line of Sects. 23 & 24
S 63 E   6.30

On the township plat the road is clearly marked; the slight breaks in the meandered line are barely discernible. Subdivisions were measured exactly; the forties consisted of 55.15 and 43.40 acres in section 23.

Winona's land office opened in early 1855. The town had become a county seat in 1854, and about a year later had 436 residents and 45 buildings, including four stores and two hotels. By December 1855 the residents numbered 815, and 24 stores and 7 hotels were among the 670 buildings. Earlier that year the proprietors had submitted a plat for approval. Essentially the same as that of 1852, the new plat showed the corner of sections 22, 23, 26, and 27 nearly coinciding with the crossing of Wabasha and Main streets; a public square drawn on the first plat (1852) still exists today. The square grid pattern, however, was along the southeast-northwest axis of the prairie. A map of the town dated 1867 used the same shaded block design that the surveyors used, but in this case the design reflected reality and the grid-pattern was tilted correctly, as Winona was planned before the survey (Fig. 5-11).[33]

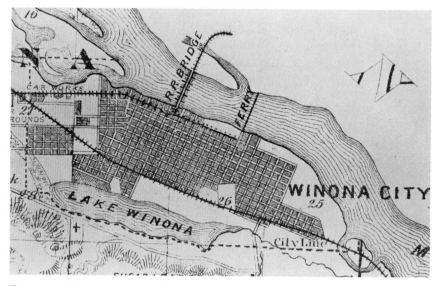

Figure 5-11. Winona City, 1867, designated by block design as on surveyor's plat (Figure 5-10), but in correct orientation. Space for public levee was maintained from the original plat of 1852. (*Bennett & Smith, Atlas of Winona County, 1867*)

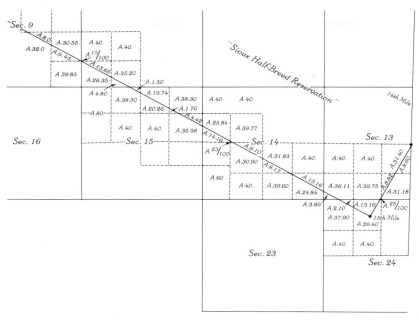

Figure 5-12. Segment of plat for T. 108 N., R. 11 W. of the Fifth Principal Meridian, showing forties divided by the diagonal boundary of the Half Breed Tract.

Wabasha and Read's Landing were two landing sites in close proximity just south of Lake Pepin and opposite the mouth of the Chippewa, which was called Buffalo, or Beef, Slough. Among the many landings that surveyors noted along the banks of the Upper Mississippi, Read's Landing is the only one which has kept the generic term as a place name.

In 1826 Wabasha was a trading post with warehouses and cabins clustered near a bayou, soon called the "Slough." The site became part of a tract reserved in 1830 for mixed-blood relatives of Sioux Indians and white men with Sioux wives.* According to Article IX of the Treaty of Prairie du Chien (1830), the boundary of the Wabasha Reservation, also called the "Half-Breed Tract," began at "a point called the barn below and near the village of the Red Wing Chief," and turned southeast as a "parallel line with Lake Pepin and the Mississippi, about thirty-two miles to a point opposite Beef or O-Boeuf River; thence fifteen miles to the Grand Encampment opposite the River aforesaid."[34] The township plat shows the right angles at the south corner of this rectangular tract (Fig. 5-12). Where forty-acre tracts were

*Some white men, however, including the Anglo-Canadian Charles Read, had no Indian wives and were illegal squatters in 1849 when Minnesota opened for settlement.

crossed by the reservation line, the size of the parcels created were noted exactly: 19.74 and 20.26 acres. 29.45 and 10.55 acres, or 36.80 and 3.20 acres. The plats were approved by the Surveyor General at Dubuque on October 24, 1855; their plane geometry and accurate arithmetic, in stark contrast to the geographic reality of the dissected countryside, was superseded by events of 1854.

In that year the half-breeds, who held no deeds for individual properties on their tract, agreed to sell their land for five pieces of scrip per person, which would allow them to claim as much as 480 acres of public land per person, either on the tract or anywhere in the United States.* The first town plat of Wabasha (1854) was enlarged by several rectangular grid additions; later all the plats but that of South Wabasha were tilted and aligned with the river front. Aside from attempts to continue the river orientation of the 1854 plat, no efforts were made to mesh streets meeting at awkward angles or ending at the slough until the twentieth century, when Hiawatha Drive along the Mississippi was improved.

In contrast, the original plat for Charles Read's Landing, also drawn in 1854, was imaginative and adjusted to the topography. It was a river-facing grid-pattern with blocks and lots of different sizes, and, instead of the usual one or two open squares reserved for public use, a central half-circle. Lots were radially arranged around this arc, a rather ingenious adaptation of a grand circular central plaza to the narrow floodplain, which was hemmed in by the bluff line. The plat stretched diagonally across survey lines and the city limits eventually extended into sections 23, 24, 25, 26 of T. 111 N., R. 11 W., and into sections 19 and 30 of R. 10 W. The town has a Water Street which does not front the river. "Read's addition," filed in 1870, covered the space between Water Street and the Mississippi with lots; sufficient alluvial deposition had taken place to warrant the partitioning of the added bench of land. Later additions were also made with consideration for river front and bluff line. Today, streets climb the bluff or are terraces, and the planned half circle is crossed by the highway and is unrecognizable. Read's Landing did not become an important river port and never had more than 700 residents; Wabasha, the county seat, was more successful.

A purely utopian plan for a landing site on the Mississippi was entertained by The Western Farm and Village Association of the City of New York in 1852. The first design, admittedly submitted "not so much for adoption as for the purpose of illustrating and setting forth the merits and pecularities" of the project, was an extreme example of "square-minded" colonization in the Western tradition. It featured four symmetrically placed parks centered in equal-sized quarters, the quarters were divided by an east-west street and

*It should be noted that two of the men instrumental in getting the scrip issued happened to be the proprietors of the site of Wabasha. Most of the half-breeds sold their scrip, which was supposedly non-transferable, and stayed around Wabasha.

by a river running north to south; the latter separated the two halves of a large central public square and was bridged.[35] In 1852 agents of the association selected a site for their town at the end of the Rollingstone Valley in Minnesota. Undaunted by ice and snow, they had investigated prospects around La Crosse without success, and had found small landings "discouraging" because of the lack of roads to the hinterland. They considered Wabasha Prairie (Winona) "prey to speculation." So, according to their report, they "hove to" and skated miles up the Mississippi from La Crosse to "a most beautiful opening" of comparatively high tableland covered with oak sufficiently large for the "entire village plot exclusive of the low land by the river."[36] But the land was not on the river; the agents unknowingly had skated up a slough. The site, bought from two claim holders, offered waterpower for a mill but no opportunities to develop a river port. A second plat designed for approximately 160 acres consisted of a square bordered by four streets with radial avenues leading to a central circle, which was to be covered with glass for a winter garden.[37] The project did not materialize and the small settlement of holders of individual tracts was incorporated as a village in 1896.

Most proprietors of landing sites who drew town plats in the expectations of the sites becoming river ports had a specific location in mind, with at least a short road already in existence that ran parallel to the shore. This resulted in plats with streets that faced the river front and cross streets that met the bluff at right angles; the orientation was rarely along survey lines. On charts dating from 1940, 102 plats can be counted between Rock Island, Illinois, and Hastings, Minnesota. Only eight have rectangular grid patterns following survey lines, irrespective of the river shoreline. Fifteen are oriented north-south and east-west, but in each case they fit the direction of the riverbank at the particular location. Sixty-five are tilted to adjust to the river. Fourteen are now towns or cities with composite grid patterns.

Many landing and ferrying points operated only for a short period. Successful development of a town by the river depended on many factors. among them a good bay, availability of wood for fuel for steamboats, level land for expansion, and the character of the hinterland. The hinterlands of the east and west banks of the Mississippi, similar as they were in physical appearance near the river, were different in two major ways: on the Wisconsin side, large rivers draining extensive watersheds offered possibilities for rafting logs from the pine timber regions north of the Hill Country to the Mississippi. On the Iowa and Minnesota side, rivers are comparatively short; their headwaters start in the rich agricultural land of the prairies. Secondly, during the 1850s, the "Western Uplands," as Wisconsins' geographers call Upper Mississippi Hill Country from the Falls of the St. Croix to the Illinois boundary, were the back door of Wisconsin (Milwaukee, the shore of Lake Michigan, and Wisconsin's southeastern counties were the front entrance to the state). But on the Minnesota side of the Mississippi from Brownsville north of the Iowa border to St. Paul, the riverbank was the front door, and the towns of Red Wing, Lake City, Wabasha, and Winona had no equivalent rivals in Wisconsin between the St. Croix and La Crosse rivers. South of the Minnesota-Iowa border, however, the influence of the lead-mining region and early settlements such as Prairie du Chien resulted in a reversal of the development along the two shores as far as Dubuque.

Another difference was the time of surveying, from 1847 to 1852 on the Wisconsin side and from 1853 to 1855 in Minnesota; in the latter area the survey coincided with a rush of land seekers on their way to the fertile land beyond the dissected country. In Minnesota claim seekers and townsite speculators preceded the surveyors in several instances only by a few months and many early towns profited from the through traffic of the westward movement. The bottomlands of the tributary valleys along the Root, the Rollingstone, the lower Zumbro, and the Cannon rivers were dotted with signs of occupance: surveyors' maps, note claims, houses, gristmills, plowed fields, and wood-choppers' cabins.

Four early settlements in the Root River valley, which presented a wide opening from the Mississippi, illustrate townsite speculation. They are Hokah, Money Creek, Preston, and Chatfield.

The town of Hokah, the first inland settlement in the Root River valley, is situated on a crescent-shaped rise of land formed by the confluence of Thompson's Creek with the Root River, which the Dakota Indians called *Hokah*. An early settler by the name of Thompson came from Illinois and pre-empted the bench by the creek in 1850, and within two years he and his brothers had erected log cabins, a blacksmith shop, a gristmill and a sawmill; a post office was established in 1854. Lumber from the surrounding region supported a small furniture factory as an associated industry; indeed, the name of a modern firm in Hokah, the Tri-State Logging Supply, referring to Minnesota, Iowa, and Wisconsin, reflects the ambition of the town to serve more than local needs. By the 1870s there were a railroad, grain elevators, wagon shops, and a boat yard in which two small river steamers were built in 1858.

The pre-emption claim for the site was entered in 1855, and the village plat, drawn up in the same year, had a Main Street curving along the bench in an approximately southwest-northeast direction with lots on either side. Two grid patterns, connected only by Main Street, were laid out at its northern and southern end in cardinal directions. A township line divided the village, extending into sections of townships 103 and 104 N., ranges 3, 4, and 5 W. In 1871 Hokah was incorporated. Main Street, which overlooks the Root River, and a lake created by a dam give Hokah an individual character of site.[38]

Money Creek—originally Hamilton—Township at the northeastern corner of Houston County is drained by a creek of the same name, a tributary to the Root River. In 1853 two New Englanders in search of a mill site followed the main valley of the Root, bypassing its south fork, and traveled upstream to the next major tributary valley—Money Creek. There they found a terrace above the bottomland on the left bank of the Creek, where they cleared two large adjacent fields. The surveyors noted these as "ploughed ground" in townships 104 N. and ranges 6 and 7 W. A gristmill was erected the next year, but its operation was intentionally delayed until the survey was completed and the land sale opened. The two claims, totaling 320 acres, were entered in 1855, when the settlement of Money Creek already had a school. The plat of 1856 was a standard four-by-five block grid pattern with one block reserved for a public square. Winter, Spring, Central, Summer, and Main streets running east-west, and First through Fourth streets (north-south) were all sixty feet wide. A survey post on the exterior township line was marked on the plat at the southwestern corner of the public square. The proprietors combined the survey's orientation and its units of measurement on their simplistic plat; their site straddled a township line. The village, which at one time had two hotels, presents only remnants of the original design today; at least half of the blocks were never occupied and three farms operate from town lots.[39]

Preston, further west on the South Branch of the Root River, is almost in the center of Fillmore County, and is the county seat as well. In 1853 a man from Pennsylvania built a cabin by a half-circular river bend where falls held promise for a mill site. The next year he sold his claim to four men who had widely searched for a site with waterpower. They platted a town with a square north-south grid, fractioning blocks along the river to fit the standardized plat into the river bend. In 1855, when the claim was entered and the town plat surveyed, Preston had a sawmill, a gristmill, and two hotels. The layout fitted the mostly level area of the southwest quarter of section 6 of Preston Township rather closely, an example of survey lines coinciding with the area inside a river bend. Not considered in the planning was a nearby hill spur, and the main north-south thoroughfare had to be curved to the northwest of the original platted area to gain sixty to seventy feet in order to reach the upland; Preston was on a stagecoach route. Additions extended Preston into section 31 of the township to the north; the block pattern was continued with two streets cutting the square blocks diagonally in adjustment to the topography. The public square was planned in the center of the bend, and major retail activities were located around the square, where a courthouse was built soon after Preston became county seat in 1856. Preston is a regular survey-oriented town to the extent valley bottomland allowed.[40]

Chatfield lies in northwestern Fillmore County; it expected at one time to be its county seat. The site was selected in 1852 by a townsite speculator from Dubuque. He staked his claim on a terrace sloping down to the confluence of Chatfield Creek and the North Branch of the Root River, paying, according to the records, $195.60 for 156.48 acres. In 1853 he erected a log cabin, and with ten men whom he had interested in his proposed town, engaged in manipulations to have Fillmore County (with Chatfield as the county seat) set off from Winona County, which was indeed large, at 3000 square miles. On December 19, 1853, the eleven claimants and a friend were the only persons present aside from a pro-tem clerk at a meeting of the commissioners of the "Root River precinct, residence of Mr. Case." The clerk recorded that Chatfield in the center of section 6, T. 104 N., R. 11 W. should be the county seat of Fillmore County. A protest meeting of the county commissioners of Winona County at Minnesota City on January 2, 1854, was indecisive.

Meanwhile the group, now incorporated, prepared an optimistic but not very accurate town plat, which was sent to newspapers in New York and Pennsylvania as an advertisement. They pursued their plans vigorously, even requesting travelers on the territorial road between St. Paul and Dubuque who wished to stay overnight at Chatfield to cut down trees on the village streets in return for hospitality. The two claims needed for the original town plat were entered in the land office at Brownsville on August 8 and 10, 1854, as the northwest quarter of section 5 and the northeast quarter of section 6 in T. 104 N., R. 11 W. On August 28, a corrected town plat was recorded in Brownsville and a square was donated to the public; a year later it had a bandstand.[41] On the square grid design, four blocks wide and ten blocks long, River, Bench, and Main streets followed the northwest-southeast direction of the terrace. The plat extended beyond the quarter-section line to the south and across the county line to the north. Division Street, the northernmost street of the original plat, lies fully in Olmsted County.

The first hope of Chatfield's speculators was defeated when in April 1856 the citizens of Fillmore County voted Preston the county seat. But that hope was renewed when in May of the same year the land office was moved from Brownsville to Chatfield. The town boomed and an addition, West Chatfield, was laid out on the other side of the valley, again with squares adjusted to the course of the Root River and not north-south oriented. Real estate dealers, lawyers, and private surveyors swarmed into town, and Chatfield became the most flourishing place in southeastern Minnesota. The business directory for 1857 listed 7 grocery and provision stores, 5 lawyers, 3 doctors, 3 civil engineers, 2 hotels, 1 livery stable, and 11 realtors—a development that was extraordinary even for the frontier. The frame building of the land office is still standing but abandoned (Fig. 5-13). Chatfield was incorporated as a village in 1857 and as a city in 1887. The speed with which the land along the western border of the Hill Country was taken up is reflected in the removal of the land office in 1860 from Chatfield to Winnebago, which lies

Figure 5-13. Abandoned U.S. Land Office at Chatfield, Minnesota, the only such structure left in the Hill Country. *(Rick Ford)*

three counties and a little more than 100 miles to the west—in prairie country.

By 1860 the political boundaries of states, counties, and townships in the Hill Country were for the most part established. Not much government land was left for sale in Upper Mississippi Country, and good land had to be purchased from private parties.

6 THE FUNCTIONAL IMPACT

Township, County, and State Boundaries

Congressional townships of thirty-six square miles were created by federal law for the sole purpose of making available easily identifiable and saleable tracts, and a county was made up of several congressional townships. Civil (legally organized) townships often but not always coincided with congressional townships, which the public called "regular" townships. Civil divisions were a result of human decisions and to some degree, geography. Their boundaries, particularly those of townships, often changed during the early years of a state's history, but most towns, townships, and counties had stable boundaries before the turn of the century and can be discussed as they appear on modern maps.

IRREGULAR TOWNSHIPS IN MINNESOTA AND WISCONSIN

Olmsted County, Minnesota has one irregular township, High Forest, in which there are twelve additional sections in the south—six below sections 31 to 36 and six more forming a panhandle south of Rock Dell Township, which lies to the west. Thus the straight line of the northern boundaries of the nine counties along the southern Minnesota border is interrupted (Fig. 1-2). The strange jog on the border came about as follows: in 1856 an attorney elected to represent Olmsted County in the state legislature found that in fact he lived in Mower County. But he persuaded the lawmakers to add twelve sections to High Forest Township from Mower County and thereby managed to retain his seat. The township road that was run through the center of the panhandle to connect it with the village of High Forest and those sections is a reminder of the gerrymander.

In Fillmore County, the township of Pilot Mound was reduced by three half-sections to permit the township to the south to gain access to the Root River. In Houston County, La Crescent Township was extended by two sections, across which a road from La Crescent village led west along Pine Creek. And between Mound Prairie and Union townships, section and half-section lines zig-zag over a ridge. The southern boundary of Money Creek Township follows the Root River more or less along section, half-section, quarter-section, and quarter-quarter section lines, which cross the river several times. The incorporated limits of the village of Money Creek (described in the last chapter) were also adjusted to the river. Houston Township, made up from parts of three government townships, was adjusted to make its village accessible to three valleys, in which most of the cultivated farms were located. In Wabasha County, the townships of Mazeppa, Zumbro, and Hyde Park are bounded in part by congressional township lines and in part by the Zumbro River. "This river rendered it so inconvenient for the people to meet, and especially so in the spring, that it was finally decided to divide the town, the Zumbro forming the boundary."[1] In addition, townships which border on the Mississippi must be irregular, because river courses almost always cause townships to be fractional. All other townships in the Hill Country of Minnesota were shaped to coincide with the thirty-six square mile congressional townships.

By comparison, irregular townships are more numerous in Wisconsin, largely a result of the greater use of rivers and ridges for delineating county boundaries (Fig. 6-1). Juneau County on the eastern margin of the Hill Country has nineteen townships, eight of which are regular. Five are rectangular and defined by section lines but not square, and six border the Wisconsin River and Petenwell Lake. At first glance the boundary between Necedah and Armenia townships appears to be the main channel of the Yellow River, a small tributary to the Wisconsin River. Closer examination reveals that only the northern segment of the township's boundary follows the course of the river; the remainder consists of section, half-section, and quarter-quarter section lines. The river meanders in a plain with many oxbows and poorly defined channels; its course was followed as closely as possible through the use of minor survey subdivision lines.[2]

Crests and divides, used by the French to define their territorial claims in North America, were also used for township boundaries in Wisconsin. An example is Lincoln Township in Buffalo County in the heart of the dissected country; its boundaries approximate the divides east and west of a stretch of the Waumandee River. The eastern boundary follows the ridge between Jahns Valley in Lincoln, and Buell and Garden valleys in adjacent Montana and Waumandee townships, respectively. The western boundary of Lincoln Township approximates the height of the Alma Ridge with Alma Township to the west. A second example of a ridge boundary is the line between Arcadia and Ettrick townships in Trempealeau County, which follows half-section,

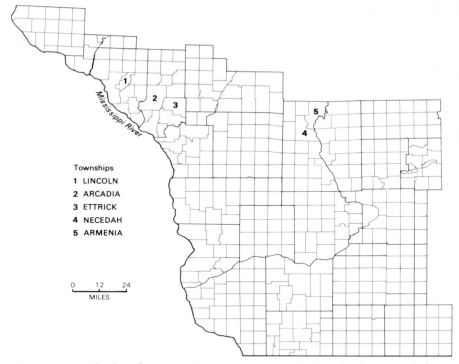

Figure 6-1. Township boundaries in southwestern Wisconsin. The boundary between Arcadia and Ettrick townships and that of Lincoln Township follow ridges. Between Necedah and Armenia townships, the boundary follows a river. Straight section-subdivision lines are used to approximate "natural" boundaries.

quarter-section, and quarter-quarter section lines. No series of straight lines and straight angles truly follows the natural features of a ridge, but through subdivision, commonly representing property lines at the time of establishment, some township boundaries were fitted very well to divides.

Irregular townships on the Wisconsin side of the Mississippi are too numerous to list. Apparently, only a small correlation exists between hilly terrain and irregularly shaped townships. To illustrate, Richland County, with twelve regular townships and four irregular bordering the Wisconsin River, is as hilly as adjacent La Crosse County, in which there were only two regular townships out of ten. And in Trempealeau County (four regular and eleven irregular townships), although a certain correlation does exist between physical features and boundaries, it is far less impressive than that between boundaries and ethnic groupings—such as the concentrations of Polish settlers in Dodge Township, Scots in Caledonia Township, and Norwegians in Ettrick Township.[3]

COUNTY BOUNDARIES

County boundaries are quite simply an expression of the order that the survey put upon the land, and north-south and east-west running survey lines (aside from rivers) constitute county boundaries in Upper Mississippi County. Generally, the drainage basins of tributaries to the Upper Mississippi are crossed by county boundaries (Fig. 6-2). Reports on the organization of new counties and the rivalry of villages striving to become county seats fill many pages in county histories. We have already described Chatfield, a village that, despite its efforts, did not become the county seat. Another example of manipulation and rivalry involved Wisconsin's Trempealeau County.

In 1852 Jackson County was set off from La Crosse County. Wisconsin's constitution stipulated that no county of an area less than 900 square miles could be subdivided, but one land speculator—a certain Judge Gale—managed to circumvent that rule by maneuvering the addition to La Crosse County of part of Chippewa County as well as parts of Buffalo and Jackson counties. With La Crosse County now large enough to be subdivided, Montoville Township (to which the parts of Buffalo and Jackson counties had been added) could be detached, and in January 1853 Gale and his group petitioned the state legislature for the organization of Montoville Township as Trempealeau County. In 1854 the enabling legislation was passed.

Although central location, irrespective of terrain, was considered advantageous when selecting a town for a county seat,* Galesville, a village platted by Judge Gale in the southern part of the county became Trempealeau's first county seat in 1855. Rivalry followed—first with Trempealeau City on the Mississippi (the oldest settlement in the county) and later with Arcadia and Whitehall. Whitehall, the most centrally located of the three, finally won out, amid much "platting and planning of county politicians, wirepullers, etc."[4]

The outline maps of counties in our region show the lower Wisconsin River to be the boundary between counties, except where the eastern border of Sauk County leaves the west bank of the river and runs straight north-south for about twelve miles. The Buffalo, Trempealeau, and La Crosse rivers are boundaries only for the last miles of their courses. West of the Mississippi no rivers serve as county boundaries.

That the square congressional townships were better suited to the prairie and the plains than to the Hill Country is obvious. In the mountainous West, straight-line boundaries are as indifferent to topography as farms delineated along cardinal directions are to the distribution of water resources, although

*For example, the location of Ellsworth, the county seat of Pierce County, Wisconsin, was determined in 1861 by crossing diagonals to find the most central spot.

Figure 6-2. The Upper Mississippi Drainage Basin north of the Missouri-Mississippi junction, with county grid.

in Oregon, some adjustment was made where county boundaries followed the divide of the Cascades.[5] In the Upper Mississippi Hill Country no attempt was made to adjust county outlines to crests or broader divides between watersheds.

STATE BOUNDARIES

In the colonial tradition, state boundaries exhibit the minimal range of choice; that is, they are based on parallels, meridians, and rivers. Parallels constitute the boundaries between Wisconsin and Illinois and between Minnesota and Iowa. A meridian and the St. Croix and Mississippi rivers separate Minnesota from Wisconsin. The Mississippi, indeed, became a boundary for the four states of our region.

The boundary between Illinois and Wisconsin dates from 1818, when Illinois pushed its border sixty miles farther north than the parallel of latitude running west from the southern end of Lake Michigan, the line suggested in the Ordinance of 1787. Illinois wanted to include the lead-mining region of Galena and an area north of Chicago. The boundary was surveyed in 1831 and 1832, by commissioners representing the United States and Illinois, and a large stone marked "Michigan" on the north and "Illinois" on the south was placed just above the high-water line on the east bank of the Mississippi at latitude 42° 30' N. The location of the marker was not entirely correct, according to measurements made in the twentieth century. From the stone a line was run east to the Fourth Principal Meridian, where an earth mound was erected. Farther to the east—on the west bank of the Rock River and 81 miles, 31 chains, and 9 links distant from the Mississippi—the boundary was found to run 54 minutes too far north. When Lake Michigan was reached, the line was half a mile north of the stipulated latitude, frequent astronomical observations notwithstanding. When Wisconsin became a state in 1846, Wisconsinites felt that their state had lost valuable farm and mineral land to Illinois unfairly.[6]

Wisconsin's northwestern boundary was also a disappointment to its citizens. In 1849 the state lost to Minnesota the territory between the St. Croix and the Upper Mississippi River. The northernmost stretch of the boundary between the two states (from the headwaters of the St. Croix to Lake Superior) was designated on the basis of Joseph Nicollet's map of 1843 with reference to the first rapids of the St. Louis River, which are mislocated on the map.[7] In 1852 a survey was made to determine their true location. Continuing dissatisfaction with the boundary finally led to a lawsuit which resulted in the resurveying of the water-inundated region near Lake Superior but in no significant change of the boundary.

Development on the west bank of the Mississippi was faster than on the east bank due to the proximity of St. Paul, St. Anthony, and Minneapolis and to numerous early settlements along the river, such as Stillwater, Marine-on-the-St. Croix, and Point Douglas. After World War II the Wisconsin side of the river was increasingly drawn into the orbit of the Twin City metropolitan region, and in 1965 the Minnesota-Wisconsin Boundary Area Commission was established by Interstate Compact. The Commission acts as a service center to advise on coordination of public policies, which is much needed in the heavily populated lower St. Croix region.

The Mississippi River boundary between Minnesota and Wisconsin was designated as the main channel of the Mississippi, or Lake Pepin. The usual practice of following the median line when boundaries run in the middle of lakes was thus circumvented, and Wisconsin claims almost three-fourths of Lake Pepin. Fish and game laws, different in the two states, are difficult to administer, especially as no well-defined natural channel exists.

In Iowa a small rectangular tract between the Des Moines River and the Mississippi was surveyed in 1832. But work in this area, called the Half-Breed Tract,* was interrupted by the Black Hawk War. In 1836, 400 square miles along the lower Iowa River were purchased by the government; in 1837 a second purchase of an area shaped like an arrowhead was made, and in 1842 and 1845 the Sauk and the Fox sold their remaining land in Iowa to the government. Later the Neutral Ground of the Winnebago, a tract that stretched diagonally from southwest to northeast across northern Iowa, was given up by that tribe. North and west of the Neutral Ground the Sioux relinquished their land in 1831 (Fig. 6-3).

Iowa became a territory on July 4, 1838. Its northern boundary had been vehemently argued between the territorial constituents and their delegates to Congress.[8] Many of the former demanded as the line a parallel of latitude through the mouth of the Blue Earth River near the bend of the Minnesota River. But the citizens' demands would have made Iowa unreasonably large and could not be supported by their own delegates in Washington, and in 1846, when Iowa became a state, Congress redetermined the border between Iowa and Minnesota as the parallel of latitude 40° 30' N. Because this parallel was also to govern surveys in Minnesota and North Dakota, it had to be accurately measured.

Under the direction of the Surveyor General at Dubuque, where the office for the surveys of the Wisconsin and Iowa districts was opened in 1838, township lines were surveyed between 1841 and 1850 up to the temporary lines of the Indian cessions, an expediency resulting in various step-like patterns.[9] The northwestern corners of the townships almost touched the diagonal line of the Winnebago tract. By 1851 the row of seven townships in the north had been subdivided. The row lies five miles south of the parallel 40° 30' N, which was to refer to the northeastern corner of the first township west of the Mississippi in the row and which was to be measured as far west as the Big Sioux River across recently ceded unexplored country that was still

*Ceded by the Sioux and Fox Indians to the half-breeds of the two tribes in 1824.

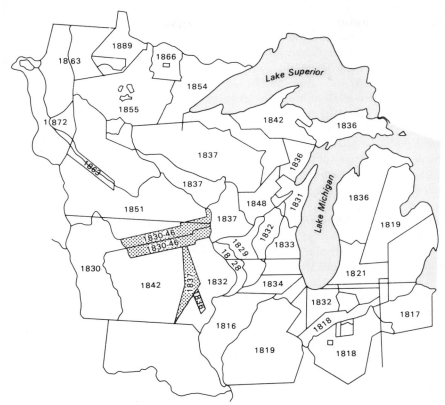

Figure 6-3. Indian cessions in the Old Northwest, prior to 1810. Note the arrow-shaped cession (1837) and the Winnebago Tracts in Iowa.

roamed by Sioux Indians. For protection of the survey party the Surveyor General at Dubuque suggested that dragoons be held ready at Fort Atkinson on the Turkey River in Winneshiek County.

Captain Lee of the U.S. Topographical Engineers established the starting point on the west bank of the Mississippi in the summer of 1849. The spot is across the road from the New Albin city dump and is marked by an inscribed cast iron pillar. In the 1960s New Albin asked to have the pillar moved from its unattractive and obscure site to a location by the Great River Road so that the public would become aware of the significance of the survey of the Iowa-Minnesota border, but the federal government refused permission and funds.

An epidemic of cholera delayed the survey, until spring, 1852, when Captain Andrew Talcott set out with a party of forty-three men: fourteen surveyors, a hunter, a doctor, an interpreter, four cooks, chainmen, flagmen, monument builders, teamsters, sod choppers, and general handymen. Their instructions were to determine the direction of the parallel by referring to the northwest corner of what became Lansing Township; that is, the corners of townships 99 and 100 north and ranges 4 and 5 west of the Fifth Principal Meridian. The point was 4¾ miles south of the parallel, and from it the surveyors struck a line straight north until it was intersected by a line straight west from the monument. This was the initial point for the survey of the parallel. The distance between the parallel and the row of townships, measured earlier, was only five miles, and sections one to six had to be left out in the townships directly south of the Iowa border. It gave land swindlers the opportunity to sell non-existent sections to unsuspecting land seekers.

The surveyors continued to the west and established points thirty-six miles apart by astronomical observation. From these points straight guide lines were run by transit sights, while offsets were calculated in adjustment of the slight curvature that a parallel of latitude more than 250 miles long shows on a flat surface (Fig. 6-4). Instructions for these calculated offsets were emphatically repeated. Eight stations were set up between the initial point and the Big Sioux River. The second point, called Station Washington, was near Chester in Howard County, Iowa, and was the first of five to be named after presidents of the United States; it became headquarters for the expedition. The surveyors reached the bank of the Big Sioux River on July 21, 1852, where a monument of Sioux quartzite was erected, of which nothing remains. At the end of the summer, when the high water of the Mississippi had receded, the last three miles of the parallel were surveyed, from the starting point east to the Mississippi. The pillar at New Albin is the only marker preserved of the more than 500 earth, wood, and stone monuments that were erected every half-mile along the 269 miles of the straight Iowa-Minnesota border.

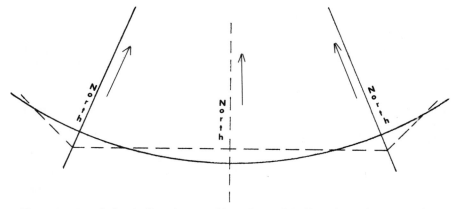

Figure 6-4. By calculated offsets the curved line of a parallel of latitude can be converted to a series of straight lines.

Today it is not possible to follow exactly the state boundary through Iowa's Hill Country by automobile. A state road runs from the New Albin pillar post by a farm three-quarters of a mile west of the town. The owner of the farm bought 200 feet of the three-mile strip left between his section line and the parallel after the survey. Beyond the farm, Allamakee County Road No. 5 branches off from Iowa State Road 26; it meets the boundary two miles farther west. During the next three and a half miles, the road winds back and forth between Iowa and Minnesota. On the ridge between Winnebago Creek and tributaries to the Upper Iowa, a marker has been moved from the center of the road to its southern edge, and an old building on the north side of the ridge is crossed by the state line. The excellent contoured farmland rolls away from the road to both sides and is laced with densely wooded valleys. Surveyors found the "surface rolling, soil clay and loam, 2nd rate and unfit for cultivation." In Houston County, the road runs on the Minnesota side, half a mile north of the state line and follows the quarter-section line in section 32 of Winnebago Township. Ten miles west of New Albin it becomes the main street in the village of Eitzen. By a right angle turn south, St. Luke's United Church of Christ is reached. Located directly on the state line, which runs through its south aisle, the church commands a good view of the up-and-down section road that represents the parallel measured in 1852 (Fig. 6-5). Children from farms on its north side go to school in Eitzen, those from farms on the south side are bussed to school in Dorchester, Allamakee County, Iowa.

West of Eitzen the surveyors described the country as "rolling, the soil first-rate and land good for farming." It still is. Soon the road veers to the south to avoid steep hills around the heads of creeks and leads into the

Figure 6-5. State Line Road running west from Eitzen Church, located in Iowa and Minnesota. To the left or south is Allamakee County, Iowa. To the right is Houston County, Minnesota.

Figure 6-6. The State Line Methodist Church. Arch over the iron gate in the background spells out "State Line Cemetery."

hamlet of Bee, the site of an early lumber mill and feed mill on Waterloo Creek. Bee has a population of about twenty people. Straddling the boundary is a store, now closed, where goods taxed in one state but not in the other were placed on the tax-free side of the building. By a small stream good for trout fishing, which is permitted in Iowa throughout the year but in Minnesota for seven months only, small signs nailed to a tree indicate which side is Minnesota and which is Iowa.

After several more detours to the north, where fine stands of maple proclaim the Minnesota Hardwood Memorial Forest in southeastern Minnesota, the roller-coaster gravel road continues straight west for ten miles to the intersection with Highway 139. At the northeast corner is a Methodist Church in front of which an iron gate proclaims "State Line Cemetery" (Fig. 6-6). A modern survey post marks the corner. Three miles on, the road detours to the north. The state line crosses eight entrenched meanders of the Upper Iowa River, where surveyors found "towering cliffs," "swift currents," and "perpendicular limestone." A road along this segment of the parallel was always impossible.

Florenceville, Iowa, approached by a section road from the south, and Granger, Minnesota, are almost directly north-south of each other. Still, a signboard on the state road announces Florenceville by pointing to the west and Granger by pointing to the east. Under the place names it is noted that the area was formerly Indian territory. West of Granger, after another curving detour to the north, the road follows the state line almost continuously to Chester on the Upper Iowa River. Less than half a mile east near its intersection with Highway 63 from Rochester, Minnesota, to Waterloo,

Iowa, a circular stone marker in the ground on the south side of the road gives the azimuth at Chester. The surveyors marked the "zenith position" on a large granite boulder which cannot be found. Here at Chester was Station Washington, fifty-five miles from the starting point in a straight line. The site of the expedition's headquarters is now occupied by a farm. The road continues straight west across land that was wet prairie or marsh with small lakes at the time of the survey. Today, much of it is drained.[10]

States tend to impress their authority on the landscape up to the very limits of their territory. The authority is visible in welcoming signs along main highways as well as through differences in road surfaces, materials used for road signs (wood in Minnesota but iron in Iowa), speed limits, and traffic regulations. Occasionally state authority is visible in human behavior, such as a motorcyclist's abrupt stop at the Iowa-Minnesota state line on the Great River Road to put on a helmet before crossing into Minnesota. Stricter liquor laws in Iowa (recently relaxed) resulted in considerable beer and liquor advertising on the Minnesota side. A State Line Inn is passed north of Chester. In Iowa fading billboards advertising colored oleomargarine remain from the years when Minnesota did not permit its sale. The boundaries of school districts, probably the most irritating enforcement of the boundary according to conversations with residents along the line, are not visible. Survey markers have to be searched for with a keen eye and are felicitously located with help from local farmers. Abraham Lincoln's words, quoted in the first chapter, are still valid: boundaries are "merely surveyor's lines, over which people may walk back and forth without any consciousness of their presence," unless one is, perchance, a student of geography.

Land Sales and Woodlots

The survey of townships and sections in the Hill Country was completed in the late 1850s. In Illinois, federal records were ready to be transferred to the state in 1860. In Iowa, the "surveying machinery was in process of being wound up," according to a report submitted to the Secretary of the Interior, in 1860, and only some isolated water-covered tracts and two townships remained to be subdivided. In Wisconsin, sizable areas remained to be surveyed only in the far northern region. Between the St. Croix River and the Fourth Principal Meridian, south of the third correction line (the latitude of Stillwater) 368 townships had been surveyed and subdivided. Southeastern Minnesota, which was surveyed between 1853 and 1855, covered 137 townships between the Mississippi and the second guide meridian west of the Fifth Principal Meridian.

The opening of land offices and public sales were announced by Presidential proclamation. The location of land offices depended on the boundaries of new land districts, which changed and overlapped depending on the prog-

ress of the survey, which in turn was affected by public demand. A map of the
establishment of land districts on both sides of the Mississippi during the
1850s shows the overlapping of districts, announced in different years, on
the Wisconsin side. Districts on the west bank of the Mississippi were
delineated by parallels in the tradition of westward expansion (Fig. 6-7).
When the acreage of land subject to private entry in any one district was
reduced to 100,000 acres, the land office and its records were transferred to
the nearest office, where the remaining unsold land was again put up for sale.

There was always a time-lapse between the Presidential proclamation of
the opening of a land office and the arrival of the appointed registers and
receivers. The transfer of records, equipment, and people took time, and
finding a suitable building was sometimes difficult. When a new office was

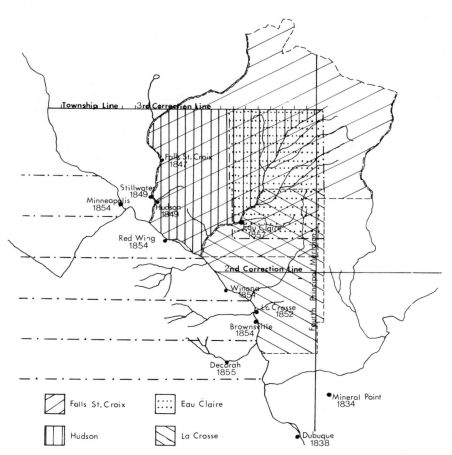

Figure 6-7. Land districts and location of land offices in the Upper Mississippi Hill Country.

opened at Chatfield, for example, the register and receiver with their wives and six children spent more than a week traveling the short distance between Brownsville and their destination over muddy roads and flooded streams. Opening dates were often postponed and the date of the first entry in the record book could be later still (Fig. 6-8).

Surveyors' township plats and notes could be studied by settlers and agents before they entered claims. Yet it is difficult to say if many of them did so, particularly in the Upper Mississippi Country, where pre-emptors had often preceded the survey. But the newcomers certainly studied the township plats *when* they entered their claims. Some of the early settlers found the claims they had staked out bisected by the surveyor's chain, and according to a county history, some squatters' claims—which seemed compact enough when originally marked out—"were sadly cut up and left laying around loose, after the compass and chain had been through them." Registers, receivers, and clerks were often ignorant of the area for sale, and deputy surveyors had stored away in their minds more than notes and plats revealed. They knew of promising sites for mills or towns, whereas only a waterfall or the fork of a road might appear on the plats. They knew where springs were located, where drainage was good, where a bench or terrace showed no flood marks. They knew the level terrain that offered a good prospect for a town. In 1837 it was charged in congressional debate that surveyors noted every valuable spot and sold the information they had acquired to speculators.[11] Such illegal transfer of information, however, was less likely to be related in pioneer diaries than were the hazards of overnight journeys to the nearest land office, the poor condition of the roads, and the names of friends, relatives, and neighbors.

The popular saying "to do a land-office business" was associated with public sales and not with day-by-day private entries. On many days nobody came to register, and often the register and receiver, who usually lived in the same building, were not on the premises. Temporary closings of the land offices, at times for personal reasons, were only occasionally announced in the local newspaper. When railroad grants of alternate sections were made, land offices officially closed for a week or more to prepare for the public sale of tracts in even-numbered sections. "The Railroad Bill has passed and the land offices are closed," noted a diarist in Olmsted County, Minnesota, in 1857. Often settlers were not able to buy their claims when a land office opened but continued to save or sought credit. Thus, some did not mind temporary closings. But while they relied on their pre-emption rights, still they feared public sales, where bidding might raise the price to more than $1.25 an acre.

Before the Pre-emption Act of 1841, settlers and territorial legislators had strongly pressured Congress to assist squatters. The Act of March 3, 1807, which interdicted all squatting, was suspended by Congress in 1838 for the

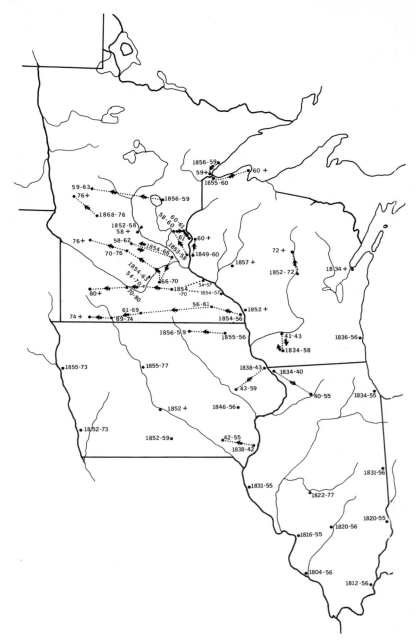

Figure 6-8. Land offices in Upper Mississippi Hill Country, with dates of openings and closings or transfer to another office.

Territory of Wisconsin, and in 1839 the legislative assembly of the Territory of Iowa re-enacted the statute.[12] The questionable legality of the authorization of pre-emption rights by a territory is not important at this point. But the timing is significant. For example, on October 1, 1838, a land office opened at Burlington, Iowa, which lay directly in the path of the westward rush of settlers. Only 220 entries had been made by October 19. But on that date, the first day of the public sale, 2000 men, all anxious to make entries, were camped around the town, among them the appointed bidders for claim associations. One of the bidders had a township map in hand, on which he and his associates had "adjusted the lines as well as they could."[13] After passage of the Pre-emption Act (1841) most claim holders in the Upper Mississippi Hill Country, with the possible exception of those who had leased mineral tracts, felt no pressing urge to begin the process of clearing their titles until threatened by the announcement of a public sale.

Reports of violence at land auctions were possibly dramatized; land offices were usually established in county seats or towns which were beginning to have orderly government. Galena had elected officials before the land office there opened in 1834. Dubuque was incorporated and its elected board of trustees had passed a number of ordinances before the Dubuque Land District was established and the land office opened on September 24, 1838. Mineral Point had been a county seat since 1829 with an estimated population of 500 in 1830.

The location of land offices was sometimes changed, for various reasons: At Mineral Point, careless selling of mineral land as agricultural tracts and a general political shake-up led to the appointment of a successful lead miner as receiver, and the office removed to Muscoda. A new register was appointed at Milwaukee, a new receiver at Green Bay, and the Surveyor General for Wisconsin and Iowa, located at Dubuque after 1838, was replaced. In 1843 the land office was moved back to Mineral Point from Muscoda.[14] At Galena, where land sold early and rapidly, the land office was consolidated in 1840 with the office at Dixon, Illinois—a move toward the southeast, not the northwest. In 1842, after 178,550 acres had been sold at Dubuque, its office was temporarily moved to Marion upon personal petition to Washington by one of its citizens. But in 1843 President Tyler ordered the return of the office to Dubuque until the Iowa Land District could be proclaimed. Iowa City was announced as the site of a land office on August 14, 1846, where the new record book listed only 575 entries during the first ten months, most of them for forty-acre tracts.[15]

Before the land office at La Crosse opened in 1853, settlers had to make their entries at Mineral Point, traveling thirty-six hours via Prairie du Chien and the Military Road. Entries during the first months were nominal, but by 1855 a force of ten to fifteen clerks was needed.[16] In that year, aside from sales covered by land warrants issued to soldiers of the Mexican War, cash sales for timbered and agricultural land amounted to $49,000 in April, $66,000 in May, $93,000 in June, $55,000 in July and $40,000 in August.[17] Keeping large sums of money and taking them periodically to the office of the Surveyor General at Dubuque was often a source of anxiety for the register, the same Swiss gentleman who was puzzled by a squatter's claim on a four-section corner at Gratiot's Grove (see pp. 66). The land office at La Crosse was open until 1866; by that time 2,500,614 acres had been sold for over three million dollars.

The Land District of La Crosse consisted of the townships surveyed west of the Fourth Principal Meridian (Fig. 6-7). The area east of it was covered by the Green Bay district. In 1848 land surveyed along the St. Croix River was offered at St. Croix Falls. This was a "detached survey"—an outlier on the frontier—and only the area close to the St. Croix River was "townshipped."[18] The register and receiver arrived in early July, the latter having had long experience at the land office in Quincy, Illinois. The first entry, made on July 24, was for 138 acres on the east bank of the St. Croix at Willow River, later called Hudson; the second entry was for 108 acres at Marine Mills on the Minnesota side of the St. Croix. The first public sale, which was publicized through handbills distributed among residents on both sides of the river, was held on August 12. A second sale took place on August 28. Both were unsuccessful. A mere $11,012 was received and 746 acres sold, most of them on the Minnesota side of the river. Only one crier (auctioneer) was engaged. The Commissioner of the General Land Office granted the register and receiver permission to leave "the distant and almost inaccessible point," provided that trustworthy substitutes were found to run the office, and in March 1849 the office was moved to Stillwater on the Minnesota side, where demand for land was greater.[19] A new land office was also opened at Hudson; there townships surveyed east of the St. Croix and west of the Chippewa were to be offered for sale.

Hudson's location was just as much a back door to Wisconsin as St. Croix Falls. "At first but a few immigrants found their way to Hudson, except such as by chance happened to stray away from Minnesota ... . The advantage of this section of the country was little known abroad, and consequently very few emigrants were attracted thither. The business of the land office was so small that there was barely one entry made in a month, and it is said, that the gentlemanly Register used to get up at nights in order to wait on a customer who came from a distance."[20] In 1860 the Hudson office was moved back to St. Croix Falls, where it finally closed in 1889.

At the northern margin of the Hill Country the land office at Eau Claire on the Chippewa River opened on July 1, 1857, a year of economic depression. After a slow beginning—only a few private entries, on land covered with hardwood and scattered pine, were made—extensive dealings in land warrants began to take place in Eau Claire. During the same time other land offices in the region also were deluged with military scrip.

The history of military bounty land goes back to the Revolution. Comparatively small acreages were awarded by congressional acts in 1811, 1812, and 1842. But under the Act of February 11, 1847, 7585 forty-acre warrants and 80,689 eighty-acre warrants issued for volunteers who had served twelve months in the Mexican War found their way to the General Land Office. Under the Act of September 28, 1850, 103,978 forty-acre, 57,715 eighty-acre, and 27,450 one-hundred-and-sixty-acre warrants were handed in at U.S. land offices in lieu of cash. And under the Act of March 22, 1852, 9070 forty-acre, 1699 eighty-acre, and 1223 one-hundred-and-sixty-acre warrants were tendered. The latter act made land warrants assignable and opened the way to speculation by absentee owners: buyers collected warrants in eastern cities and agents selected tracts in the west. Under the Act of March 3, 1855, warrants were also issued for 10-, 60-, and 100-acre tracts, which enabled any participant in a war of the United States, including those who had received warrants for less acreage earlier, to enter up to the new minimum of 160 acres. Proof of only fourteen days of service or of participation in one battle was needed, and 49,491 warrants for 80-acre tracts, 97,096 for 120-acre tracts, and 115,783 for 160-acre tracts reached the General Land Office.[21] Iowa led the nineteen states which had to accept military land warrants; Wisconsin was fourth in total receipts by 1879. Land offices in southeastern Minnesota opened in the mid-fifties, at a time when the speculation was peaking.

At Eau Claire there was no need for agents; former soldiers, now employees of lumber companies, sold their claims directly to their employers. In 1859 the Fox-Wisconsin River Improvement Company, after receiving a land grant for building a canal at Portage, urged that land be purchased by warrants only. Trading of warrants contributed to the turmoil in Eau Claire, where in the same year the land office was robbed and its safe dynamited. Yet the local historian commented: "The United States government now has the best system for surveying land ever adopted, and had the system for the sale and settlement of the Government domain been equally judicious much of the suffering and many of the hardships of the early pioneers would have been materially lessened.[22] The land office at Eau Claire continued to operate well into the twentieth century.

Military warrants were less frequent among early entries in northeastern Iowa. But they were numerous in the Turkey River Land District office, which comprised six rows of townships south of the state line and as far west as Chester. The office was opened in Decorah on December 23, 1855. Business was reportedly so brisk that land seekers bribed head clerks to enter claims during the night. Prairie land was most in demand. By the following summer the office moved west to Osage, a location reportedly selected by the register and the receiver because they had an interest in the townsite and its surrounding land. From Osage the office records were moved to the State Land Office at Des Moines in 1858.[23]

The establishment of offices in southeastern Minnesota at Brownsville, Winona, Red Wing, and Minneapolis was announced in 1854. In 1857 the office at Brownsville was moved to Chatfield and the offices at Red Wing and Winona to Faribault.

By 1860 all the land offices in the Upper Mississippi Hill Country, with the exception of La Crosse, had been moved farther west. At the end of the nineteenth century, Illinois no longer had a government land office; Iowa had but one—at Des Moines; Wisconsin had three—at Eau Claire, Wausau, and Ashland; and Minnesota had four—at Marshall, St. Cloud, Crookston, and Duluth. In 1859-60 only 47 acres were sold at Dubuque, 302 acres at Osage, and 856 acres at Chatfield. But in Wisconsin 1167 acres were sold at Hudson. At La Crosse, from which land in northern Wisconsin was also sold, 3043 acres went for the regular price of $1.25 an acre and 4468 acres for $1.00 an acre [24] (the price for lower-quality land that had been on the market for more than ten years was reduced through the Graduation Act of 1854).[25] At Eau Claire 1427 acres sold for $1.25 an acre in 1859-60. These three offices (Eau Claire, Hudson, and La Crosse) together accounted for 10,106 acres out of a total of 11,400 sold in that year in all of Wisconsin, but little of this land was in the Hill Country.

In the Hill Country west of the Mississippi Winona was the fastest-growing river port in the 1850s. Its land office, opened in early January 1855, had listed 748 entries by October 28, some as far west as Rice County. Yet sales were slow during the first few months. The first two claims, dated January 17 and 29, were for tracts in Wilson Township adjacent to Winona Township. Only seven more claims were entered up to April 2, one of which was farther inland on the prairie of Winona County, southeast of Rochester. During April most entries covered tracts around Rochester and along the Middle Branch of the Zumbro River. By the end of May the plat of Winona Township was nearly covered, and during June the western half of Olmsted County was dotted with entries. Some bottomland in the valleys of the Rollingstone and Whitewater rivers northwest of Winona was also occupied.[26] The Whitewater Valley offers an excellent example for the study of sequent occupance* in the Hill Country, beginning here with land entries. In Chapter 8 we shall see how settlement transformed the land.

The Whitewater drainage basin, which extends over parts of Winona, Olmsted, and Wabasha counties, covers over 320 square miles. The Middle Fork of the Whitewater is joined by the North Fork at the beginning of the

---

*Derwent Whittlesey, in an article entitled "Sequent Occupance" (*Annals* of the Association of American Geographers, June, 1929) created this term for human occupance of land, which according to Whittlesey, "carries within itself the seed of its own transformation."

main valley about two miles south of the town of Elba and by the South Fork directly north of the town (Fig. 6-9). After heavy rains, the location of drainage outlets for the major part of the watershed creates severe flood conditions between Elba and Beaver Creek in the main valley, where the bluffs come close together and form a bottleneck. Yet exploring claim seekers could hardly have been aware of the hydrological pattern. Their approach was from Winona along the upland territorial road through short side valleys where creeks followed steep gorges cut into the sedimentary rock by glacial streams. The many small rapids and falls along these valleys provided attractive but rather secluded mill sites. The plats for townships 107 and 108 N., R. 10 W. of the Fifth Principal Meridian (Elba and Whitewater townships), covered the main stretch of the valley with its bluffs, ridges, and adjoining upland. West of Whitewater township is Quincy Township in Wabasha County. Let us follow the entries in the Winona Land Office Record Book for this central part of the Whitewater drainage basin.[27]

The first claim in the Whitewater basin was made on May 22, 1855, for 160 acres of bottomland, a square quarter section on a branch of the North Fork in Quincy Township. Three days later, 120 acres were entered for a tract along Beaver Creek in Whitewater Township by a settler whose descendant still resided on the same tract in the 1950s. Claims on the upland between the South Fork and the territorial road followed. An entry numbered 168, another quarter-section claim on the North Fork in Quincy Township, was scribbled in the small space allowed for the column called "Section and part of" as follows: "W½ of NW¼ + NW¼ of SW¼ of Sect. 2 + NE¼ of SE¼ of Sect. 3." This quarter-section consisted of one 80- and two 40-acre tracts in two sections along the northern township line, toward which "deficiencies and excesses" were pushed during surveying. Thus it was recorded as containing 159.09 acres and selling for $198.86 ¼ at $1.25 per acre. The tract was subsequently subdivided, but one can reconstruct the claim on the plat of the county atlas of 1896 (Fig. 6-10).

The first entry on the township plat of Elba was numbered 238 and made on August 13 for 160 acres of river bottomland on both sides of the North Fork (Fig. 6-9b). It was described in the record book as "NW¼ of the SE¼ + N½ of the SW¼ + SW¼ of NW¼ of Sect. 25," T. 107 N., R. 10 W. A week later, the second entry in Elba Township, numbered 432, was for 120 acres, composed of three forties and shaped to extend over bottomland along the South Fork east of Elba. On October 6, a claim numbered 440 comprised two adjacent 80-acre tracts on the upland in sections 32 and 33. On October 15 and 17, claims 506 and 546 were for 80 and 120 acres in the valley at the spot that became the town of Elba. On October 19, claims 571 and 572 extended across the river in the broad valley bottom south of Elba. Claims 579 and 580 were 120- and 80-acre tracts on the upland in sections 34 and 27. On October 20 and 22, claims 606 and 609 were 40-acre tracts on the North

Fork, undoubtedly selected for the location of Fairwater Mills later on. Most of claim 666 covered the bottomland along the South Fork east of Elba. It was another quarter section composed of forties and described as "NE¼ of the NE¼ of Sect. 10 + NW¼ + E½ of the NW¼ of Sect. 11," T. 107 N. R. 10 W. Claims 721 and 722 on October 26 were for 120 and 80 acres adjacent to claim 579 on the upland, which left one 40-acre tract vacant between the two claims. The sixteen claims entered between August 13 and October 26 comprised a total of 1720 acres.

These examples, selected from many, must suffice to prove that quarter sections were not necessarily square from the start. All the forms that 160- and 120-acre tracts can take when they are composed of forties appeared among the first 748 entries at the land office in Winona in 1855. It is obvious that claimants knew which land they wanted and that they shaped their

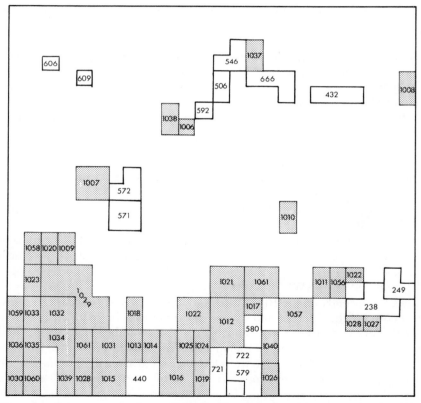

Figure 6-9a. Private entries and tracts (shaded) sold in 1855 at public auction in Elba Township (compare with opposite map).

claims to fit topographical conditions. The composite or irregular quarter sections spelled out above merely illustrate three possibilities under the law of 1832, which authorized the sale of 40 acres as the smallest unit. In the Hill Country, settlers were challenged to compose as many forms as possible in order to adjust to bluffs, to meandering streams and valley bottoms, to terraces above flood-prone bottomlands, and to gorges with promising mill sites. The tracts had to be aligned with cardinal directions and had to be contiguous; that is, they could not merely touch each other at the corners, but had to be adjacent. Thus the number of adjustments the quarter-section claimant could make was reduced to nineteen variations for 160 acres, to six

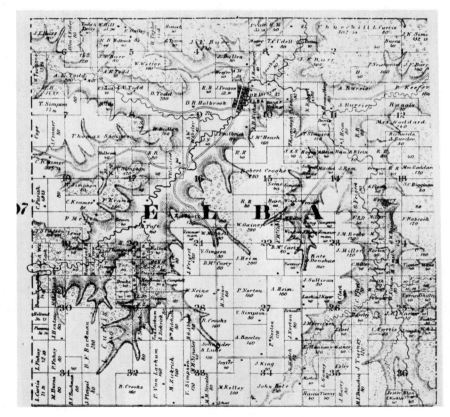

Figure 6-9a. Plat of Elba Township, Winona County. The Middle Fork of the Whitewater is seen running diagonally from section 30 (lower left) to section 3 (upper right). The South Fork (lower right, section 36) joins the main stream near the village of Elba in section 10. In sections 30, 29, and 32 is the Curtis Tract, mostly upland. Ten-acre woodlots are found in section 25. (*Bennett & Smith, Map of Winona County, 1867*)

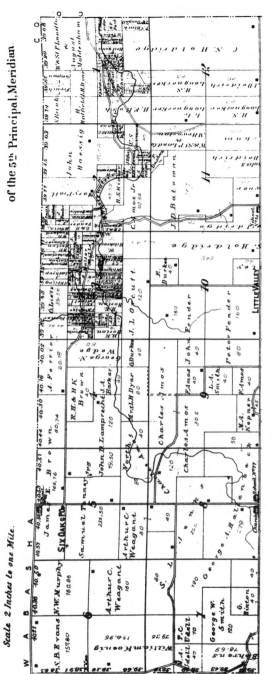

Figure 6-10. Pioneer farmers divided forties in woodlots along the North Fork of the Whitewater River. Deficiencies and excesses of acreage appear as exactly measured 40-acre tracts, called government lots, along northern and southern township lines.

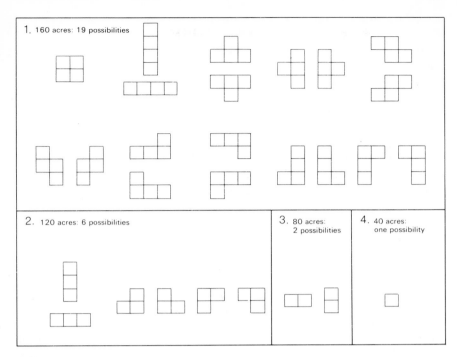

Figure 6-11. Possible layout of land claims, ranging from one possibility for a 40-acre tract to nineteen for 160 acres.

for 120 acres, and to two for 80 (Fig. 6-11). The forty as a modular unit is characteristic of the survey in the Hill Country. Square quarter sections were frequent only on township plats that covered level country.

Decisions regarding the townships and sections to be offered at public sales of land were often rather arbitrary. At the first public sale at Winona in November 1855, the unclaimed land was offered only in eight townships, none farther west than Elba and Whitewater townships and none in Wabasha and Olmsted counties, although the latter were equally desirable and also partially claimed. During the first two days of the sale, 126 tracts were sold, only two tracts on the third day. Of the entries numbered 749 to 1022, forty-one were for tracts in Elba Township. The first sixteen sales were for upland tracts in the southern sections, most of them for 160 acres or less. Two sales were for 240 acres, numbered 1012 and 1016 in Elba Township. No land sold for more than $1.25 an acre on November 1. But on November 2, upland tracts in sections 31, 32, and 33 were sold for $1.70, $1.85, $2.50 and $2.75. Four hundred acres represented the largest sale of a contiguous tract to one party, Lyman Curtis, entry No. 1029, whose name appears also in sections 30 and 32 on the map of 1867 on a contiguous holding of 640 acres (Fig. 6-9). Mr. Curtis owned a section—but by size, not by form.

The largest acreage sold at the public auction was on the upland. In the valley north and south of Elba only three tracts adjoining earlier claims were sold. Subsequent to the sale during the remainder of 1855 and 1856, private entries almost filled the northern part of Elba Township. On the township's plat, as on most other plats of southeastern Minnesota, five numbers appear after or below "LW" (land warrant) which almost efface the faintly written entry numbers for tracts. It would be very difficult to establish the chronological sequence of entries from a filled-out township plat. Once a plat was covered with entries it became a document for the "stouthearted" student, as one scholar of public land policy put it.[28]

WOODLOTS

In 1867, when the first county atlas of Winona County was published and ten years after Winona's land office had been moved west to Faribault in Rice County, a few forty-acre tracts were still public land in Elba Township. But, being in the gorges, those tracts were inaccessible. Ten-acre tracts, the result of dividing forty acres, appear in sections 20 and 25 of the map of Elba Township in the atlas. These were woodlots. Wooded land could not be bought from the government in tracts of less than forty acres, and, since most farmers did not need forty acres for personal use, timbered land was often subdivided and resold soon after the date of its first sale. Two cases, one in Elba and the other in Quincy Township will serve as illustrations.[29]

On September 20, 1856, the southeast quarter of the southwest quarter of section 19 in Elba Township became private property. On October 3, ten of the forty acres were sold. The description of ten acres by metes and bounds; that is, by rods, chains, and links, took three nine-inch lines, and will be spared the reader. Three years later twenty acres "with the privilege of raising a dam" were sold off from the remaining thirty acres for $750, and in 1861 the same twenty acres were resold for $799. In 1863 a small parcel was sold off from the remaining ten acres for $37.50. In Quincy Township, where the claim of a composite quarter section was described earlier, an 80-acre tract entered in 1855 was sold and resold in 1856. One year later two five-acre woodlots from the same tract were sold for $100 each, and in 1860 fourteen more acres—ten at $100 an acre and four at $36 an acre—were sold (compare to Fig. 6-10). Pioneer farmers with $50 to spare for an extra wooded forty at $1.25 an acre could make a 300 per cent profit by dividing it into eight five-acre woodlots at $5.00 an acre. This was hardly land speculation, merely capitalism at work on a small scale. Woodlots generally sold for $5.00 an acre in Minnesota and Iowa during the 1860s, but in southeastern

Minnesota, an acre could fetch $10.00 depending on accessibility, the quality of the timber, and the demand for wood.

Most farmers gained additional income from hauling and selling wood. Every winter during the 1860s the St. Charles newspaper carried notices of the scarcity and high price of wood. Hauling could be difficult during December and January due to the "January thaw," which made use of sleighs hazardous. Alternate freezing and thawing caused a thin crust of ice to form on the snow; draft animals could break through this crust easily. One settler on the broad prairie ridge between the Whitewater and Zumbro rivers who had searched for several months for a wooded lot noted that in September (1856) he had his "40 of timber run out [surveyed]" near Beaver in the Whitewater valley. In December he recorded that he had started to draw a load of provisions for a Wabasha man, but, after waiting a day because of rain and hail, was forced to stop at a tavern. The next day he could move his team only a few rods: "The crust was so sharp it cut the feet and legs of the oxen very badly." So he sheltered them, returned home, and started out again the next day with five yoke of oxen and ten men, who, by shoveling and "with their own feet" broke a road. For the rest of the winter he was unable to haul logs because of bad roads, and two years later he bargained his wooded forty at Beaver for a land warrant. Thereafter he helped himself to wood from what he mistook for a vacant lot, later paying fifteen dollars to the woodlot's owner for damages. "So much for meddling with what is not your own" were the words he entered in his diary on March 12, 1858.[30]

Such regret was not typical. The practice of cutting wood on land of absentee owners was widespread. Local residents near West Liberty, Iowa, helped themselves to many loads of wood from privately owned land along Wapsipinicon Creek, which they called "Canada." By the use of this term the residents admitted the theft of wood, since they associated Canada with the place to which "bigger rascals" escaped after committing crimes.[31] In fact, everyone used unsold government land for grazing livestock, cutting hay, and procuring wood, considering it de facto communal property, comparable to the legalized commons in colonial New England. With regard to stealing timber from the Public Domain, the U.S. Land Commissioner wrote in 1865: "When Community interests conflict with law and when public opinion is in conflict with its enforcement, it becomes virtually inoperative." [32]

In southeastern Minnesota and northeastern Iowa, woodlots were most frequent along winding streams. Private roads leading to and along the edge of the woodlots dated from the early years of settlement. Some are still used for hauling wood for fireplaces in nearby towns. Today the timber is second growth. Some "personal," as they were called, woodlot trails still exist in central Iowa.[33] Old wire fences along the closely spaced property lines cannot be readily seen when driving through the valleys, where today the woodlands look "natural." Yet the woods consist of many parcels, each of which has its own history of usage and ownership (Fig. 6-12).

With the first change of ownership after the purchase of a tract from the land office, the work of surveyors under contract with the government was over. Private surveyors or the men who bought or sold tracts and lots paced off the parcels themselves: 250 paces, double steps, were the usual surveyors' unit measures. Federal legislation and rules for deputy surveyors did not require that the interior center (the crosspoint of lines in a quartered section) of sections be marked by a post. County surveyors were later required by state rules to designate forties by placing new posts equidistant between half-mile section posts. It was expected that if the government division overran or fell short, each portion would gain or lose proportionately. The difference between distances measured by plumb lines as seen from the air, described in Chapter 4, and distances paced off on steep slopes could be considerable. "He farms 160 acres on his forty," says the vernacular. This is a partial explanation of the discrepancies between the sizes of tracts as described in surveyors' records and the surface acreages reported by farmers.[34]

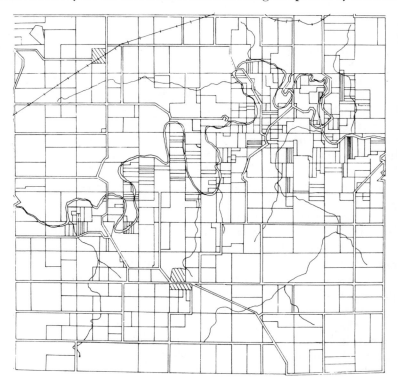

Figure 6-12. On a plat map of 1930 the early woodlots along the North Branch of the Root River indicate the presence of heavily dissected land in Pleasant Grove Township, Olmsted County, Minnesota.

Settlers could rarely see the lines of their properties in hilly wooded country. But they had seen their tract on the township plat. An illiterate could watch his particular tract being outlined by a clerk in the appropriate section or sections. The vision of the lines guided a man when he paced off distances between equidistant points. He must have imagined his forty acres to be a square unit, but he could not have thought of or seen a composite quarter section as a square. Yet the squares of the checkerboard became the popular image of the landscape of the Middle West. The origin of this stereotype merits explanation.

The Checkerboard Image

The definition of "chequer" in *The Oxford English Dictionary* is "to divide or partition into square sections by crossing lines." Nineteenth century author and artist George Catlin probably was referring to crossplowing or rectangular fields when in 1841 he wrote: "I have seen the rich Louisianan checkering out his cotton and sugar plantations."[35] Catlin may have imagined the plan of a plantation or fields and lines, but of course it was highly improbable that he had ever seen a bird's-eye view of a checkerboard landscape.

The term "chessboard" has often been used by Europeans in descriptions of the Middle West. About seventy-five years ago, a French scholar of the U.S. Land Survey referred to *jeu de dame*—chequers—in speaking of the rectangular landscape. More recently a British geographer captioned an air photograph of a Middle West landscape with a quotation from Lewis Carroll's *Through the Looking Glass:* Alice, in looking over the country, says: "I declare, it's marked just like a large chessboard," and a Swiss geographer has titled a chapter in his book on the United States, "The Chessboard Structure of the Modern American Cultural Landscape."[36]

North Americans prefer the term "checkerboard" to "chessboard," but the meaning is the same. Both terms are applied loosely. For example, textbook writers use "checkerboard" in describing air photographs of farm-land where the lines are section roads crossing at right angles but where fields are variously proportioned rectangles and not alternate light and dark squares. And we can hardly assume that alternate light and dark squares are in the soil conservationist's mind who writes: "There are no agronomic and other technical programs adequately tailored to meet the unique needs of areas heavily checkerboarded with agricultural and urban land use."[37]

The alternation of squares for the parceling of land goes back to the Ordinance of May 20, 1785, which stipulated that townships sold entire be alternated with townships sold by lots. When the system of the plan is drawn (Fig. 3-2, p. 45) it resembles a checkerboard. The purpose of alternation was to attract both large and small buyers. We cannot prove another consideration; namely, that improvements made on small tracts adjacent to large, extensively worked holdings might increase the value of the large tracts. The idea fits John Locke's theory that land has no value without labor and that it attains increasing value with the progress of settlement. It also agrees with the modern thought that change in the value of occupied areas will change the value of interspersed vacant areas. Also, during the nineteenth century, railroads and canals were expected to increase the value of alternately located tracts, an expectation that was reflected in a series of acts granting land to companies and states for internal improvement.

The first of these acts gave to Indiana a nineteen-foot right-of-way on each side of a projected canal that was to connect the Wabash River and Lake Erie. An additional grant in 1827 allowed "a quantity of land equal to one-half of five sections in width and reserving alternate sections for the United States." The Pre-emption Act of 1841 stipulated that the minimum price of $1.25 per acre for government land should be increased only when Congress granted alternate sections to states for construction of canals or railroads or other public improvement. The government had "the right to raise the minimum price on any land reserved to the United States alternate to other sections."[38] After 1827, eight land grants were made for canal construction; Wisconsin received one for the Fox-Wisconsin River canal in 1848. One stipulation of these grants was that alternate sections held by the government were to be sold for $2.50 an acre, twice the minimum price asked elsewhere. As John Calhoun had pointed out in 1846, the government would receive the same amount of money that way. Half the number of sections sold at twice the minimum price would yield the same sum as if all sections were sold at $1.25 an acre. Some settlers objected to paying twice the usual sum for government land to subsidize the railroad, but apparently many more were willing to pay the price. The first large grant was made to the Illinois Central Railroad in 1850; the line sold about half of its grant, more than a million acres, for more than fifteen million dollars during the first three years, and the sale of alternate government sections proceeded proportionately.[39] The sale of alternate sections at $2.50 an acre became general policy and a standard provision of railroad grants.[40]

In 1852 John Murray Forbes of the Chicago, Burlington, and Quincy Railroad commented on abuses suffered by immigrants on their way from ports to the interior. "The railroads which are at last chequering the West in all directions," he wrote, "will give a new element of certainty to Emigrants."[41] Forbes must have referred to maps of projected railroad routes, along which alternate odd-numbered sections inside the six-mile limit were shaded, crossed, or otherwise marked. If he had no such maps in hand, he must have envisioned the sections. And certainly his vision was not affected by the concession of "indemnity selections" or "lieu lands," tracts that railroad land agents had selected within fifteen miles of the rail line to compensate for acreage already occupied in odd-numbered sections inside the six-mile limit.

An example of how the problem was dealt with is found in the "Act making a grant of land to the Territory of Minnesota in alternate sections to aid in the construction of certain railroads in said territory," dated March 3, 1857. It granted land "for a railroad from Winona via St. Peter to a point on the big Sioux River south of the forty-fifth parallel of north latitude every alternate section designated by odd numbers for six sections in width on each section of said road. But in case it should appear that the United States should have ... sold any sections or any parts thereof granted as aforesaid ... it should be lawful for any agent ... to select ... from the lands nearest to the tiers of sections above specified so much land in alternate sections or parts of sections as should be equal to such lands as the United States had sold."[42] The amount of land to be granted was specifically defined by sections, not by square miles: "a quantity of land not exceeding one hundred and twenty sections for which each of said roads and branches and included within a continuous length of twenty miles of each of said roads and branches might be sold." The state of Minnesota executed the trust on March 8, 1857, authorizing the Transit Railroad Company to select land. But in southeastern Minnesota square-mile sections could be found only in rough land close to the Mississippi. Because so much land had been sold previously, widely dispersed tracts, many of them forty acres, were selected to make up the total acreage of "lieu land" (see Fig. 4-5). In areas farther west, where railroad grants had preceeded settlement, vacant odd-numbered sections in the six-mile limit were generally available. Yet even there, a few earlier entries of eighty or forty acres made it necessary to go beyond the six-mile limit for additional small tracts. An example is the location of 252,356 acres deeded to the Winona and St. Peter Railroad Company in 1872 in Redwood County, Minnesota (Fig. 4-5, pp. 68-69).

Maps illustrating the checkerboard pattern are usually from the West, where the section landscape was much less disturbed by previous claims. A good illustration is a map of alternate holdings by sections in Paullin's *Atlas of the Historical Geography of the United States*, which shows the tracts held by the Weyerhauser Timber Company, the state of Washington, and the Northern Pacific Railway in 1914.[43] The starkness of the pattern was a function of timing. Regular or interrupted, the pattern visible on maps was not visible in reality.

One cause of settlers' opposition to government railroad grants was that lands were withheld from regular sales until railroad agents had made their selection of lieu lands, often the best tracts. An additional complication arose when limits of the grants inside which railroads were selecting land overlapped. An illustration of the sequence of entries is T. 26 N., R. 11 W. of the Fourth Principal Meridian, L'Eau Galle Township in Dunn County at the northern margin of the Hill Country. In section 36, surveyors in 1848 noted "L'Eau Gallé Mills" and a field dating from pre-survey years. The plat was approved in 1849 and received by the register at Hudson in August of the same year. An early entry for 120 acres is drawn in and shaded with unusual care in section 1. At Hudson the register was not rushed. Entries up to 1856 were not numerous; there were as many in even-numbered sections as in the odd-numbered sections. Most of the latter were traversed by the Eau Galle River (sections 11, 13, and 25) or by a tributary stream (sections 9, 21, and 23). Six entries in section 11 were paid with land warrants, all of which were issued in 1855. In 1856, Wisconsin received a grant in the township for the Chicago, St. Paul, and Minneapolis Railroad, and later a line was drawn on the plat to indicate the southern limit extended to ten miles, inside which odd-numbered alternate sections were designated as "RR" land. Only five odd-numbered sections were fully free of entries and available to the railroad. The even-numbered section inside the six-mile limit granted to the railroad was offered for sale in 1859. A checkerboard pattern can perhaps be recognized only in the northwestern corner of the original document.

In T. 27 N., R. 15 W. northwest of Eau Galle Township there is a clearer checkerboard pattern. Far fewer settlers had taken land in its odd-numbered sections before a grant was made to a railroad (Fig. 6-13). This area was close to Hudson where, in 1857, the government still held one million acres—land that was to be opened to private entry "as soon as the lines of the land-grant railroads were permanently located. [44] It is doubtful that buyers were impressed by a checkerboard pattern on township plats in government or railroad land offices; "checkerboard" did not seem to be part of the vocabulary of contemporary writers.

But township plats in county atlases and on county wall maps contributed to public awareness of section lines and numbers. County land-ownership maps hung in offices, dry-goods stores, banks, and other gathering places. They were based on government township plats and supplemented by information—often hastily gathered by a surveyor who had been commissioned by a publisher—on houses, woods, orchards, bridges, and the like. About 1000 copies, usually at $5 each, were usually printed and distributed to subscribers, who had been convinced of the wisdom of owning such a document by canvassers or by ads in newspapers or by the endorsements of county officials, bankers, and other prominent local persons. When a subscriber's establishment appeared in a small lithographic view along the margin of the map, he paid between $36 and $60 for the privilege. Including their ornate borders, these maps, printed on four separate sheets, were between five and six feet square. Often they were colored by hand, mounted on cloth, and protected with a coat of varnish.

The firm of Henry Francis Walling of Boston, which published many such maps for the eastern states, also published some for the Hill Country, such as that of Grant County, Wisconsin, the earliest county map for that state held by the Library of Congress. County maps were also produced by two

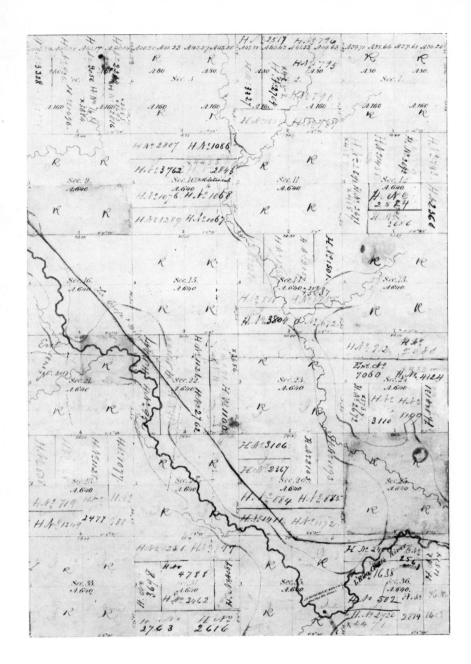

Figure 6-13. Checkerboard pattern on the plat of T. 27 N., R. 15 W. of the Fourth Principal Meridian formed by the "RR"-designated sections reserved for the Chicago, St. Paul and Minneapolis Railroad.

Figure 6-14. Residence of a subscriber to the *Illustrated Historical Atlas of the State of Minnesota*, 1874.

government agencies, the Confederate Army Engineers and the Texas General Land Office. The township plats in county atlases were printed from earlier county maps at scales ranging from 1:3960 to 1:600,000.[45]

Every atlas had a full page devoted to the explanation of the U.S. Land Survey, more informative than the occasional appendix on the survey in geography textbooks today. Owners of atlases and their visitors poured over these volumes in the family parlor; in them they could see their names in print inside the rectangular outlines of their holdings, next to a section number in heavy print (Fig. 6-10). They probably studied their property lines on the township plats very closely. On county maps in state atlases the subscribers could see a small facsimile of their houses (Fig. 6-14)

COUNTY HISTORIES

In county histories hundreds of pages were filled with "biographies," much of the information obtained through interviews. The format hardly varied from county to county in the nineteenth century. In the preface publishers thanked local officials, newspapers, and citizens for their help. Townships were listed alphabetically, but the residents of each township were listed in no discernible order. The first part of a biographical sketch identified the location of settlers by section numbers; those persons who immediately settled in a town and bought no land at all were rare.

The following notations are typical: "He surrounded some land in section thirty-four." "He is now on the line of sections twenty-four and twenty-five." "He surrounded a farm in section five and he still stands guard over it." "He resides on the northeast corner of section 30, where he settled in 1853." "He purchased eighty acres of his farm from Jonah Seaman, eighty acres from A. C. Daley, and forty acres from C. C. Woodman. His farm now contains 210 acres. He resides on section 9, town 6, range 6 west" (identification by congressional township data was necessary when a civil township extended into more than one government township). "On July 1, 1856, he came with wife, niece and nephew, settling in section 21, town 10 north, range 4 west, where he still lives. He entered forty acres of his farm, and bought forty acres ... making all the improvements himself." "He made a claim of a quarter section of land, forty acres on each of the four sections numbered 22, 23, 26, 27." "The three located on section 30 live in town 14 range 3 west, where they erected a sawmill on the Kickapoo River.[46] "Linemindedness" is evident throughout, reflected in such phrases as "he is now on the line of sections twenty-seven and twenty-eight," or "he pre-empted 160 acres in sections twenty-seven and twenty-eight."

Only rarely is a geographic feature mentioned. If one is mentioned, it is likely to be the name of a spring near a mill or of a major road on which a tavern or hotel was located. Occasionally phrases such as "next to a fine spring," or "near a bluff," crop up. After about 1910, when compilers of these volumes relied heavily on histories written in the last quarter of the nineteenth century, the phrasing changed slightly; townships and places were identified by name and by more graphic descriptions of locations of people. The following examples indicate the transition: "In 1856 he located on a homestead of 160 acres in section five, Saratoga Township. From a neighbor, Mr. Russell, he purchased 160 acres." He "owns and operates the old farm of his parents in Jefferson Township." In 1894 "he came to Bee on the state line between Iowa and Minnesota. He bought forty acres of land in 1899 in the vicinity, all but six acres of which had been broken. He also added to his land four acres." In the 1960s, locations are brought up-to-date. For instance, he "came to Eau Claire in 1855. He farmed on the Truax Prairie until 1867. He bought a farm on what is now Rudolph Road and Benton Avenues where his descendants still live." After the last two sentences the writer mentioned the township, range, and section numbers of Oak Grove Township and added, "Today (1960) the boundary line may be more graphically described as running from the Chippewa River through the Courthouse Square westerly, and through the side of the old high school."[47]

Did early settlers when reading about themselves and their friends think of section numbers as places? Did readers of biographies think of people "on the other side of the ridge," "farther up the valley," or "on hogback" when they read section numbers? Farmers say "I live in the coulee" or "on Hoosier ridge" today. Were section numbers comparable to street and house numbers in towns or similar to our use of numbers for highways? "They live in the 3800 block," and "then you come to the second alphabet" are examples from Minneapolis. Today we drive to Madison, Wisconsin by "going 94," or we "change to 14 at Rochester to get to Winona" or we "take 61" along the Mississippi. Roads are either lines with numbers (on a map) or signs with numbers. In pioneer times, section numbers were carved on posts and trees and certainly were observed by settlers when they cleared the land. The numbers were not conspicuous and did not last long, but they were very important to their owners, who had secured title to their land and improved it by hard work year after year.

I have not found the word "checkerboard" in pioneer histories of the Upper Mississippi Hill Country, but I have not read all of the dreary volumes that exist. Nor have I heard farmers use the word today. But the use of "section" instead of a "square mile" to indicate the size of a tract has entered the vernacular, carried over from the survey and from legal documents. Farmers also use the term "quarter section" for 160 acres, although many talk of their holding in multiples of "forties." This means that their quarter section is not a square-shaped quarter of a section. While (in the words of John Fraser Hart) "the common notion that the Middle West is a checkerboard of 160 acre homesteaded farms divided into four square-acre fields has little basis in fact," the idea is still publicized.[48]

Some writers use the stereotype discerningly. Joseph Schafer, Wisconsin's agricultural historian, wrote in 1926 that "older Wisconsin was checkered by the surveyors' townships." He obviously had in mind a map showing exterior township lines as on Figure 5-6, p. 99). A mental reservation can also be reflected by quotation marks; Griffith Taylor used them when he wrote of "the universal checkerboard plan of the township." In modern textbooks the term is a cliché, such as the title "checkerboard" for an air photograph of wheatfields in Montana or western Canada. The pictures of long strips of cultivated fields alternating with strips of fallow land—light and dark or on colored photographs, yellow and brown—remind observers who are less pre-conditioned than Americans; of stripes on an awning. The squares of a checkerboard as a perception may fit the landscape of section roads to some degree. However, they do not describe the agricultural landscape of the Upper Mississippi Hill Country.

In 1852, when Mr. Forbes found the railroads "chequering the West," field borders and fences were spottily distributed on the frontier. As visible phenomena the survey lines emerged gradually, through plowed fields, fences and roads, and fundamentally, through the deeply ingrained urge of people to observe property lines.

7 EMERGENCE OF THE SURVEY LANDSCAPE

Agricultural Technology and Clearing

In 1860 population density in the lead-mining region was 18 persons per square mile, based on township averages, and by 1870 most townships in the Upper Mississippi Hill Country had reached the same density. Several rural townships in the lead-mining region and La Crosse and Monroe counties in Wisconsin reached the peak of their population in the same census year, but in most townships of the Hill Country the population peaked in 1890 and 1900. River valleys and ridges were occupied fairly continuously by 1870. A lower rural population density in the less dissected parts of the region derived from larger farm holdings. In general, the Driftless Area was less productive than the glaciated part—not so much because of poor soils but because steep slopes and rough land impossible to cultivate made up a proportion of individual farms.[1]

Pioneers preferred to settle in valleys and on rolling upland as close as possible to roads and timber. Some settlers may have paid more than $1.25 an acre for land sold at auctions or for land in even-numbered sections inside the limits of railroad grants, but over-all, they paid the same for government land irrespective of location and soil quality. In 1860 the Commissioner of the General Land Office wrote that the minimum price of $1.25 an acre "received no complaint from the citizens" and added: "The system is perfect, the price moderate, and the settler is secured in his improvements."

The improvements needed to give the pioneer farmer a feeling of security were, first of all, a shelter. Shelters varied considerably. Occasionally, a family used their wagon during the first season. Some shelters were dugouts excavated in the side of a hill and supplemented by logs; others were log

151

cabins chinked with mortar. Chimneys were made of stone, at times of brick, with stovepipes brought along from the East. Animal shelters consisted of crotched posts with sticks and branches laid across for a temporary roof. Barns were also made from crotched poles placed eight or ten feet apart in three rows, the center pole being the highest. Long poles were laid on top of the crotches, and leaning posts were set against the long poles. Before straw was at hand, prairie grass was piled up for walls.

As soon as possible, the second improvement was undertaken—clearing the natural vegetation and breaking the soil for a first crop. The small fields of the first subsistence crops—potatoes, rutabagas, or other root crops—and grain, which served for food and as the first cash crop, had to be fenced in immediately. Clearing techniques changed little during pioneer times. It is estimated that the average rate of clearing was five acres a year; a single man could not break a larger area besides tilling and harvesting the land he had already cleared. Occasionally a pioneer biography mentions that a farmer cleared ten, even twenty, acres in one off-season; this was most probably oak savanna, called "oak openings." First clearing never included stump removal.

The main tools used in clearing still were those of colonial times, a felling axe, a one-or two-man crosscut saw, a cant hook for rolling logs, and log tongs ("come-alongs"), used for carrying the cut logs. After girdling—the complete removal of bark to deaden the tree—and burning, rudimentary tillage was possible. But the dead trunks had to be cut down and burnt soon to create a clearing. Stumps still remained, of course. Stump removal, a pioneer's heaviest work, is not treated explicitly in early literature, possibly because the disagreeable task was performed gradually over the years. Sometimes the stumps merely rotted away. No satisfactory stump-puller was on the market, although a tripod-like rig with pulleys and ropes that were tied around the stumps and pulled by oxen, came into fairly wide use toward the end of the nineteenth century, when logged-off lands in north-central Wisconsin were up for sale. The use of dynamite was dangerous and practical only for very large stumps.[2]

In the driftless part of the Hill Country, boulders and heavy stones were practically absent. Where glacial drift covered the northern margin, farmers gradually removed stones from the fields, piling them into fences or heaping them at the corners and in the middle of their fields. Some piles overgrown with brush can be seen from Highway 12 in the middle of fields in St. Croix and Dunn counties, Wisconsin.

The clearing of prairie tracts was easier and faster. One drawback was the seasonal nature of the work. If the sod was turned over too early in spring, prairie grasses might re-root. Thus the chore had to be done during a short period between late spring and early summer when it did not compete with other work. Prairie plows consisted of a wooden moldboard to which were attached metal sheets or a cast iron plowshare. The latter weighed as much as 125 pounds, and the plow had a fourteen-foot beam to which as many as five or six yoke of oxen were hitched. At least eight oxen were needed to pull the plow through the heavily matted and deep-rooted cover of the prairie soil. Few individual farmers owned that many oxen, so most of them hired "prairie-breakers"—crews of about eight, including local boys who ran errands and had the early morning chore of searching in the dew-laden grass for oxen who had wandered away during the night.[3] The prairie-breakers' oxen, as other livestock, grazed on unfenced land owned by the government or private parties while the crews trekked from job to job. As early as 1856 grass along main roads was reported to be scarce, especially in Iowa.

After the initial breaking of the sod two or three more plowings were required to fully prepare a field for planting. For small grain the soil was smoothed by harrowing, with branches as the first primitive tool, then with a peg-tooth, spring-tooth, or disc harrow. It is very difficult to reconstruct exactly the layout of first fields and the direction of the furrows, but we can surmise that plowmen were "line-minded" after their experiences of staking and entering claims. Clearings which were close to the shelter were progressively extended, whereas in dissected country, fields might be separately adjusted to the terrain. Woodland clearings were less rectangular than on the prairie. Large breaking teams may have dictated slightly S-curved furrows at first to allow for the turning of the multiple yokes of oxen. Such curves have been documented for the long strips that during medieval times in England replaced squarish fields whenever heavy plows were used instead of the early scratchy plow.[4]

In imperfectly cleared ground where small grain would not thrive, corn could be planted in spots. On improved clearings, corn was seeded "in check" (crossplowing at right angles with seeds dropped at the crosspoints). The practice of "checkering" was continued after corn-planting machines were available and after hillers and cultivators, adjustable to the width of growing plants, replaced hoeing by hand (Fig. 7-1). During the early nineteenth century, farmers still seeded by broadcasting, cutting their grain with a scythe; the next advance was the grain cradle, which was used standing upright to cut or reap.[5] When in the 1860s wheat became the major cash crop in the Middle West, the mechanical reaper became popular. Its invention is usually associated with the name of Cyrus McCormick, who first patented his machine in 1834.[6] By the 1860s, eight or nine different models competed with McCormick's, with the Marsh harvester generally considered the best. Invented by the Marsh brothers of De Kalb, Illinois, it had a square platform on which two men bound the cut grain into bundles. New machines were demonstrated at agricultural fairs, where interest usually ran

THE BROWN CORN PLANTER IN OPERATION.

Figure 7-1. Advertisement for a cornchecker. (Illustration from a book entitled *American Agricultural Implements*, 1894)

high. One firm, showing a self-rake reaper and mower costing $225 at a Minnesota fair in 1867, received more orders than it was able to fill immediately.[7]

Individual farmers adopted mechanization selectively. The acquisition of time-saving machinery depended not only on their financial ability and personal attitudes but also on the suitability of machines for specific locations. The farmer who used an iron plow drawn by oxen or planted by hand might well harvest his grain with a mechanical reaper. One farmer near Rochester bought only a cradle in 1857. His neighbor, who bought a reaper in the same year, spent an additional $87 only a few years later to buy a horse-drawn grain driller when grain-stealing carrier pigeons began to appear in great numbers. The machine, he hoped, would "put the grain deeper and quicker than the harrows."[8]

The average value of machinery per farm in the United States in 1870 was approximately twice that of 1860. A manpower shortage and high prices for grain during the Civil War had contributed to the increase.* Furthermore, the major manufacturers were located in or close to the Upper Mississippi Country—Chicago, Moline, Rockford, and Minneapolis were the most important centers—and many smaller firms operated at Galena, Dubuque, Prairie du Chien, Winona, Rochester, and Owatonna. And John Deere, who perfected the self-scouring plow, had established his company (still the largest manufacturer of steel plows) at Moline, Illinois, in 1837.

---

*Many farmers, however, were tempted to buy on credit, and some became "machine-poor."[9]

Old advertisements for machines in agricultural journals such as *The Independent Farmer*, *American Agriculturalist*, and *Farmer and Gardener* show a Marsh harvester, an Elward self-binding harvester, a McCormick binder and self-raking reaper, an S. L. Allen horse-drawn walking cultivator, to name a few. All the machines are pictured in operation not on hillsides but on level ground, with the faint outlines of hills serving only as background. A threshing operation illustrated in *The Independent Farmer* (November 1879) shows a totally flat landscape, possible in Minnesota's Red River Valley or on the central prairies of Iowa or Illinois, but not in the Upper Mississippi Hill Country, not even on the rather level Military Ridge or on the flats along the Wisconsin River in Grant and Iowa counties. The handling of complicated machinery was difficult for the bush farmer, who worked hilly land. His machines broke down more often and repairs were costly. Blacksmiths were always in demand for repairs, and when agents and dealers in towns were not able to supply spare parts, the village blacksmith was called upon to forge the parts.

The rate at which clearings and cultivated fields were extended varied from region to region and from farm to farm. Published data of improved and unimproved acreages do not reflect the progress of clearing on individual farms and groups of upland farms as compared with hill-and-valley farms. The manuscript agricultural census is more revealing.

Let us take a look at three townships in Winona County, Minnesota, one comprising level prairie upland, another dissected bottomland and upland, and the third mostly dissected land. St. Charles, Elba, and Whitewater townships are congressional townships, each 36 square miles in size. Their settlement began simultaneously and proceeded equally. The agricultural census of 1860 listed forty-eight farmers in St. Charles; their holdings ranged from 40 acres, of which 12 were improved, to 1416 acres, of which 336 were improved. In Elba Township, five of nine acres on the smallest holding were improved; on the largest holding (420 acres) 110 acres were improved. In Whitewater Township, the smallest holding (22 acres) was completely improved; the largest (500 acres), which was owned by a lumberman, had only 8 improved acres. The rate at which improvements covered a property and thereby reached survey lines can be seen by comparing the declared improved and unimproved acreages in 1860 and 1870 (see Table 1).

In St. Charles Township with 122 farm operators in 1870, seven reported their holdings as 100 per cent improved. These improvements amounted actually to 3, 40, 74, 80, 85, 160, and 161 acres. Thirty-nine had more than 75 per cent of their acreages improved, and forty-seven more than 50 per cent. Twenty-four had less than 50 per cent of their land improved. In Elba Township, where eighty-five farmers reported, five had their holdings of 10, 40, 40, 50, and 100 acres completely improved. Nineteen farmers had improved 75 per cent and forty-five farmers less than 50 per cent of their

Table 1. Farm Sizes and Percentage of Land Improved in
Three Townships, Winona County, Minnesota, 1860 and 1870

Townships		No. of Farms	Minimum and Maximum Size in (Acres)	Lowest and Highest % of Acreage Improved	Average % of Acreage Improved
			Farms of 0-80 Acres		
St. Charles	1860	8	40-80	18-36	24
	1870	35	3-80	14-100	69
Elba	1860	8	9-80	9-100	36
	1870	30	10-80	5-100	55
Whitewater	1860	6	22-80	19-100	36
	1870	31	30-80	13-100	52
			Farms of 81-239 Acres		
St. Charles	1860	33	120-210	17-90	30
	1870	68	85-230	9-100	65
Elba	1860	12	90-200	8-66	20
	1870	46	84-220	12-91	46
Whitewater	1860	12	145-212	7-37	16
	1870	41	85-220	3-100	35
			Farms of 240 Acres and Over		
St. Charles	1860	7	240-1416	9-30	21
	1870	19	240-1360	19-79	61
Elba	1860	5	240-420	9-50	22
	1870	9	240-460	4-91	51
Whitewater	1860	3	400-500	2-19	9
	1870	4	260-460	25-63	35

land. In Whitewater Township with seventy-six farmers, five with 30, 50, 50, 65, and 220 acres reported 100 per cent improvement. Five farmers reported 75 per cent or more acres improved and thirteen 50 to 75 per cent. Fifty-two farmers had less than 50 per cent of their land improved.

Table I shows that the largest percentage of land cleared was on small farms. St. Charles, the upland township, shows a greater gain, absolutely and proportionately, of cleared land during the 1860s than Elba and Whitewater townships. More land was cleared on 40- and 80-acre farms than on the 80- to 239-acre and on over 240-acre holdings. It is evident that the survey-derived property lines must have been reached by many clearings in 1870. Following the directions of the non-varying grid became a way of life for the pioneer farmer.

The agricultural census used the same definition for improved land with only minor modifications from 1850 to 1920: improved land included regularly tilled and mowed land; tilled or cleared pastures; land lying fallow or occupied by farm buildings; and gardens, orchards, vineyards, and nurseries. Unimproved land included woodland in 1860, but in 1870 woodland was listed separately. A "clearing" might be strewn with stumps or it might be fully broken prairie sod. Fields could be diminished by the roads that occasionally cut across them or, if they bordered on a creek, by flooding. Such variations are reflected in the farmers' reported cultivated acreages in wheat, oats, or corn, which they recorded with precision in fractions such as 8.2, 14.9, or 17.8 acres. But the *sums* of their improved and unimproved acreages were usually divisible by ten because the tracts they had in mind were derived from survey measurements. The discrepancy between township acreages—improved, unimproved, and woodland— reported by farmers and those reported by surveyors is considerable in some dissected townships. Obviously, some hilly land generally used for grazing was being tilled (Fig. 7-2). Farmers in Quincy Township, which is very dissected,

Figure 7-2. This 400-acre farm occupied bluff and bottomland in the Whitewater Valley around 1875. Note the rectangular fields along survey lines in the background and the road (now Highway 74), which cuts through the farmstead itself. The traveling artist, charged to render an exact likeness of the farm for its owner, placed himself and a lady in the foreground. (*Illustrated Historical Atlas of the State of Minnesota,* 1874)

reported a total of 26,358 acres, but according to the surveyors the township contained only 23,976 acres. There is some justification for the saying that "he farms 160 acres on his forty."

Fencing

Fencing, still an important tool in modern land management, was necessary for the survival of pioneer farmers.[10] The word is derived from "defense," and in England enclosures were hedged or fenced to restrain sheep and cattle from free grazing. In America, fences had the opposite purpose. Unfenced land was considered free for pasture, and common law ruled that it was the responsibility of the owner to fence cropped land. The animals—cattle and hogs, but especially oxen—were a constant menace to cultivated fields, which offered the delectable fodder of root crops, sweet sorghum, grain, and corn.

In New England, clearings were protected against roaming stock by stone walls topped with split rails (cross-and-rail fence). When fields were abandoned the rails rotted away, but sections of the walls remain in many second-growth woods today. The rails were eleven feet long. Fence viewers—elected officials who supervised the upkeep of fences and settled small disputes between landowners—could estimate at a glance how large a field was, provided it was approximately rectangular. They counted the rails and apportioned six rails to one Gunter's chain (66 feet). Three rails were two rods.

Split rail fences were the rule in the South, where they consisted of rails stacked alternately between two stakes driven into the ground (stake-and-rail). To eliminate stakes and the labor of digging holes, pioneers in the Southern colonies also built zig-zag fences, stacking rails alternately at angles. This fence earned the name "worm" or "snake" fence. With or without stakes, split-rail fences (Fig. 7-3) were as American in the eighteenth century as hedgerows were English. Pioneers were addicted to fencing, as is illustrated by a contemporary photograph from Wisconsin (Fig. 7-4).

In 1780 a London paper criticized the American "mania for enclosures," noting: "The stripping of forests to build fortifications around personal property is a perfect example of the way those people in the New World live and think."[11] Visitors from northwestern Europe looked upon American fences as a great waste of wood; they did not consider that hedgerows, while possibly prettier, required the labor of clipping and constant watching for holes. Nor did they consider that hedges grew to a width of several feet, taking over land that had been cleared for tilling.

Westward-moving settlers carried with them the idea of the split-rail fence to mixed prairie and forest regions. They spent enormous amounts of labor in building their fences, sometimes hauling wood from as far as twelve

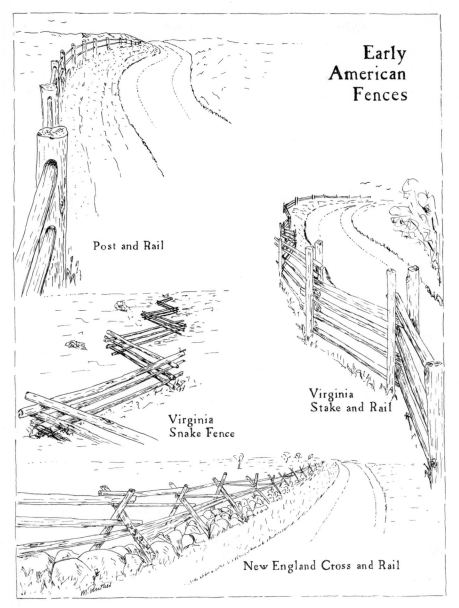

Early
American
Fences

Post and Rail

Virginia
Snake Fence

Virginia
Stake and Rail

New England Cross and Rail

Figure 7-3. Variety of wood fences used in the Middle West during the nineteenth century.

Figure 7-4. Alexander Smith farm, *c.* 1875, in Richland County, Wisconsin, near Lone Rock. Field borders follow survey directions; fences are fairly well aligned with them. (*State Historical Society of Wisconsin*)

miles away. In Minnesota one settler calculated that he needed 6720 rails (fourteen to a rod) and 1920 stakes to fence eighty acres. Splitting the rails took him sixty-seven days.[12] Still more labor was spent on post-and-rail fences (Fig. 7-3), which required digging post-holes and boring or chiseling holes in the posts. Because it was neater than the split-rail, the post-and-rail fence was more often built around the farmstead than as a border between field and unimproved land. Neither fence was very practical in the woods, unless a swath was cleared earlier, and both were awkward to build on steep slopes. Still, farmers erected them straight uphill along the "lines" (Fig. 7-5).

Fences were a national problem. They were very costly; in 1871, on the basis of returns from 846 counties, it was estimated that 1748 million dollars had been spent on the construction of 1,619,199,428 rods of fences existing in that year in the United States.[13] Farmers had invested as much in fences in that year as they had in farm animals. Nobody contested the need for fences, but everyone disliked the labor connected with them. It is doubtful that early settlers were as sentimental about rail fences—"mule high, pig-tight and bull-strong"—as was an observer in the 1930s who protested against wood-burning trucks, which were then consuming outdated rail fences: "Was there ever a finer school for civil and political training than the old rail fence, that fertile generator of thought, that unsurpassed promoter of friendly interest?" During the early years, however, it is doubtful that farmers had time to sit on fences and think. In fact, an observer of midwestern agriculture in 1867 found that "farmers work too hard and think too little."[14]

Fences contributed to the appearance of rectangularity in the landscape. At first, the alignment of a pioneer fence was usually no more precise than the border of a clearing. But a crooked fence was nothing to be proud of, and eventually straighter fences appeared on the landscape. Undoubtedly the use of the stake-and-rail fence enforced some straightness. Even the cleared patch surrounded by a split-rail fence without stakes near a log cabin on the Historical Farm in Des Moines, Iowa, is square. So are the fields on the Mississippi bottomland in Seth Eastman's watercolor (Fig. 1-1, p. 9). Herbert Quick, author of books on pioneer farm life in the Middle West and

Figure 7-5. Up-and-downhill fences parallel survey lines on a farm in Wabasha County, Minnesota. (*A.T. Andreas, Illustrated Historical Atlas of the State of Minnesota,* 1874)

a good observer, mentions the "quadrangular raft of tillage" on the prairie.[15] We saw on the early photograph of a Wisconsin farm how the size and form of fields are emphasized by the more or less straight lines of fences.

To the old problem of the cost of labor the new problem of the availability of wood was added when the westward movement began to reach the prairies. A substitute was eagerly sought and, for a while at least, hedges were thought to be the answer. Even surveyors began to seed hedges. On the western prairie margin of the hilly country, in Elgin Township, Wabasha County, where soil was "first or second rate" and the land "gently rolling with the surface of superior quality but being deficient in timber not valuable for general agricultural purposes," the surveyor's party planted osage orange seed along the section lines. Osage orange was also seeded along most lines in the eastern part of Plainview Township, although the occurrence of some timber—black and bur oak and aspen—was noted. And in Eyota Township, Olmsted County, with "rolling soil," and some "wet marsh" another surveyor planted cherry and plum seeds.

Sections in these townships were surveyed in 1853, and then settlers also planted hedge fences. In 1854 a farmer could contract for osage orange for 12 cents a rod for the first seeding, 5 cents a rod for servicing the rows during the second and third year, and 15½ cents a rod (the balance) during the fourth year, when the hedge was expected to be established. Expectations ran high, and many farmers suffered from "hedge fever."[16] But after the winter of 1856-57, one of the worst in the Middle West, most of the young plants were found killed by the cold. Particularly damaging had been the sharp winds across the wide, flat ridges. "The osage orange appears to be gone, think it will never be profitably grown here," wrote a settler on the Greenwood Prairie in Wabasha County in the spring of 1857.[17] As early as 1847 the *Prairie Farmer* declared that the great problem of fencing could be solved through planting hedges of Virginia thorn, and as late as 1867 a writer in *Iowa Homestead* believed that if Iowa was to be "densely populated, there would be need of the planting of timber belts and serried squares of hedged fences."[18]

Hedge fencing had failed, but then there never had been a real need for it in Upper Mississippi Country—the last region of the Middle West frontier where timber was locally adequate for traditional wood fencing. By the end of the 1850s the pineries of Wisconsin were supplying timber to the river ports, which also served the hinterland on the west bank of the Mississippi. In southeastern Minnesota the finest hardwoods—basswood, oak, black walnut, hickory, and maple—were used for rails, and light ash and cherry, now at a premium, were much in demand for posts.* Virgin timber was much preferred for fences; it lasted about ten years, much longer than fences

---

*I saw cherry-wood fence posts strung with barbed wire in the late 1950s, and a farmer once told me that he found a load of cherry-wood rails, never used, in his barn.

cut from second-growth. In 1866 there was still a full supply of good wood for fencing in the Upper Mississippi.[19]

Another "fencing" material in good supply was hazel brush (then considered an indication of excellent soil and preferable to pure grassland), which was often piled up against stakes, making rail fences a more effective barrier against oxen.

The rate of increase in miles of fences during the early 1870s was slower than during the 1860s: oxen had begun to decline in number with increasing use of agricultural machinery, and livestock was not the main concern of those farmers who produced small grain. Without fertilizers and scientific crop rotation, wheat yields decreased during the period of exhaustive wheat production in the 1870s. Then a wheat-destroying pest, the chinch bug, crossed the Mississippi from Wisconsin, actually forcing the farmers to change to diversified farming. The better-capitalized farms became stock-farms, and greater attention to breeding once again brought greater need for fencing. The hazards that railroads and precipitous slopes presented to roaming livestock also meant more fencing. Vacant land was becoming scarce and complaints about unrestrained cattle more frequent. Some villages had herd laws as early as the late 1860s, and in 1873 the governor of Minnesota stated that the "vexed question" of fencing cattle in or fencing cattle out was to be settled on the county and township level.[20] Whatever local rules were made in a state regarding the payment of damages, the hours when cattle could roam free, or the strength of fences required, the results of the rules were always more fences. The grazing of cattle in woods continued, and fences began to extend into timbered land. In 1884 a writer commented on past and present: "The more sensible practice for requiring each farmer to fence his stock rather than his crops resulted in the speedy disappearance of fences, which are almost wholly unnecessary in a country exclusively devoted to grain raising. The introduction of stock raising on an extensive scale is, however, calling for the restoration of fences. The old Virginia rail fence had had its day, however, and wire is being successfully substituted."[21]

The "wire that fenced the West" was invented by Joseph Glidden, a New Hampshire schoolmaster who moved west to farm near De Kalb, Illinois and filed the patent for his invention of 1873.[22] In a legal desposition in 1874 he stated that he "put up some 30 rods of said fence along the public roads of his farm." Glidden was proud of his great new fence, which he purposely erected where the public would notice it from the road. Along midwestern roads, where fences are seen by the public, fences were and still are better maintained and also the sturdiest because danger to livestock is greatest.[23] Types and distribution of fences were by no means uniform on a farmer's property. Near farmsteads, where functions were concentrated, fenced-in units were more numerous and smaller than for the farms as a whole. Close to the residence more costly board fences, sometimes painted, eventually

Figure 7-6. Five kinds of fences surround this Iowa farmstead, counting four-, five-, and six-board fences. (*A.T. Andreas, Illustrated Historical Atlas of the State of Iowa, 1875*)

replaced rail fences. Better residences had picket fences around the front yard, and most farms had a variety of fences (Fig. 7-6).

By the 1880s most towns had dealers who regularly stocked boards, pickets, and posts; after wire began to replace the rails, it was still strung from the wooden posts for many years. Field borders and fences gradually became straight lines, coinciding with property lines to a far greater degree than did the winding roads in the dissected part of our region. Only along the slopes in the valleys, where the plowmen lost orientation between the steep hillside and the winding streams, might field borders veer from cardinal directions. Otherwise survey or property lines dictated fence and field lines as they had had earlier in Ohio and Indiana.[24] These field lines remain visible to the present although the fences may have been removed (Fig. 7-7).

In the space left along the field borders where plows were turned, lines of shrubs and trees eventually developed (Fig. 7-8). Along rural roads, trees that from a distance appear to stand by themselves in a field are simply growing along a field border. One can judge the direction of a curving road from the angle it forms with the lines of fences; for example, a territorial road runs straight east-west or north-south for a stretch across a ridge when its angle with fences is 90 degrees. On the face of hills, fences crossing at right angles also help in orientation. People who live in what once was Public Domain usually can tell cardinal directions; their orientation is aided by section roads and fence lines.[25] Students from areas where the metes-and-bounds system prevails learn quickly on field excursions, and have found the help of fences for orientation "neat," as one group recently put it.

Roads in the Middle West were aligned with survey directions as much as

Figure 7-7. Right-angled corners between woods and fields are characteristic in Hill Country today and are maintained even after fences are removed. *(Lynne Bly Takemoto)*

Figure 7-8. Tree growth along fence lines in the Chippewa Valley, south of Eau Claire, Wisconsin.

the rail fences were and coincided to a large degree with property lines. Norman Thrower found in his sample area of the rectangular survey in Ohio that in 1955 only 0.3 per cent of the farmland was half a mile or more distant from public roads.[26] A number of outside forces, among them the change from animal-drawn to motor-powered vehicles and improved road technology, have converged to create the section-road landscape of the twentieth century in the Middle West and over much of the Upper Mississippi Hill Country.

The Section Roadscape

Good roads in 1878 were "the exception in all states," in the judgment of the U.S. Commissioner of Agriculture. Even territorial roads dating from pre-survey years were allowed to deteriorate after railroads replaced stagecoaches and wagons in overland transportation. A Madison attorney told the Wisconsin Agricultural Society in 1893: "For the last forty years the energy and capital of this country have been devoted to the building of railroads … . In this rush for better railroads, our common public highways have been wholly neglected and forgotten. They are in the same condition as forty years ago; 'managed' in the same shiftless, expensive, and unscientific way."[27] Rural roads were left to local and personal maintenance; state aid to township roads was impossible under the laws of Wisconsin and Minnesota. At the beginning of the twentieth century the dean at Iowa State College at Ames declared that America had easily the best railway system in the world and at the same time the most inferior public highway system of all leading and progressive nations.

SECTIONS AND ROADS IN CANADA

A short discussion of the section road system in Canada is indicated at this point because it appears to be very much like that of the United States. But there was one basic difference: the Ordinance of 1785 and subsequent survey legislation included no space allowance for roads, while the survey of Dominion lands in Canada's western provinces included road allowances. In 1869 Lieutenant Colonel J.S. Dennis, later the Canadian Surveyor General, openly criticized the American system because it forced settlers to give up land for roads. The Minister of Public Works concurred, but proposed sections of 800 acres, with each settler assured 200 acres and an additional 5 per cent for roads. But in the House of Commons a debate arose over the merits of square sections of 640 acres versus rectangular sections of 800 acres and whether roads should be 66 feet (one chain) or 99 feet (one and a half chains) wide. In Manitoba, for example, existing roads often were two chains wide, the large width facilitating complete turn-arounds; also, when roads became muddy from rain and melting snow, Red River carts had room to shift to firmer surfaces along the sides, away from deep ruts. Finally decided upon was the square section, and by Orders in Council (1871), the size of sections became 640 acres and roads between all sections 99 feet wide. In 1881 road allowances were reduced to 66 feet; only alternate east-west section roads were to be spaced out.[28] The Dominion Land Surveys Act, as it later became known, provided for roads along all north-south section lines and along alternate east-west lines at two-, four-, and six-mile points. Inevitably not all of the road allowances were used, and many became incorporated, illegally, into the farms—along straight lines, of course.

STRAIGHT ROADS VERSUS CURVED ROADS

Road experts in the United States did not always recommend straight roads. New York Governor De Witt Clinton declared that straight roads, unless on level land, were merely bad roads because "straightness means up and down." On the other hand, William Mitchell Gillespie, author of an 1847 textbook for civil engineers (10 editions by 1871) preferred straight roads, observing that in the past, too many roads had been built "not so much on mathematical as on social principles,"* meaning that too few roads followed the shortest, straight route.[29] In principle, Gillespie urged that "every road, other things being equal, should be perfectly straight." It should be level, and one rod (pole), or sixteen and a half feet wide generally. Thirty feet, he noted, were "fully sufficient for driving," adding, however, that since a road could rarely be at the same time straight and level, the two requirements would often conflict.

So Gillespie, who preferred what he called "Hogarth's line of grace" (namely, curved roads) for pleasure drives anyway, resolved the conflict by conceding the need for winding roads in hilly country and even criticized the section road system with its restriction to only two directions.

> The mathematical axiom that 'a straight line is the shortest distance between two points,' is thus seen to be an unsafe guide in roadmaking, and less appropriate than the paradoxical proverb that 'the longest way around is the shortest way home.'

> The evil is now perpetuated by the unwillingness of farmers to allow a road through their farms in a winding line. They attach more importance to the squareness of their fields than to the improvement of the lines of their

---

*An early example of yielding to "social principles" was Thomas Jefferson's reluctant consent in 1808 to let the National Road deviate from a straight route to detour through Uniontown in western Pennsylvania.[30]

roads—not being aware how much more labor is wasted by them in travelling over these steep roads, than there would be in cultivating an awkward corner of a field.

This feeling is seen carried to excess in some of the new states in the West, in which the roads run along 'section lines,' and as these sections are all squares with sides directed towards the cardinal points of the compass, a person wishing to cross the country in any other direction than North, South, East and West must do so in rectangular zig-zags.[31]

In the dissected parts of the Hill Country many roads still lead "the longest way around." When the state geologist of Wisconsin made a thorough investigation of roads in the state around the turn of the century he received many complaints, among them the following: "This thing of following arbitrary lines and climbing hills at an angle of forty-five degrees will never give good roads. I have lived in hillier countries, but never had to climb such hills as where they lay roads on section lines." The arbitrary location of roads was also expensive, for steep crests had to be cut down and depressions filled up. West of Richland Center, for example, one straight road followed the sloping side of the valley; it had a comparatively good grade but that was achieved by "an almost continuous series of cuts and fills." The right of way, according to the geologist, could have been purchased only a short distance away from the slope at a fraction of the cost of the cuts and fills needed to construct the section road.[32]

On the upland, roads at first "went into all directions," "ran diagonal," "branched regardless of section lines," and "were developed without work," in the words of local historians. Gradually, however, the "roads were put on the lines," and up-and-down sections roads across the swales and rises of the fertile undulating prairie furnished proof for the saying "the better the soil the poorer the road." In Iowa, which was famous for its mud roads, engineers deplored that "even animals display more engineering skill in the trend of their trails and paths than we have in locating our roads."

MAINTAINING ROADS

Many bridges and stretches of corduroy road were needed to keep dirt roads in hilly country passable. Young trees, as uniform and straight as possible, or ten-foot rails of oak or ash were laid side by side across the road in boggy spots. Sometimes bridges consisted only of "stringers" (trunks laid lengthwise). Corduroy roads were constantly in need of repair. This was costly, and near towns, improvements were sometimes financed by subscription. For example, the road between Winona and Minnesota City was graded at a cost of about $800 in 1857, and in 1861 Winona raised an initial $8000 and an additional $10,000 for the road between Wabasha Prairie and

Stockton via Minnesota City.[33] Short floods often damaged or washed out the numerous small bridges; in the summer of 1863, for example, heavy rains washed out practically all bridges in the Zumbro River watershed. By 1865 a special law permitted townships in Minnesota to assess a local tax for bridge building. Years later (1881) Preston Township did manage to collect $600 to bridge the Root River at Rushford, but usually towns were too poor and waited for counties to act. In Wisconsin, Trempealeau County was an example; its earliest appropriations of funds for roads were made in 1858, exclusively for building and maintaining bridges.[34]

Counties in turn relied on voluntary self-help in townships or on town supervisors. For example, after 1854 Houston County, Minnesota, town supervisors were ordered to "view" the roads, which at times could be found obstructed by fences. (Settlers were known to run their fencing not only across county roads but even across state and territorial roads.) County supervisors could be called in for help in relocating survey markers,[35] but most of the time, townships received no assistance.

Everywhere in the United States, administrative and engineering tasks exceeded the talents of county road supervisors and the financial resources of townships. Conditions in Wisconsin were typical. Elected highway "commissioners" served as road overseers for township districts—districts that changed with every town-board election and where some men were elected as a joke. A commissioner's duties were "to regulate the roads already laid out, and to alter such of them as they shall deem inconvenient." In each township district, according to the revised statutes of Wisconsin in 1849, male inhabitants between 21 and 50 years old—excepting "persons of color, paupers, idiots, and lunatics"—had to pay, in addition to assessed taxes, 75 cents poll tax for which they could substitute the work of an eight-hour day. Seventy-five cents per day was also credited "for every cart, wagon, plow, scraper, yoke of oxen or span of horses furnished." In 1858 the credit was $1.00 for one day of labor, 50 cents for a team of oxen, and $1.25 for a span of horses. Not until 1893 was statutory labor abolished in the state and were all road taxes required to be paid in currency.[36]

The motley crews who gathered with their poorest tools, oldest wagons, and weakest animals to repair rural roads became the object of ridicule across the country. All but five states in the Union employed the "corvee," or labor tax. The system of elected district road officers and the labor tax was a traditional institution introduced from England and was simply outdated. Counties needed good dirt roads before expensive macadam roads (which were already understood technically) could be proposed. Township roads needed most of all to be leveled, a hard task unless machines were available, and few townships could afford to buy steam rollers at a cost of some $5000.

Although no rights-of-way had been reserved when the surveys were made in the United States, there were no legal complications regarding the use of privately owned land for roads. In the nineteenth and during the first decade of the twentieth century, owners generally did not protest losing to the public two rods (33 feet) along their side of a section line for a road that would also serve them. The thought that private property should be acquired under eminent domain did not occur to them at that time. In the dissected country, where section lines could not serve as roads, many of the early roads developed by trappers, scouts, and pioneers simply persisted. "They worked themselves out" was the vernacular saying. These roads were usually adjusted to the terrain and much the better for it.

ROADS AND SECTION LINES

By 1889 eight out of forty-six states or territories had provisions stipulating that section lines were to become roads. In California private roads were to run along a section or half-section line wherever practicable. In Texas a section line might be declared a neighborhood road upon application to the commissioners, and in Florida all new roads were to run "as near as may be upon section lines and subdivisions thereof." In the Dakotas, Nebraska, Kansas, and Michigan, section lines were simply declared public roads and were neither surveyed nor viewed. In Minnesota all section lines became public roads after 1873; Illinois, Wisconsin, and Iowa made no special provision.

Section lines did not directly connect towns and villages as did the railroads. The custom of following survey lines for roads was found "very natural" but wasteful and inconvenient in a study of American roads made in 1889: "The distances from place to place can be easily reckoned; the farms lie in compact form. Clearly, however, it is not primarily the purpose of roads to perform these subordinate functions." The author of the study recommended a plan, based on a German treatise of 1869, that proposed an overlapping pentagonal circulation system, in which first- and second-class roads never ran along cardinal directions but connected existing places. He warned that a country that looked only to roads along cardinal directions might need, when it was fairly well settled, "diagonal" roads—in spite of the complaints from farmers whose land would be "thereby cut into irregular shapes."[37] This was a prophetic comment! To illustrate, in 1935 the General Assembly of Iowa prohibited the Highway Commission from purchasing right-of-way, grading, bridging, or surfacing a new system of diagonal highways around Des Moines. (In 1963, however the rule was repealed because it interfered with potential interstate routes.) Through the years other plans for diagonal roads in Iowa, projected from Des Moines to Sioux City and to Burlington, were "killed due to their disruption of farming and safety arguments about diagonal intersections with previously existing roads."[38] and as late as 1973, an appeal against constructing a diagonal section of road from Des Moines to Marshalltown was before the Circuit Court of Appeals.

The roads that were shifted to the survey lines were at first neither as straight nor as stark in appearance as section roads are today. Their edges were poorly defined; they had no side ditches and they curved around obstacles such as the headwaters of small streams or gulches. They climbed uphill with uncertain bends and veered around undrained patches in wet prairie. Straw, stones, planks, and brush were used to fill in the holes on the earth-colored up-and-down roads. Limits to maximum grades, design of horizontal curvature, and consideration of soils in relationship to road construction were unknown. And many more small bridges had to be built, for in the Middle West stream patterns are generally dendritic. Roads that defer to topography need fewer bridges than straight section-roads, which may cross the same winding stream several times. The need for more bridges under the rectangular survey system than for roads under the unsystematic survey has been demonstrated by careful comparison elsewhere.[39]

THE "GOOD ROADS MOVEMENT"

The National League for Good Roads was organized in 1892 by citizens' groups and strongly supported by the Grange and the nation's railroads. The latter were concerned with the cost and uncertainty of shipping goods to rural residences as well as the farmers' inability to haul produce regularly to railroad depots over poor dirt roads. Most urgent however, were the needs to abolish a township road system that relied on untrained labor and to establish statewide standards on road quality. Several other forces supported the so-called "Good Roads Movement," and finally, at the end of the nineteenth century, the resignation with which rural residents had usually accepted their poor roads changed to action which led to state road legislation. The first state highway department was set up in Vermont in 1892. Others throughout the country followed; departments in the Hill Country were established in 1904 (Iowa), in 1905 (Minnesota and Illinois), and in 1911 (Wisconsin).

Among the reasons why farmers began to demand better roads were new developments in the dairy industry. It is a myth that home-made butter, for which every farm wife had her own method, was dependably good. Merchants alternately complained about the miserable product or advertised an occasional good shipment as "unusual." The importation in 1882 of the cream separator from Europe, the invention of the Babcock cream tester, (by which the proportion of butter fat in milk was determined), and the organization of cooperative creameries combined to transfer butter-making from farms to factories during the 1890s. To shorten the haul for patrons, skimming stations were installed outside of towns so that only cream needed to be delivered to the creameries. Still, the delivery of cream was in jeopardy as long as roads were so bumpy that the liquid would become butter from too much shaking. This was a serious problem for dairy farmers in Minnesota and Wisconsin, states known as the butter and cheese states of the Union.

On the national level, another impetus for good roads came from the League of American Wheelmen, the national organization of bicyclists. In 1896 four million bicycles were used in the United States. Manufacturers, who had been producing 6000 bikes a year, gave strong support to the League, whose members were agitating for improved roads near cities and towns. Still another, and by far the most powerful force to bring all farmers into the Good-Roads Movement, was federal legislation implementing Rural Free Delivery (RFD).

In 1890 nineteen of seventy-six million people in the United States had mail delivered to their doors in the cities. The rest received their letters when the head of the family took a trip to the post office in the village, where according to one farm woman, men and boys were often "tempted to spend time and money in the billiard rooms and other similar places while waiting for the mail."[40]

The first experiment in the East with Rural Free Delivery (1891) was immediately supported by the press—which hoped to increase subscriptions for newspapers—and by the Grange and Farmers' Alliance clubs, who sent urgent requests for the service to their congressmen. In 1893 Congress appropriated $10,000 for further experimentation, and when the money was not used, Congressmen from rural districts rebuked the Postmaster General for favoring free delivery in cities. An additional $20,000 was approved in 1894, and $40,000 in 1895. By 1897, eighty-two pioneer routes had been laid out, and by 1900 many counties in the Hill Country had a first mail route, usually connecting county seats with towns along major roads.

In 1899 the Post Office Department announced that rural routes and rural free delivery would be established only where roads were passable and maintained year-round, and that petitions for rural routes had to be accompanied by maps of roads. The maps, wherever possible, were to designate roads as running east, south, west, and north; the number of miles had to be added along sections. Petitions, however, were often hastily prepared on Grange nights and then rejected because the roads were in fact found to be impassable. To prod the public into action and upon urging by the National League for Good Roads, Congress established in 1893 the Office of Public Road Inquiry, which publicized better road-building techniques, sponsoring, for example, the widely publicized "Good Roads Train," which toured the South staffed with the personnel of road-building equipment companies. Most important among the train's demonstrations was an improved road drag that left the road slightly raised in the center to provide better drainage to both sides (Fig. 7-9). Such practices were slowly adopted in the Hill Country and helped farmers in obtaining RFD.

Figure 7-9. Road at margin of Hill Country in Sauk County, Wisconsin. Improved by road-cut (leveling) in foreground and slight raise in center to provide better drainage. (*State Historical Society of Wisconsin*)

In 1903 the battle for the permanent establishment of Rural Free Delivery was won. Occasionally routes were vehemently denounced by patrons who objected to the location of mail boxes, which for some farmers often were as much as a quarter of a mile away from the farmhouse.[41] Soon the silvery-gray mailbox, approved by the Postmaster General as a stamp on every one certifies, became a symbol of rural America along country roads.

The mailmen kept constant watch over their routes of about twenty-five miles, talked to farmers about the condition of the roads, reporting their findings to the supervisors of the postal system in each county. Many counties and townships, however, were still unable to meet the road standards of the postal services. In regions of great local variety, such as Upper Mississippi Hill Country, some farmers were able to afford the labor and capital to improve their roads, while others, in the same township and along the same rural route, were not. In 1904 only a small percentage of roads in the Middle West were gravel surfaced.[42]* Gradually, however, the states

*In Illinois of a total of 94,141 miles of road, 6800 were surfaced with gravel and 1106 with stone; in Minnesota of 79,324 miles, 6179 with gravel, 67 with stone; in Iowa of 102,448 miles, 1403 with gravel and 241 with stone; and in Wisconsin of 63,593 miles, 9900 with gravel and 733 with stone.

Figure 7-10. Up-and-down section road, looking straight east between sections 6 and 7 in T. 106 N., R. 10 W, Winona County, Minnesota.

passed laws to permit funds collected by special taxes or money from their treasuries to be used for the development of public highways and enacted laws to aid counties. But the pressure for federal aid continued.

In 1908, President Theodore Roosevelt's Country Life Commission reported among other things, that rural highways usable the year around were essential for marketing agricultural products and that the rural free delivery of mails should be extended as rapidly as possible to correct the social sterility of farm life. In 1912 promoters of improved rural roads drafted a bill in which the federal government was to pay annual rental fees of $25 per mile for macadam roads, $20 per mile for gravel roads, and $12 per mile for dirt roads used by the U.S. postal services. The American Automobile Association was instrumental in the defeat of this bill; its members were urged to write their senators, opposing the "Knights of the dirt roads." The Federal Highway Act, which President Woodrow Wilson signed in July, 1916, assured assistance to states for road-building projects.* Thus the Good Roads Movement had culminated in a law intended to help farmers. But the motor-vehicle interests proved to be stronger.[43]

The automobile needed firm and smooth surfaces. Its power permitted straight uphill and downhill travel; greater speed of travel made it difficult to manipulate curves. In the Hill Country, with the exception of ridge, bluff,

*In 1921, however, the act was amended to exclude local rural roads, and not until 1936 was it amended again to permit federal aid to rural roads.

and valley roads, roads were straightened out wherever possible, even crossing slopes over 15 per cent steep. (Fig. 7-10). On large-scale highway maps the presence of dissected land may be discerned from winding roads; on a map of six townships in Iowa's Allamakee County, for example, the section-road pattern prevails west of Waukon on the upland prairie, but to the east roads are curved. Figure 7-11 illustrates the transition as well as the persistence of early roads with their curves now straightened out. Straightening, graveling, and paving have made the survey lines visible on a grand scale.

When diagonal wagon tracks from farms to villages—"farm-to-market" roads—were replaced by right-angled roads, the road mileage per square mile in the United States was increased. And after World War I, in spite of a loss of rural population, the continuation of the same dense road system was promoted through school consolidation.[44] Farm-to-market roads represent about four-fifths of rural roads under local control; of these, a report by the Bureau of Public Roads in 1950 considered one-fourth "non-essential."

An extraordinary mileage in roads remains available to drivers in the Middle West. But in rural areas, where local politics have long focussed on roads, residents will rarely concede that a road is non-essential. For example, in Farmington Township, Olmsted County, it was found that 22 per cent or 13.25 miles of the township's road system—amounting to eighty acres taken for right-of-way—could be abandoned with no hardship to residents. But the farmers have insisted that every existing road be maintained because their farms, while larger, have become more fragmented in recent years.* In fact almost half of the township's farms include more than one tract scattered over several miles along the section roads. Indeed, the enlargement of farms was made possible in the first place by the dense section-road system, which has enabled farm operators to reach their tracts with heavy modern machinery.[45]

In the 1970s, a decreasing rural population and an increasing number of abandoned farmsteads in the Middle West have contributed to the increase of rural crime; in fact, the dense road system, which provides a quick getaway, has been of special benefit to cattle and hog rustlers.[46]

In hilly country a dense section-road system, of course, is not possible. A map of rural road density in the "Central Interior States" shows the Driftless Area with a density of less than .7 miles surrounded by a density of 1.4 to 2.0 per square mile. Similar differences exist between the Ozarks, the Flint Hills in south-central Kansas, and the Sand Hills of Nebraska, and the surroundings of these three hilly areas. In open country everywhere, not only in Wisconsin, Iowa, and Minnesota, road mileage has decreased gener-

*Between 1930 and 1960 the average farm size in the township increased from 183 acres to 219 acres. Size and form of the tracts did not change, but the number of non-contiguous holdings increased, and only 52 per cent of the township's farms were contiguous in the 1960s.

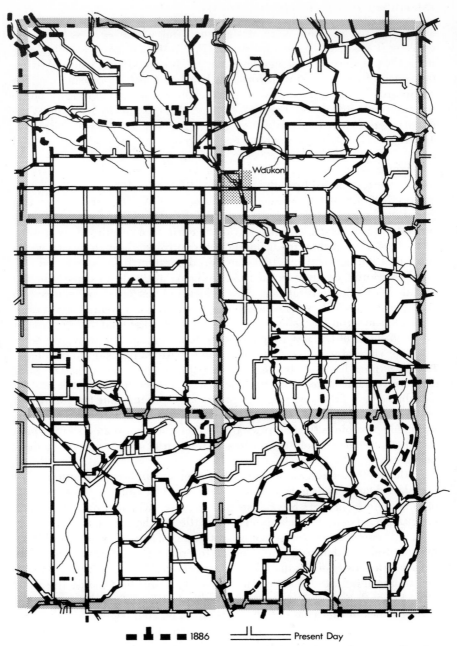

■ ▬ ■ ■ ▬ ■ 1886   ⌐⌐╌ Present Day

Figure 7-11. Section and valley roads in six congressional townships in southwestern Allamakee County, Iowa. Early road bends were replaced by straight roads with sharper corners. No road was abandoned, some road mileage was added between 1886 and 1969. (*Based on Allamakee County Atlas, 1886,* and *Iowa State Highway Commission map, 1969*)

ally much less than the rural farming population. Furthermore, the mileage is unlikely to decrease in the future, for consolidated school systems use the roads, as do increasing numbers of non-rural residents in the open country. They too now benefit from the original plans, implemented a century later.

While section roads date from the late 1800s and the early 1900s, historical, terrain-dictated roads often are more than 100 years old. They may cut directly across a farm or, usually in valleys, even run between the buildings of a farmstead.[47] "You feel you are driving across their front yard," commented one resident of Trempealeau County recently.

It is often difficult to establish the legal survey line for section roads. But now that section roads are graveled or paved and lined with ditches, it is apparent that the lines often are not as straight as they appear to be on maps. As early as 1855 William Burt observed, "Measurements with the chain and tally pin are often very imperfectly performed by the chain men and much more error is made than is generally supposed.[48] County surveyors expect considerable error when they trace original lines for re-surveying.

Roads along section lines generally covered the survey markers, and today most of the original markers cannot be found. New markers, sited by measurements with modern instruments, have frequently been moved "across the road," from the center to the ditch. However, the property lines along the originally surveyed section line remain inviolate along the section roads. Although historical, terrain-dictated roads are being shifted from their original locations through straightening of curves, improved location of bridges, and widening, modern section roads reflect the original design of 1785, creating the "grid-paper" landscape admired by the foreign-born pilot in 1950.

The American public is probably less aware of the section-road landscape in the age of interstate highway travel. But many voices are raised in criticism of monotonous grid-pattern towns, a criticism that began as early as the end of the nineteenth century.

Grid Pattern Towns and Main Street

In 1871 Horace Cleveland, a noted American landscape architect, wrote of western towns:

> The monotonous character of their rectangular streets, which on level ground is simply tedious in its persistent uniformity, becomes actually hideous when it sets at defiance the plainest suggestion of natural topography and sacrifices every feature of natural beauty and every opportunity for picturesque effect in its blind adherence to geometrical lines.[49]

And in a 1965 edition of Cleveland's *Landscape Architecture as Applied to the Wants of the West*, the editor commented that "pervasive gridiron plat so efficient for purposes of speculative subdivision and barter and so inefficient for most other purposes, personified the antinaturalism which influenced nineteenth-century urban form.[50] In Cleveland's time the opposition against rectangular planning was tied to a back-to-nature movement that produced two major "substitutes for nature" on the American scene, landscape parks and suburbs. The former, skillfully and artificially constructed, were designed with romantic assumptions about nature and featured curved roads and peaceful, informal scenes; the latter, sometimes with similar features, were often given names such as Oak Park, Forest Park, or Elmwood Park.

The rapid expansion of suburbs proceeded by tracts which indeed could often be dubbed "suburban life by the square mile."[51] A real estate textbook warned in 1926: "The old gridiron arrangement of blocks in uniform row upon row is obsolete because it is ugly, inconvenient, deadening, and sometimes expensive."[52] Indiscriminate use of the rectangular system in the layout of cities was regretted by a historian of the U.S. land survey as "a most unhappy corollary of the system."[53] Rural towns were no different from the cities and thus were rejected by nineteenth-century American romanticists, who saw beauty in a picturesque landscape. Grid patterns were simply not painterly. But how far the survey should be blamed for their extensive use is debatable.

The grid-pattern town is not American or exclusively western in origin. Straight streets and rectangular or square blocks are the simplest way to attain lots of equal size and streets with easy two-way turns for vehicles. It is an archetypal settlement, both in practical colonization and on utopian plans. In 1811 the proposed plan for Manhattan included this observation:

> One of the first objects which claimed their [the Commission's] attention was ... whether they should confine themselves to rectilinear and rectangular streets, or whether they should adopt some of those supposed improvements, by circles, ovals, and stars. They could not but bear in mind that a city is to be composed principally of the habitations of men, and that strait sided, and right angled houses are the most cheap to build, and the most convenient to live in. The effect of these plain and simple reflections was decisive.[54]

Furthermore, the square or plaza as an ingredient of the grid pattern is ubiquitous, the most popular American version being the Philadelphia plan (simple central square), which served as a model for towns[55] such as Lancaster, Ohio, and Lexington, Kentucky. It is not surprising that a colonization of unparalleled speed and extent produced grid-pattern towns across American in the nineteenth century. Yet non-varying directions, the peculiarity of the U.S. survey, certainly were not characteristic of the midwestern towns and villages, nor were they prevalent in the East. In Pennsylvania rectilinear towns of the nineteenth century frequently conformed to directions of turnpikes and rivers.[56] And in the Upper Mississippi Hill Country, grid-pattern blocks did not dominate the towns and villages as much as they did in cities like Chicago, Salt Lake, or Houston. Many pre-survey settlements were planned on a grid, as we saw earlier, but on a grid that was often adjusted to sites with dominating physical features—landings along the Mississippi, the Chippewa, and the St. Croix rivers, for example.

Surveyors took pride in accuracy and in following rules. They contributed to the standardization of units of measure, for instance, by allowing 66 to 99 feet for the width of streets and by dividing 40 acred plots two or three times down to 5-acre blocks. The sizes of lots varied in the expectation that towns would need both compact business blocks and residential blocks. Later, when a village or town incorporated, survey lines were used as boundaries. On most maps the incorporated limits of settlements are shaded, giving the impression that the towns are compact squares or rectilinear tracts. But the direction of streets and built-up areas do not necessarily conform.

Sections and multiples of forty acres were implied in federal acts, usually called "townsites acts," which legalized the reservation of land for townsites and town pre-emption rights between 1824 and 1877. According to the Townsite Act of 1844 the party interested in founding a city first had to file with the county recorder a plat of not more than 640 acres, describing its boundaries according to the lines of the public surveys. By 1867 and after various additional acts, towns of between 100 and 200 inhabitants could occupy 320 acres; of 200 to 1000 inhabitants, 640 acres; and over 1000, up to 1280 acres (two sections). In 1877 the maximum any townsite could occupy was four sections.[57] *The Manual of Surveying Instructions of 1947* described the typical townsite:

> The blocks may be made 300 feet square, and usually not over 320 feet by 400 feet, with a 20-foot alley running the long dimension of the block. The principal streets are usually made 80 feet in width, though frequently as much as 100 feet where the greater width appears to be needed or desirable, and the less important intersecting streets are seldom given a width of less than 60 feet. An alley is usually placed in each block, 20 feet in width and paralleling the principal street system. The normal frontage of the lots is 50 feet, which run back in rectangular form to the alley. Unless planned differently, the whole system is laid out on cardinal directions, and in all town sites the blocks are given serial numbers, usually beginning with the northeast block and proceeding with the numbers alternately to the west and to the east. The lots are given serial numbers within the block.[58]

Only five towns in the Hill Country, all in Minnesota, filed their plats of more than 160 and up to 400 acres under townsite pre-emption rights: St. Charles, Winona, and Minneiska in Winona County, Oronoco in Olmsted

County, and Mazeppa in Wabasha County.[59] Minneiska, known as the "town where the sun sets at three o'clock," illustrates the difference between a typical grid-pattern townsite and an actual block plan. Its corporation limits follow section and quarter quarter-section lines and the Mississippi shoreline, exceeding the area of the built-up town. On the plat of 1854, lots and blocks were laid out to curve around the bluff, nearly 400 feet high. Later, the Milwaukee, St. Paul, and Pacific Railroad tracks were squeezed between the shore and the houses that fronted, on both sides, the one road at the base of the rocky bluff. There is no correlation between the survey lines and the one-street town that developed into little more than a thoroughfare.

Corporation limits on the Wisconsin side of the Mississippi correspond equally little with the areas actually occupied by the towns: Fountain City, Buffalo, and Alma—all in Buffalo County—are triangles formed by survey lines and the southeast-northwest running shoreline. Alma's city limits comprise two such triangles, which extend inland for six sections in one township and five in another. Buffalo's town limits, platted on the nonvarying grid, spread over a wide prairie, which the town has never filled; and Fountain City, with a flatiron center formed by Front and Main Streets, has a steeply climbing North Street lined by culverts and ditches cemented against washouts. Cross streets are terraces, the lowest being Main Street. Heavy rains in Fountain City "make the radishes roll down from the vegetable gardens into the streets," according to residents of rival Buffalo. The town of Alma, "plastered up against the bluff" in local parlance, is one mile long on Highway 35, its main street a thoroughfare for one-eighth of a mile at the foot of the bluff, which rises more than 500 feet above the valley. Only one steep street goes straight up from Main Street to Second Street. County Road E, which goes up at an angle, continues to wind its way to the top of the bluff. Other "streets" are staircases. The courthouse, churches, and the old Buffalo County Teachers College of 1902 are on the terrace of Second Street. These examples of river towns illustrate how town platters fared when they played out the grid pattern in a real environment against water and hill—the two "perpetual wild cards,"[60] according to Ivor de Wolfe, architect and imaginative interpreter of the Italian townscape.

Shorelines, blufflines, roads, terraces, and railroad tracks influenced the orientation of plats at least as much as survey lines in the second half of the nineteenth century. Illustrating the variety of townsite plats found in many counties are four railroad stops along the Mississippi in Vernon County, Wisconsin—Stoddard, Genoa, Victory, and De Soto. Stoddard's main street ran parallel to but did not face the tracks of the Chicago, Burlington, and Northern Railroad. In Genoa, Water and Main streets paralleled the river and the railroad, which ran approximately northeast. On Victory's plat, tilted northeast along the bluffline, the railroad cut across lots and blocks. De Soto's plat, which extended into Crawford County to the south, deferred to topography; the main street angles up to the table of the hinterland through a coulee. Elevator, warehouse, and railroad depot down by the river were built just north of the coulee's opening toward the Mississippi. These four small settlements in the same county shared the same function in very similar physical surroundings but all had different original grid patterns.

The largest town in Vernon County at the end of the nineteenth century was the county seat, Viroqua. There the corporation limits extended over 1680 acres into four sections, forming a perfect square, its main street followed a north-south section line, and the grid consisted of standard square blocks. In Hillsborough, in the same county, the main street followed the South Fork of the Baraboo River in southwest-northeast direction. Directly to the north Ontario had a plat that straddled section and county lines at an angle but fitted into the junction of the Kickapoo River and Brush Creek. Westby, to the northeast of Viroqua, followed the direction of the early ridge road. Its main thoroughfare, called the "Sparta to Viroqua Road" on the plat, led northeast and was crossed at an oblique angle by east-west running streets. The diamond-shaped outline of its first corporation limits, in defiance of survey lines, was later changed to follow the lines.

In the late 1890s five of thirty-three post office corners in Vernon County had small plats affected by a river, mill pond, or road junction. Only three of the corners later developed into villages, one of which, Avalanche, still shows "some evidence of a street pattern distinct from the highway" along which it is now located.[61] The original plat looks more ambitious, but—as in all cases—it should be carefully scrutinized with reasoned imagination. The houses of other hamlets were located radially around a crosspoint of winding or straight roads, or they lined the road near a bridge, an early mill, or a cheese factory.

In county atlases, the blocks and lots of townsites are colored in; the "original plat" and the "additions" with somebody's name printed in heavy letters. Schools, churches, and hotels are black rectangles which stand out clearly. Wagonsmiths and blacksmiths, mills and cheese factories are designated in small print; their ground plans are shaded grey. So are all the residences. It is from the location of these inconspicuously drawn structures that the imagination must reconstruct the appearance of the place, not from the colored blocks of the plat—which reflect at best the ambitions for a settlement. Scattered buildings surrounded by cleared land and roads were the reality. The short lineup of commercial structures at uneven distances from the board-covered walks barely created a town-like appearance. The precision of the plats was in stark contrast to the disorder of the scene.

Local historians did not specify that towns were platted on the grid pattern; their statements were simple: "The original plat of Hokah included Main Street with lots on either side." "He platted the town and erected the first house at the corner of Front Street," "The village was surveyed in

February, 1855, but the first frame house upon the site was erected in 1854."

Anybody who wished to plat a tract could do so. On the average about thirty places were platted in a county; in Winona County, Minnesota, thirty-four villages and towns were platted between 1852 and 1901. Of those places, only Winona, the riverport of 1852, is thriving. Beaver, a valley town founded in 1856, had a mill at a road junction; floods contributed to its disappearance in swamps. Altura, platted in 1866 in conformity with the survey as the terminal of a branch of the Chicago and Northwestern Railroad, still has its elevator and also a modern turkey-processing factory. Factors that contributed to a townsite's success or failure seem apparent in retrospect; but each place in its own time envisioned a glorious future. But the future was not glorious except in a few places, such as Rochester with its Mayo Clinic.

MAIN STREET

European geographers' classifications of rural settlements in Europe are complex. For instance, in Germany separate farmsteads, linear villages, compact and irregular forms of settlement have been subclassified on the basis of origin, state of development, and ground plans.[62] Yet rural settlement in the Middle West is commonly characterized by American and European geographers as consisting of grid-pattern towns and dispersed settlement of single farmsteads, with little attention paid to individual sites.* "Courthouse Square" towns have been investigated, but others deserve attention as well. Many grid-pattern towns not only have plats tilted in adjustment to physical features, they often have a sense of place due to site, which plats do not reveal. Bluff, valley-junction, and riverfront towns are among those that deserve recognition. But public interest, including that of geographers, in a discriminating typology of rural towns in the Middle West has been delayed immeasureably by Sinclair Lewis's novel, *Main Street*, which created for Europeans and Americans alike the "typical" midwestern town.

Lewis never conceded that the Gopher Prairie of his novel was Sauk Centre, Minnesota, but his description of several buildings in his Gopher Prairie closely fits a few existing buildings in Sauk Centre—and most certainly the fictional town and the real one are the same in the public mind. Sauk Centre, which is located on the prairie west of the Mississippi, was staked out near a gristmill on a glacial moraine in 1857. It was platted in 1863 and incorporated in 1876. Its main street, now called "Original Main Street," runs straight north-south and dips about 20 feet at its northern end toward the Sauk River, where the gristmill stood. Around the lake created

*Central place studies might be cited, but they usually reveal little about site and appearance.

Figure 7-12. Main Street, Sauk Centre, Minnesota. (*Minnesota Historical Society*)

by the mill dam, the city established a park in 1882. The St. Paul, Minneapolis, and Manitoba Railroad reached Sauk Centre in 1878 and cut diagonally across the grid, which after additions, extended into six sections. Only one small subdivision, the industrial area close to the depot, is oriented toward the tracks and not along the survey's cardinal directions. Today as in the past, Sauk Centre is a retail center for goods and services, most of which are offered along two blocks on Main Street and along one-half block on a cross street now called Sinclair Lewis Avenue. It is this pattern—a north-south main street with about two blocks of business establishments crossed by a shorter business street in a grid-pattern town that has become the prototype of town and village settlement in the Middle West.

Many readers came to accept as a truism Lewis's words: "Main Street is the continuation of Main Streets everywhere" (Fig. 7-12). The novel was translated into many languages, and its title, now part of the international vocabulary, came to stand not only for a settlement but for a way of life as well. Fifty years after the book's publication a reporter for the *Saturday Review* selected Mason City, Iowa, (where the main street is called Federal Avenue, not Main Street), to check on the social and cultural qualities of *Main Street*. He found that they had endured through half a century.[63]

Throughout the novel are passages that reflect Lewis's inclination, shared by many Americans, to use European derivatives as standards of aesthetic values. Carol Kennicott, the heroine through whose eyes the reader sees the environment, regrets "the excessive breadth and straightness of the gashed streets, so that there is no escape from gales and from sight of the grim sweep of land, nor any windings to coax the loiterer along, while the breadth which would be majestic in an avenue of palaces make the low shabby shops

creeping down the typical Main Street the more mean by comparison."[64]
Indeed, derivative American taste built châteaus fashioned after European
models above the Hudson River, which was compared to the Rhine just as
were the Ohio and the Upper Mississippi.

Lewis, who was born and raised in Sauk Centre and educated at Yale
University, worked for newspapers in Waterloo, Iowa, New York, and San
Francisco. He had been exposed to three contrasting American environments and was also influenced deeply by Hamlin Garland's *Main-Travelled
Roads* before he brought off *Main Street*. Through writing the book he freed
himself of "The Village Virus," the title of the first twenty thousand words he
wrote on the theme of Main Street. His painstaking preparations also
included map-drawing. One manuscript map, carefully lettered, was of
Pony Valley, North Dakota, with square-shaped counties and a straight
east-west line for the Northern Pacific Railroad. Trust the genius and industry of the creative artist to absorb the survey, then not say one word about it
in the novel that he intended to stand for square-minded America!

If, in the perception of the public, midwestern towns are Main Street
towns lacking the picturesque, winding village streets of Europe, the image
should also embrace "Elm Street." Tree-lined residential streets of sufficient
width for comfortable sidewalks might well be considered an asset of small
towns, albeit they have no European equivalent. In fact, Europeans find the
Elm Streets of midwestern towns attractive. But Lewis ignored such features, noting only that Gopher Prairie's main street was disproportionate in
comparison to the widths of streets and heights of buildings in eastern
American cities and in European towns. In the late 1830s Fredrick Marryat,
an astute observer from England wrote: "Americans are very judicious in
planning their new towns: the streets are laid out so wide there will never be
any occasion to pull down, to widen and improve as we do in England."[65]
Main Streeters have no parking problems in the 1970s and many build new
homes between older houses on spacious lots along their "Elm Streets." But
to call midwestern towns "Elm Street" towns would be as much a stereotype
as calling them "Main Street" towns.

EUROPEAN SETTLEMENTS

One might expect that the many different groups who helped to settle the
Middle West contributed to variety in the appearance of towns as much as
geographic sites. This is not so. European settlements in the Upper Mississippi Country are rarely distinctive in layout, for immigrants often took over
towns platted earlier or drew their own plans of square blocks—another
indication that man instinctively uses the simplest geometry when he becomes a colonizer. One exception, however, was Spillville (originally Spiel-
ville) on the Turkey River in Winnesheik County, Iowa, platted in 1860 by

Bohemians. Long lots of the proportion of 1:15 bordered both sides of its north-south main street. One cross street ascends gently from the square at the northern end of Main Street straight west to the church, which was reported to have "commanding eminence overlooking the town."[66] Anton Dvořák on a visit in 1893 was enchanted with the town's "tidy streets and well-kept walks." Today the original long lots are no longer apparent in the town. Another exception was the Amana colonies of Iowa, where German Inspirationists built stone houses along two winding streets in one, but only one, of the six villages. But New Ulm, where leaders of the Cincinnati and Chicago Turnverein platted a fine utopian town, had four symmetrically placed public squares on a grid following the axis of a terrace above the river. And in Guttenberg, Iowa, attractively surrounded by bluffs, a German settlement association from Cincinnati bought 365 lots, adding streets named after Goethe, Schiller, Herder and other poets, on a composite grid pattern. New Glarus on the banks of the Little Sugar River in Wisconsin was platted in 1845 along cardinal directions by Swiss emigrants; in an attempt to emulate a Swiss village, the town has become somewhat commercialized. For the convenience of tourists the New Glarus grid is painted on a sign-board on the main street opposite the Greyhound bus stop, which is only functionally identical with a *Gasthaus zur Post* of the post-coach era in Swiss villages. New Glarus' bus stop is pure American Middle West, like its grid (Fig. 7-13). The town of Lindstrom, set back from the western bluff of the St. Croix, with a monument of Oscar and Kristine, the Swedish couple of fiction and film fame, is a regular "Main and Elm street" town by a lake. Westby, in Vernon County, Wisconsin is "Norwegian" but the only indication to the outsider is the *Welkom* sign at the entrance to the town. And New Prague in Minnesota is an undistinguished grid-pattern town. Some of the mining and river towns have more Old World atmosphere than most towns associated with ethnic traditions.

To repeat, it is usually a distinctive geographic site that makes a place "interesting." But the location of structures can contribute a great deal. For example, Roman Catholic churches in many Hill Country towns were sited with an eye to the environment. At Elba the highway leading into town leads directly to the door of the Catholic church, which sits at the base of a steep hill on a street running at right angles to the highway. The effect is that of a "T-trap."* In Trempealeau County, the Polish church at Independence occupies a slight rise by a lake at a road crossing. The site of the Catholic church at Arcadia is more commanding than the Protestant counterpart. On the upland in Iowa, the steeples of several villages, notably of Luxemburg and New Vienna in Dubuque County, outsignal the ubiquitous water towers which usually accentuate the modest skylines of rural towns in the Middle West.

*"T-trap" implies an element of surprise—often experienced in Italian towns—where on certain streets one expects a dead-end but finds streets to both sides at the end.

Figure 7-13. Consecutively numbered streets and avenues of New Glarus, a grid-pattern town that features ethnic tradition as a tourist attraction. *(Lynne Bly Takemoto)*

Thus sites and orientation, in addition to location of architecture, create variations in the grid-pattern and Main Street environment. Courthouse Square towns encourage further efforts toward a taxonomy that considers site and layout.[67] All county seats have courthouses, but not all have a central courthouse square.[68] Lancaster, Grant County, Wisconsin, kept its courthouse square intact and built a modern annex in one of the surrounding blocks. In Austin, Minnesota, an annex was placed next to the courthouse, destroying the latter's independent central place on the square. Durand, Pepin County, with three courthouses, offers three architectural styles directly next to each other. But the square is not the center of the town. Its main street, parallel to the neglected riverfront of the Chippewa River, prevents the courthouse square from giving the town its sense of place.

A discriminating locographic classification would acknowledge the early modification of a single grid by composite grid patterns. It would distinguish for example, ridge towns, where the thoroughfare follows a divide and is not always straight. River towns might be a group restricted to level terrain offering space for expansion—Prairie du Chien, La Crosse, Winona, and Lake City would be classified as such. Bluff towns would be those that could only expand lengthwise, and railroad towns would be flat places with main streets facing the tracks or leading straight to them. Valley towns would be those adjusted to valley junctions. The term "Main Street town" might apply to towns where main streets are level thoroughfares and conform to survey lines, straight north-south or east-west.

Main Street will not soon lose the somewhat derogatory associations bestowed on it by a Nobel prize winner. All the more we should not overlook two special assets of several towns in the Upper Mississippi Country: the commanding sites of rich families' residences overlooking a town—called "Quality Hills"—and the hilltop colleges. The finest "Quality Hill" is in Galena. Decorah, Iowa, has a number of superb nineteenth-century mansions on "Quality Hill," a Main Street thoroughfare, a courthouse on the first terrace above it, and Luther College, founded in 1861 on a hilltop site second to none (Fig. 7-14). Mount Vernon, Iowa, west of Cedar Rapids and close to Cedar River, is unequivocally a hilltop college town. At Northfield, Minnesota, a broad main street competes for attention with St. Olaf College's hilltop to one side and the campus of Carleton College, which includes an arboretum, on the other. In Wisconsin, Eau Claire's composite grid, characteristic of mill towns in Upper Coulee Country, includes a

Figure 7-14. The surroundings of Decorah. The hill-and-valley site, not the grid pattern, gives this town with a main street, courthouse square, and hilltop college its sense of place. (A.T. Andreas, *Illustrated Historical Atlas of the State of Iowa*, 1876)

hilltop college, the University of Wisconsin-Eau Claire, with footbridges across the Chippewa River. The ground plans of hilltop colleges are the antithesis of standard grid patterns.

In the twentieth century, the layout of additions and subdivisions of towns and cities was strongly affected by survey lines, and the ugly aspects of "rectangular" expansion imparted new ardor to the early criticisms of the grid pattern. In contrast, the rural landscape began to diminish its rectangularity. The new curvilinearity was achieved through the contour plowing and planting of fields, to be discussed in the next chapter.

PART III
THE TWENTIETH CENTURY

8 LAND AND WATER MANAGEMENT

Contour and Watershed

The supremacy of cardinal directions in the rectangular survey had a strong impact on land-use patterns. Field borders and furrows were rarely adjusted to the lay of the land, and farmers usually plowed straight up and down hill. The linearity of the survey landscape was further accentuated by the linear arrangement of orchards and plantations, so that, as one observer noted, "Forested groves became right-angled plantations."[1] And along straight field borders there grew straight rows of weeds, saplings, or trees. Such pervasive rectangularity was more appropriate for plains than for hilly lands. In this chapter, we will discuss survey-derived problems of land and water management in the Hill Country and the first attempts that were made to improve agricultural land, notably drainage. Our emphasis will then be on the three fundamentals of conservation—land-use capability, contour plowing, and watershed management.

IMPROVEMENT THROUGH DRAINAGE

During the early years of settlement, farmers, when planting corn on wet prairie, avoided the damp patches in swales. But about 1870, farmers began to drain their land, and the once-varied landscape began to take on a uniform appearance. If drainage ditches were to follow natural gradients in "survey country," many would have to run diagonally across fields—an obvious impediment to farming. In addition, it was often difficult for an owner of wet land to secure permission from other property owners to cut ditches across their land. This hastened the adoption of tiling, and between 1880 and 1910 thousands of miles of tiles were laid in the Middle West, usually in channels three feet deep. This improvement made tiled land and land capable of being drained rise in price, and the owners of large, level tracts that were now completely cultivable benefitted. In Wisconsin, for example, only about 44 per cent of the sharply dissected Driftless Area was in crops in 1910 compared to 63 per cent in less-hilly glaciated country.[2] The higher percentage was, of course, due to tiling, but it was also due to the hopes—which were high around the turn of the century—for farming the swamplands in the counties of the northern borderland of the Hill Country. Expectations, however, continued to be thwarted.

Under the Swamp Land Act of 1850 the federal government granted the states the acreage of "swamp and overflowed" land on the condition that the income from sales would be used for reclamation. Wisconsin, receiving 1,500,000 acres of such land, much of it in the seven counties bordering the Hill Country, collected almost a million dollars in sales by 1860. Most of the money, however, although it had originally been set aside as a special fund for reclamation of swampland, was spent for public works, with very little redistributed to the seven counties. During the 1880s, drainage projects were delayed even further. Prompted by declining wheat yields in the Hill Country, the owners of wet lands decided to try their hand at grain farming. Yields were high, especially in the early 1890s, when drought caused crop failures in Kansas and other wheat-growing areas, and the subject of drainage was forgotten until after the dry years had passed. But then there were other problems: most of the settlers (many of whom were from central Europe) had no experience with drainage, and, with no help from the Swamp Land Fund, the drainage districts that were formed ran heavily into debt. By 1924, the fifteen districts organized since 1900 (with 338 farms) had only 722 miles of ditches.[3] The floods of 1911 (which almost destroyed Black River Falls) and the high acidity of the soil in the area further aggravated the situation. The northern borderland east of the Mississippi became a depressed agricultural region, and today much of the landscape is that of forests and abandoned farms. The area is regaining its diversity; the roads are widely spaced. West of the Mississippi, however, the tiled prairies are intensively cropped. The landscape is of man-made uniformity, served by the section-road grid.

Tiling was not necessary on strongly sloping fields that drained directly into the valleys of the Hill Country in eastern Iowa and Minnesota. There, crops aggravated the runoff from fields, which were extended as close to the edges of the slopes as possible; this increased sedimentation in valley bottoms. The asymmetrical slopes of the valleys in Wisconsin had their own transportational processes; soil creep was considerably more active on lower than upper slopes.[4] This, too, affected bench and valley-bottom farms adversely. Soil erosion became serious in the Upper Mississippi Hill Country after World War I, when silt loams on the ridges began to show erosion rills and gullies. Partially cleared and grazed, woodlands on hills and bluffs lost their absorptive capacity and the runoff during heavy rains caused floods that covered formerly fertile alluvial valley bottoms with upland soil, sand, and gravel. On alluvial terraces, gullies tore into the fields. The properties of soils as well as erosion were understood after intensive soil surveys made during the 1920s in several counties.[5] But preventive measures needed changes in farming habits as well as technical knowledge and capital not available on the local level.

THE SOIL CONSERVATION SERVICE

In 1928 a booklet emphasizing the physical aspects of water erosion and relating lessened soil productivity to the loss of topsoil was published.[6] Entitled *Soil Erosion, A National Menace*, it received nationwide attention. Its author, Hugh H. Bennett, was a soil scientist whose ceaseless work eventually led to Public Law No. 46, which established the Soil Conservation Service (SCS) as a permanent agency of the Department of Agriculture in 1935, 180 years after the Ordinance of 1785. It was through the efforts of this agency that contour strip-cropping was introduced, the first new formative element in the American agricultural landscape since the establishment of the survey in 1785 and 1796.

Hugh Bennett, the first Chief of the SCS and one whose strong personality elicited admiration as well as criticism, made contour plowing and conservation overused household words.[7] One of his followers was Aldo Leopold, author of *Sand County Almanac*, who warned in 1949: "In our attempt to make conservation easy we have made it trivial." The achievements made through contour strip-cropping and other conservation measures became widely known through two demonstration projects, one in South Carolina and one in Wisconsin. They were visited not only by agricultural experts from the U.S. and abroad but also by civic groups, business firms, schools, and youth organizations.

In Wisconsin the Coon Creek Erosion Control Demonstration Project covered roughly 92,000 acres of ridge and valley land in the driftless area of Vernon, La Crosse, and Monroe counties (Fig. 8-1). The technical and scientific input was enormous: the University of Wisconsin, U.S. Geological Survey, Weather Bureau, Agricultural Extension Service, Bureau of Plant Industry, and U.S. Biology Survey cooperated with the SCS in the first five-year plan (1933-38). By 1938 the field layout of 40,000 acres in the watershed had changed the area's appearance (Fig. 8-2). Tillage on the contour covered 15,362 acres; 1772 acres were protected by 132 miles of terraces. About 1650 trees per acre were planted on a little over 12,800 acres, and 2760 rods of fences were built, very few along survey lines. About one-third of the cultivated acreage was turned into pasture, woods, and permanent cover. The Coon Creek project, "The First Watershed Project of

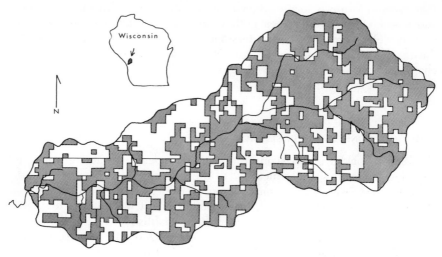

Figure 8-1. The Coon Valley Erosion Control Demonstration Project, Wisconsin. Cooperating farms (dark-shaded areas) practice conservation. All tracts show rectangular borders.

Figure 8-2. Contour stripping and water control structure in the Coon Valley Watershed, Wisconsin. *(USDA, Soil Conservation Service)*

the Nation" according to a sign on the highway, remains a showpiece of a conservation landscape to the present.

LAND-USE CAPABILITY

Three concepts, none totally new, were integrated in the treatment of individual farms in the Coon Creek project: land-use capability, contour strip-cropping, and watershed management. Land-use capability implies land classification. From the beginning of federal land legislation a few not-very-successful attempts were made to classify land. Mineral land was the first that surveyors were required to identify. Swampland had to be designated as swampland by 1850. And after 1876, when the Desert Land Act was passed, deserts too had to be classified.* The designation and appraisal of the value of timberlands, already urged in 1874 by the commissioner of the General Land Office, began in 1878 through an act that dealt with the sale of timber in the West. It was extended to all states in 1892, stipulating a minimum price of $2.50 an acre for timbered land. But many timbered acres, worth $100 each, also sold for only $2.50 per acre, which in fact became not the minimum but maximum price paid for timbered land. Such were the meager attempts to classify public lands until 1906, when the U.S. Geological Survey began to classify coal, oil, gas, phosphate, and potash lands, and potential reservoir sites—all subject to withdrawal from public sale to private parties.[8]

The concept of land capability as a definitive characteristic of land is debatable because of changes in scientific knowledge, and in economics and geographic conditions. But the land-classification system created by the SCS in the 1930s remains in use today. Eight classes were designated: (1) level land needing no special practices, (2) gently sloping land cultivable with simple conservation practices, (3) moderately eroding land needing complex practices, (4) land unsuited for continuous cultivation, (5) land suited for grazing and forestry only, (6) land in need of careful management for grazing or forestry, (7) very steep and eroded land needing complex management for forestry, and (8) land productive only for wildlife. In the Upper Mississippi Hill Country only the first five classes apply.

Technicians of the SCS were needed to make land-use capability maps for individual farms. On the basis of these maps, farm plans were developed assigning each acre (as much as possible) to its best possible use under good conservation practices. The plans themselves were striking: the curving borders of the fields designated for contour strip-cropping were in stark

*Arid land was sold cheaply and in large quantities under the condition that the buyers irrigate the land. But, because of excessive speculative buying not followed by the hoped-for irrigation, the Desert Land Act was discontinued in 1902.

contrast to the survey-derived property lines of the farmsteads. The public interest was not much aroused by land-use capability maps, but erosion control measures, particularly contour* plowing, soon could be seen throughout the countryside.

CONTOUR PLOWING

Following the contrary direction by plowing up and down hill was criticized by Pliny in Roman times (but as far as we know, without result). Horizontal plowing with a special hillside plow was known in early modern times as "hill culture" in Europe, notably in Switzerland; a Hessian soldier-settler is reported to have practiced hill culture in Pennsylvania. Toward the end of the eighteenth century, when sloping fields with row crops such as tobacco and corn showed severe gullying, the possibility of plowing on the level was being discussed by observing Americans. In 1790 the Philadelphia Agricultural Society tried to elicit advice from its members for "recovering old gullied fields to a hearty state," and in 1811 the Richmond Agricultural Society asked for information on the best mode of preventing land under the plow from washing. George Washington and Thomas Jefferson were among those who blamed the manner of cultivation rather than exhaustion of the soil for low yields and gullies; as early as 1810 Jefferson was convinced that "horizontal furrows arrested the water after heavy downpours." He later noted: "Our country is hilly, and we have been in the habit of ploughing in straight rows whether up and down hill, in oblique lines, or however they led.... In a farm horizontally and deeply ploughed, scarcely an ounce of soil is now carried from it. In point of beauty nothing can exceed that of the waving lines and rows winding along the face of the hills and valleys."[10] In 1817 he wrote from Monticello describing how guide lines conducted horizontally around the hill were "laid off with a rafter level of ten feet span" and how he marked steps on the level followed by a plough to mark the trace. "The work," he stated, "when once done is forever done." On his farm Jefferson noted that he generally "levelled a field the year it was put into corn."[11]

Horizontal plowing was next tried in Mississippi, where Nicholas Sorsby, influenced by ideas derived from Jefferson and T. M. Randolph, Jefferson's son-in-law, began to practice "level culture." He wrote a book on the subject in which he opposed "checking" (plowing crosswise) corn and cotton—a habit farmers were unwilling to give up, he said, because "they like to plow both ways." Sorsby's plan for erosion control, which included straight, short

---

*Contour means literally "to turn together or around"; the word is used in American cartography to mean a line that connects points of equal elevation. European cartographers call such isolines "isohypse."[9]

ditches and required abandonment of all up-and-down hill furrows, was probably adopted by a few farmers after the Civil War, but it was too complicated for most. His drawing of a plan for farming in "diversified hills" is not unlike the farm plans of the SCS designed in the 1940s.[12]

In the Hill Country, a few settlers practised strip cropping as early as the 1860s. In fact the SCS labeled an area north of La Crosse in Mormon Coulee as America's "Cradle of Strip Cropping"; there, shortly after the Civil War, a German immigrant plowed straight, narrow strips of 25 to 35 feet along a hillside that happened to parallel a section road. In 1876 a Swiss immigrant in Houston County, Minnesota, farmed his two forties, which extended over a narrow valley floor and alluvial terraces, in alternate bands of hay or meadow and cropland no wider than 90 feet; strips of corn were never wider than 75 feet. Eighty-four of 198 acres were strip cropped on the same farm in 1937; on neighboring farms, however, entire fields of sloping land were still being plowed "at once." During sixty-one years, the successful practice of this highly respected farmer—he had also started a cheese factory in Hokah—spread only into one adjacent valley.[13]

Up-and-down hill plowing, regardless of slope, was simply a habit. Farmers took pride in plowing straight furrows, and a man's ability to plow straight determined whether he was considered a good farmer in his community. Plowing matches, in fact, were a regular event at fairs where "Straightness of furrows and even land ends were of primary importance on the judges' score card." And they still are in Minnesota, where a farmer recently hoped to gain the world's title at an international plowing match in England by plowing "straight as a shot."[14]

Perhaps the straight furrow is another instinctive expression of man's desire for order. The explanation of an English observer around 1900 (who wondered why so ordinary and ubiquitous a task as plowing should elicit extraordinary application of perfectionism) deserves mention: there was little else in the lives of most farmers, so they took pride in this major chore.[15] Midwestern vernacular called the man who strip-cropped in curves a "crazy-quilt farmer." The conservation-minded countered with the "square-minded farmer" or "square farming on round land."[16] Contour plowing had to be glamorized and that fact was recognized when in 1941 the First Dairyland Contour Plowing Match was held in Mormon Coulee before 2000 spectators. The six finalists had won in elimination matches at Eau Claire, Alma, Virginia, and Mount Horeb in Wisconsin; at Lewiston in Minnesota; and at Garnaville in Iowa—all in the Hill Country. A year later a "singing plowboy" who plowed "crooked to win" was featured in a magazine article,[17] and when in 1957 the Gillmore Valley Watershed Project in Winona County celebrated its 25th anniversary, the state contour plowing matches were followed by the election of the "Queen of the Furrow Tractor Driving Contest."

Figure 8-3. Wisconsin strip farming. Contour strips are set into former rectangular fields on upland; a tree (lower right) indicates the center of a section.

Responsible for conservation in the Hill Country was the La Crosse Agricultural Experiment Station, which in the 1930s and 1940s developed specific cultivating practices for twelve million acres of grayish-brown, hilly silt loams in southwestern Wisconsin, southeastern Minnesota, northeastern Iowa, and northwestern Illinois—one of the most severely eroded farming areas in the United States. That plowing with the property fence lines and not with the land had caused a considerable amount of erosion was admitted.[18] Yet I have never heard anyone from the SCS mention that the survey was responsible for those property lines.

Survey lines in the conservation landscape remain recognizable today not only in the Hill Country, but everywhere. Contours do not mesh along field lines even when fences are pulled down between adjacent fields (Fig. 8-3), and section lines have persisted as roads in most projects, including Coon Creek. One reason for the "durability" of survey lines is that conservation practices vary from one farm to the next; through the years, field personnel, technology, and farmers' economic conditions have changed. Also, because of a great diversity of slope, the actual layouts of strips, terraces, and diversion dikes may vary between adjacent farms. Thus, along the borders of many 40- or 80-acre tracts, contour strips of different widths meet woods or another curving field along a straight line. When farms on which conservation practices had been applied in the 1940s were later enlarged, the layout of fields contoured earlier was maintained and remained separate from newly contoured fields. For example, in Trempealeau County, an aerial photograph of a 360-acre farm (whose owner in 1973 described his land as consisting of "nine forties") shows the persistence of lines apparent between subdivisions (Fig. 8-4).

Figure 8-4. A 360-acre farm in sections 15 and 22, T. 22 N., R. 10 W., Trempeauleau County, Wisconsin, consists of nine forties recognizable through abruptly stopping contour-stripped fields. (*Courtesy Terry Williams, County Surveyor*)

WATERSHED AND SOIL CONSERVATION DISTRICTS

A watershed, or drainage basin, comprises the land area that is drained by a river at its mouth. The area can be a few square miles in the case of a creek or very large, as for example, in the Tennessee Valley project. The boundaries (divides) of these natural regions are always curved. Chief Bennett of the SCS, who preached "farming with nature," held watershed management as gospel. During his tenure and in the following years, several drainage basin projects were set up, among them four in our region.

The Coon Creek Project, already discussed, was one of them. Another was the McGregor Project (1935), which consisted of thirty-two cooperating farms (out of forty) and the town of McGregor in a watershed of 2500 acres; floods and soils washed down from cropped hogback ridges had caused considerable damage there. The Gillmore Valley Project of 1935 included fifty-five farms, most of them on hills drained through Gillmore Creek into Lake Winona. All but one farmer applied to participate in the project, which was designed to protect Winona against overflow from the lake through streambank stabilization, culverts, terraces, diversion dikes, contour strips, grassways, fenced woodland, long-term crop rotation favoring cover crops, not corn, and dairying rather than hog production. The Farmersburg Watershed Project (1935) covered 11,500 acres, a part of which was included in the Clayton County Soil Conservation District in 1940. Straight-lined townships, however, do not coincide with watersheds (Fig. 8-5).

Soil conservation districts were originally meant to be identical with watersheds and to be initiated by farmers who through district supervisors would cooperatively seek assistance from the SCS. The supervisors were to be comparable to county commissioners and to act as a board, not as individuals. But after the late 1930s, soil conservation districts were organized and named by counties, not by watersheds; the reason for this can be largely attributed to the vital role county attorneys played as legal advisors to soil conservation districts. Thus it proved impossible to bypass, let alone to override, the political power of the county.[19]

The districts, however, did not have the power to enforce conservation measures. Persuasion and neighborly cooperation were not always successful, and at times a non-cooperating farmer could jeopardize the labor and capital invested by an adjacent operator and the SCS. Protective measures could disappear when a farm was sold to or inherited by parties who neglected maintenance or reverted to earlier, harmful practices. Land could not be entailed and property rights remained inviolate, so that an owner's freedom to manage his land as he wished was maintained. "The whole conservation movement might have been unnecessary if the laws of waste had been more effective and had applied to owners as well as holders of lesser estates. In society's effort to establish the freest tenure the pendulum probably swung too far toward complete freedom.[20]

LAND AND WATER MANAGEMENT201

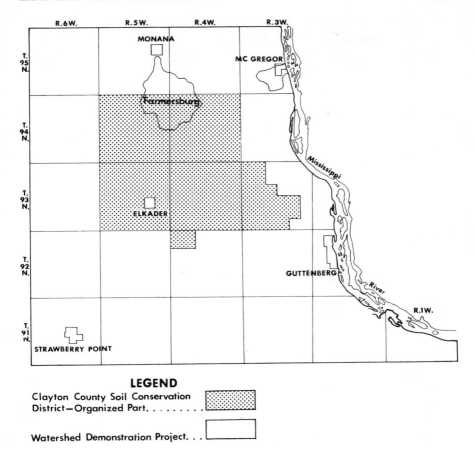

Figure 8-5. The Clayton Soil Conservation District of 1940 consisted of 4 1/2 congressional townships. The outlines of the Farmersburg and McGregor watersheds contrast with the straight-lined boundaries of townships and sections

Less enthusiastic farmers were probably persuaded to cooperate in early demonstration watershed projects through heavy SCS subsidies of improvements on their farms. Mere appeals to be good stewards of their land would not have generated the high measure of collaboration needed for managing such projects, which often covered several thousand acres. Occasionally counties organized coordinated programs, such as that covering the Forestville Lake drainage basin, which extends into four Iowa counties: Delaware, Clayton, Fayette, and Buchanan. Each county soil conservation district appointed a commissioner to serve on the Four District Soil Conservation Watershed, organized in 1948.

Between 1937 and 1947 around 1750 soil conservation districts were organized in the United States. By 1962 approximately 92 per cent of the land in farms and 96 per cent of all farms and ranches were located in such districts, which encompassed over 945 million acres and about 4,200,000 farms—"better than two-thirds of the farms and ranches in the nation," according to the SCS. But this estimate is based on the total area of participating counties (districts); the acreage under conservation by participating farmers in these districts was much less and not computed by the SCS. Let us be reminded again that conservation districts identical with counties cannot have boundaries that are also the divide between watersheds. American society ignored this concept, which is very important for land and water management, in the drawing of civil boundaries. The significance of the watershed has been learned only after bitter experience.

WATERSHED ASSOCIATIONS

Federal legislation led the way toward a greater national awareness of the need to consider watershed management as part of preventive flood control measures. The Flood Control Act of 1936 recognized the need for flood control through retardation of runoff from small upstream watersheds. Three watersheds in our region—the Root, Whitewater, and Galena—were surveyed for improvements; their plans were reported to the Secretary of Agriculture by 1949 but not authorized or funded. In 1953 President Eisenhower stated in a message to Congress that a more logical division of responsibilities among federal agencies was needed to achieve the greatest efficiency and the least duplication; comprehensive river-basin planning with the cooperation of state and local interests was required. Congress responded by appropriating five million dollars to begin sixty-five pilot projects, among them one on the West Fork of the Kickapoo River in Vernon and Monroe counties, Wisconsin, and another on East Willow Creek in Fillmore County, Minnesota. At the same time and somewhat unexplained (unless the declared desirability of strengthening state and local influence was acceptable as an explanation) the Secretary of Agriculture announced in 1953 the abolishment of the regional offices of the SCS. This aroused strong protest from the National Association of Soil Conservation Districts, whose members were aware of the value of the regional offices as training institutions of loyal SCS men. Functions of seven regional offices were to be dispersed among forty-eight state offices.

   In 1954, Public Law 566, an act usually cited as the "Watershed Protection and Flood Prevention Act," was passed. Watersheds not exceeding 250,000 acres were to be managed through the teamwork of local organizations under the supervision of state agencies. Conditions for obtaining federal assistance stipulated that easements and rights-of-way be acquired locally and without cost to the federal government and that local organizations assume an equitable share of the cost of installing improvements.[21]

The first National Watershed Congress in December 1954 was sponsored by twenty-four national organizations, among them the National Grange, National Farmers Union, National Association of Soil Conservation Districts, Izaak Walton League, Wildlife Management Institute, American Federation of Labor, and National Association of Manufacturers. The national interest in drainage basins had been aroused, and water and soil conservation were proclaimed as interdependent and essential for rural and urban regions.

Small watershed projects were local undertakings with federal help. In severely eroded Buffalo County, Wisconsin, local watershed associations were organized in the Alma-Mill Creek and South Nelson watersheds in 1959. The Garden Valley Watershed, with 121,000 acres, and the Beef River Watershed, extending over 140,000 acres, were organized in 1960, leaving only two principal watersheds to round out the county. That year Buffalo County was cited as "the most watershed-conscious county in the State of Wisconsin."[22] And west of Monroe the Smock Valley Watershed Association, organized about 1952, made fast progress, causing a reporter in 1956 to wonder "if the watershed association will replace the threshing ring."

While the threshing ring can ignore county boundaries, watershed associations have to work through county districts. In the French-Beaver Creek Watershed, organized in 1954, the headwaters of North and South Beaver Creek are crossed, straight north-south, by the boundary between Jackson and Trempealeau counties. By 1973 the creeks still did not have the six dams proposed in the original plan. And a pamphlet published by the directors of the project in 1972 listed the need for, among other measures, roadside erosion control along five miles, tree plantings on 6500 acres, streambank protection along 116 miles, 390 flood-water control structures, and contour strip-farming on 21,802 acres. The completed work in each category amounted respectively to 5, 12, 14, 23, and 84 per cent of what was needed. Proportionately by far the highest achievement was the adoption of contour strip-farming. The reason, of course, is that while change of field layout on farms can be brought about by individual decisions of farm operators, collaborative measures in watershed management must begin with petitions by county boards of commissioners to state resource boards. In short, progress depends upon the cooperation of many and upon agreements and assistance from several state and county agencies.[23]

Further progress of conservation measures is being delayed by the curtailment of funds from the Agricultural Stabilization and Conservation Service.[24] Indeed, some strip-cropped curving fields and grassways on small ridge and bench farms in the Hill Country may disappear. But the new layout of larger farms has been achieved at great expense, and the many

farmers who gave up their former habits of straight plowing simply are not
going to change again. They grew up with contour farming.

TERRACING, MULCHING, AND SHELTERBELTS

Contouring along slopes, which requires the tilting of tractors and plows,
often does not retard soil erosion satisfactorily. Terracing, a recently recommended practice, requires still more technical and scientific expertise
than contour stripping, and on some slopes an effective terracing system is
almost impossible to construct. While the appeal to "plow with nature" was
simply good propoganda, terracing is even more than contouring a "rational
use" of land, as a French agronomist calls modern conservation practices.[25]

Aside from contouring, the replacement of deep plowing by shallow disk-
harrowing also contributed to a new look in the American survey landscape.
When shallow plowing was recognized as "the great error of American
agriculture" in the beginning of the nineteenth century, deep plowing,
resulting in tidy-looking fields in which farmers took great pride, became the
custom.[26] That habit, however, was broken through the enormous influence
of a book entitled *Plowman's Folly*, which sold 355,000 copies; it advocated
shallow disk-harrowing for small grain crops.[27] This method left crop residue
as surface mulch and thus reduced the effects of wind erosion on the "dirty"
fields.[28]

Wind erosion in the Hill Country is a serious problem in sandy outwash
and loess-blown areas along the northern margin. Shelterbelts, usually of
jack pine, are numerous on the level stretches of upland and wide river-
terraces, for example, along the Chippewa River north of Durand in
Wisconsin's "Caddie Woodlawn" country. They are planted in north-south
and east-west rows. So are windbreaks around most farmsteads; they rarely
cluster or curve around the northwestern corner of a farmstead. Questioned
on the reason for only two directions, farmers, technicians, and scientists
usually give the same answer: Nobody likes to break up a field and change
"lines." Since wind erosion is prevalent over large, flat areas where survey
lines rule supreme, mature shelterbelts further enforce the influence of the
non-varying grid. They are marvels of rectangularity in the Great Plains and
in the Red River Valley. In Pepin, Dunn, northern Trempealeau, and
Jackson counties they are rows spaced at various intervals. Conservation
legislation has indirectly subsidized shelterbelts and tree plantings by making seedlings available from state nurseries.

It is difficult to change traditions in agriculture, particularly where field
borders are concerned.[29] In many parts of the world, farmers are extraordinarily resistant to any alteration of field lines—far more so than to the
adoption of crop rotation, new technologies, or new patterns of ownership
and tenancy. So the process of changing the rectangular field layout of a

midwestern farm to contours and terraces—an impressive spectacle in itself—becomes all the more significant. During the 1950s, when soil conservation districts staged "conservation days," crowds of several hundred people watched crews tearing out fence posts, rolling up the wire fences, setting new posts, plowing along contour lines, and leveling terraces. The movement of machines and the personnel involved in changing the face of the land was formidable.

It remains to discuss the disappearance of survey lines when land is returned from private to public ownership—usually for recreational purposes. In southeastern Minnesota the Whitewater Watershed is one such area; its study also offers an opportunity to observe a sequent occupance.

Recreational Land Use

The purpose for which the Ordinance of 1785 reserved four out of every thirty-six square miles was not spelled out. Perhaps the Founding Fathers had forests in mind, such as we find on eighteenth-century utopian plans—areas that we call "open space" today. No provisions for open space were included in the Act of 1796.* In the 1970s U.S. planners consider recreational space a necessity for society and they recommend, although not unanimously, a minimum of ten acres for each 1000 persons. Had the stipulation of the 1785 ordinance been carried out, a county such as Winona in the Hill Country would have had seventy square miles reserved, which in 1900, when the county had 35,686 inhabitants, would have amounted to 100 times the area of open space now considered a desirable minimum. But by the turn of the century no publicly owned recreational areas existed in the Hill Country. In fact, with the disposal of the public domain nearly complete, no national parks or forests had been set aside in Illinois, Wisconsin, or Iowa. In Minnesota Superior National Forest and Voyageur National Park were eventually established, but they are far to the north. Little has changed. In Wisconsin seven small scattered tracts called the Ice Age National Scientific Reserve are federally controlled, and all four states have a share in the Upper Mississippi Wildlife and Fish Refuge. It is the states that have carried the main responsibility of providing recreational space for the public.

STATE PARKS

In the East, New York was the leader of the state park movement; in the Middle West it was Minnesota, acquiring land around the headwaters of the

*In 1802 Congress granted section 16 in each township to states for the maintenance of schools; in 1848 another, section 36, was added to the grants of school lands. The acreage turned over to the states was sold in Illinois, Iowa, Wisconsin, and Minnesota, and no public space remained reserved in the townships.

Mississippi for Itasca State Park in 1891. The land for St. Croix Interstate Park was bought by Minnesota and Wisconsin in 1895 and 1900 respectively. Wisconsin's State Park Board, founded in 1907, acquired 3641 acres of woodland, Peninsula State Park, near Green Bay in 1910. In the Hill Country 2538 acres near Devil's Lake in Sauk County were bought in 1917. Very little clearing had taken place in the rough country around Devil's Lake, and much of the acreage was covered by natural forest. In 1917, the state also bought 1671 acres for Wyalusing State Park near Prairie du Chien; in the following year 1027 acres for Perrot State Park were deeded as a gift. And in 1919, Tower Hill, an old shot-tower near Helena dating from the lead-mining period, was acquired as a historical site. Dewey Nelson State Park, the site of the governor's first plantation near Cassville, became a historical site in 1935, and in 1957 Black River State Forest, consisting of 59,000 acres of marshland and jack pine, became the most recent addition to Wisconsin's state park and forest system in the Hill Country.

Iowa in 1919 bought 1600 acres for Backbone State Park, a scenic area of rock ledges, caves, boulders, rock formations, and a high limestone ridge called the "Devil's Backbone" above the Makoqueta River at the southern end of the Hill Country. Illinois, which bought only 315 acres for Starved Rock State Park in the Rock River Hill Country, was more interested in historical than scenic sites until the 1920s, when conservation groups began to exert their influence. Among several park sites in the Driftless Area proposed by a Chicago group known as the "Friends of Our Native Landscape" was the Apple River Canyon east of Galena, which became a park in 1932.[30]

THE WHITEWATER VALLEY

Along the Whitewater River, a tributary to the Upper Mississippi, pale yellow Jordan sandstone is exposed at the base of some rock cliffs and above it ocher-colored Oneita dolomite forms turret-like outcrops so typical along tributaries of the Upper Mississippi. Lookouts such as Flat Iron Rock, Chimney Rock, and Signal Point rise 200 feet and more above the river. The beauty of such rock scenery stirred private citizens in southeastern Minnesota to work for a public recreation area in the Whitewater Valley as early as 1912. In 1917 residents of St. Charles tried to raise funds for a park by selling a book illustrated with photographs of the valley,[31] but a bill for the park was vetoed, and it was not until 1919 that the state appropriated $10,000 to buy land in the valley. By 1923 a total of 668 acres, covering a winding gorge and an abandoned valley of the Middle Fork of the Whitewater, had been acquired. The Whitewater State Park, today only 20 acres larger, is still short of the 1000 acres recommended in a 1937 plan.

Outdoor enthusiasts in Winona and Olmsted counties wanted more than a

Figure 8-6. Denuded pastures on a slope along the South Branch of the Whitewater River (1949). *(Clarence O. Bergeson)*

small state park. In 1931 the Minnesota Division of the Izaak Walton League* filed a petition with the Conservation Commission of Minnesota for the establishment of a game refuge and public hunting ground in the Whitewater Valley. After the petition's immediate approval the commission bought sixteen tracts totaling 950 acres, one of which was Crystal Trout Springs in Elba Township (which had attracted city people as early as 1890 for its trout fishing)[32] for $15,000—more than half of the total sum spent for the acreage acquired in 1932. In 1933 eight tracts (1034 acres) were added to the refuge; one was a farm of 360 acres close to the village of Beaver, where the valley floor narrows.[33]

The 1933 acquisition was an unfortunate one from the point of view of timing water management in a flood-prone valley. After the floodplain was no longer cultivated in the refuge area, brushy growth held up floodwaters and increased sedimentation upstream. Lateral cutting of streambanks along the Whitewater's three forks continued (Fig. 8-6). By 1938, 2525 acres of farmland in the bottoms and on adjacent ridges had been removed from production, and deterioration continued.

*The league itself had been founded in 1922 by a Winona City resident and soon became a national conservation organization.

Minnesota's Conservation Commission had investigated flood hazards in
the valley as early as 1920, proposing to straighten the main channel of the
Whitewater from Elba to its mouth, but it lacked funds for such a project.
Tax delinquency on valley farms increased greatly during the 1930s, and
when the Army Corps of Engineers surveyed the drainage basin between
1937 and 1941 they found that the cost of flood-control measures would
exceed benefits. At about the same time the Soil Conservation Service
surveyed the watershed and found the cropland riddled with gullies and no
less than 90 farms and 110 village residences subject to flooding. The Service
suggested new farming practices but also recommended that about 32,000
acres, consisting largely of woodland and cropland, be turned back to public
ownership, stressing scenic beauty, trout fishing, accessibility, and proximity to large rural and urban populations as assets of the watershed.[34] But the
acquisition of so large an acreage for a wildlife area called for federal funds.

In a study of national planning and public works as they relate to natural
resources (1934), the National Resources Board in Washington found that
recreational areas were concentrated in the West, unrelated to the demands
of population centers in the East. The board also noted that state parks,
containing altogether less than one-fourth of the acreage in national parks,
were visited by far more people from lower-income groups than were the
national parks. The time had come for federal support of state efforts to
acquire recreational space and for the restoration of "natural" areas in
heavily populated regions. At about the same time that the Resources Board
announced its findings, it was suggested by the President's Committee on
Wildlife Restoration that submarginal farmland be withdrawn from production by outright purchase[35]—a proposal that led to the Wildlife Restoration
Act of September 2, 1937.* The act stipulated that one-half of the federal
sales tax on firearms and ammunition be set aside, with one-half of that fund
to be allocated to states in proportion to the number of hunting licences sold
in each, the other half in proportion to its area. State game and fish departments were to submit to the U.S. Fish and Wildlife Service projects for
purchasing land,[36] and, after approval, the federal government would contribute three-fourths, the state one-fourth of the land-purchase cost. The
concept behind this law is traceable to the English tradition that wild animals
are subject to the crown. The idea to combine wildlife protection with
erosion control on surrounding farmland, however, was contributed by the
American conservation movement.

The purchase that the SCS recommended had earlier consisted of 11,418
acres along the three forks of the Whitewater and 20,554 acres in the main
valley and the tributary valleys of Beaver and Trout creeks. In 1943 the

*The Act, often cited as the Pittman/Robertson Act with reference to Pittman/Robertson funds
was sponsored by Senator Key Pittman of Nevada and Representative Willis Robertson of
Virginia.

Secretary of the Interior approved a project for the acquisition of 10,940 acres, and within five years 5560 acres had been purchased and 1363 acres optioned. Together with the land bought earlier by the state, the publicly owned land now amounted to more than 10,000 acres. Of the purchase Minnesota's Director of Game and Fish wrote: "In spite of inflated land values resulting from unprecedented demands for agricultural products, these lands were so badly depleted that no difficulties were encountered in purchasing or optioning 7023.23 acres at prices comparable to those determined by appraisers of the United States Fish and Wildlife Service."[37] Because of its initial success, the project was extended to cover over 39,000 acres through a second agreement in 1948. Figure 8-7 illustrates the influence of survey lines on the proposed boundary of the refuge.

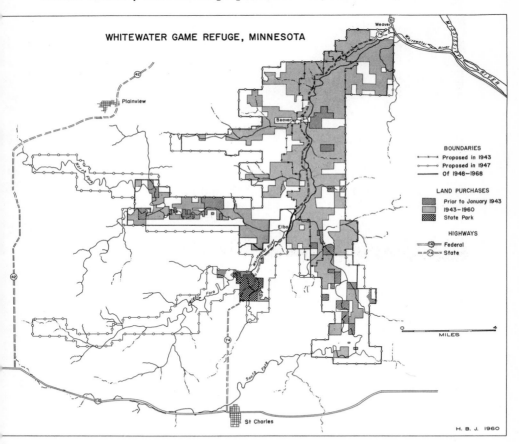

Figure 8-7. The Whitewater Game Refuge, Minnesota.

Figure 8-8. Hill-and-valley farm of 270 acres and 22-room residence, sold for $4000 in 1944. (*U.S. Fish and Wildlife Service*)

The acquisition program proceeded rapidly up to 1950 through the purchase of several large farms. Between 1950 and 1960, however, most of the transactions were for forty acres or less and added just under 800 acres. The first three purchases in 1943 amounted to 881 acres; in 1955 nine out of fourteen tracts were acquired with the help of condemnation procedures, an indication of the difficulties encountered.[38] Large farms offered for sale by indebted owners were processed first. The acquisition of woodlots, which were wanted to fill small gaps between large tracts, required much preparatory field and legal work. Still, acquisitions throughout the 1950s were "reasonably handled and not overpaid," according to the U.S. Fish and Wildlife Service. Prices for a farm tract, which ranged from $6.25 an acre in 1945 to $118.18 an acre in 1956, depended upon the condition of buildings, the degree of erosion on fields, and the deterioration of grazed woodlots. Examples are a valley farm of 360 acres, sold for $1998 in 1933, and the Appleby Farm, a former showplace of 270 acres (Fig. 8-8), sold for $4000 in 1944. A 440-acre farm on the ridge between the Whitewater and Trout Creek, partially tiled, went for $12,600 in 1950.* On the narrow valley of the South Fork, $750 was paid in 1959 for thirty acres. All parcels were described according to the survey system, which continues to serve in the vast

*In 1974, some good, tiled land sold for $1000-1500 an acre on the uplands of our region.

majority of abstracts. The measure of rods and description by metes and bounds have been used for only a few very small irregular tracts along winding roads. These parcels, often less than ten acres, had changed hands through 100 years only for better adjustment to roads, not to the river's course.

Most valley farms extended across the road and the river and included bluffs and upland. Some consisted of separate tracts, adjusted to topography. For example, one property of 302 acres, sold for $7750 in 1949, consisted of two parts: one, a tract of five forties, stretched for 1¼ miles along the slope of a small valley and the other, a tract of 80 acres, had been enlarged by two acres to gain more frontage along the main road. In keeping with the rules of survey history, the 80 acres consisted of two forties straddling a section line. In 1925 the county surveyor had found there the quarter corner of section 28-33 "evidenced by a sound old stake and monument of stone and both government stumps."

Tracts had to be purchased for the refuge where and when they became available; some transactions were protracted through legal difficulties with several heirs; others through owners who were not dependent upon farm income. But by 1960 most of the main valley north of Elba had been purchased, and gaps remained only between Elba and Whitewater State Park (Fig. 8-7). Dealing with three counties also created difficulties. But even without the Middle Fork, the refuge still extended into three counties, in which conservation districts were to bring about remedial land treatment on upland farms so as to diminish runoff and floods in the valleys. Interviews with farmers in Quincy Township and on the upland in the southeastern part of the watershed revealed a variety of personal and economic reasons for their reluctance to adopt such practices. One man put forth the idea that the state or federal authorities should redesign farm units into valley and upland farms, "leaving the rough land alone."

In the 1960s the acquisition of land came to a near standstill. Today the state owns 24,771 acres in what is now called the Whitewater Wildlife Management Area and 14,400 acres are still to be acquired. Federal funds are still available for land purchases, and the Sierra Club is expected to introduce a bill appropriating $500,000 in state funds for continuing acquisition of land. Included in the Area are the state park, a small wildlife sanctuary near Beaver, secluded tracts in side valleys that also provide refuge for wildlife, and leased land under cultivation.

Management of the Area has included the construction of 38,700 feet of dikes to impound pools for waterfowl, the leasing of land to farmers (under the condition that they leave grain plots unharvested to provide winter food plots for wild animals), the planting of some 400,000 trees, the removal of nearly 125,000 yards of fencing and the construction of 16,500 yards of new fences, streambank control through diversion channels, and the posting of

Figure 8-9. (1) Farm residence in Beaver, Minnesota, June 1918.

(2) The same house in 1950.

(3) The house site in 1967.

forty miles of boundaries. Because the state could not assume risks for injuries incurred by trespassers on "an attractive nuisance," nearly 140 old building complexes were destroyed; stone houses were wrecked and wooden structures were sold for removal. Since 1959, however, cemeteries have been maintained in "proper and decent manner," in accordance with legislation passed under pressure from relatives in neighboring towns. Management of the Area is difficult not only because of heavy public use, but because 35 miles of road remain under township control; thus motor vehicle traffic is not restricted. Furthermore, there are thirteen access roads.

Easy accessibility, argued by citizens of St. Charles in 1917 as one reason for creating a state park in the Whitewater Valley, has caused very heavy usage by local, regional, and national clientele. Some of the foreign visitors heard of the Whitewater when they were patients at the Mayo Clinic in Rochester. Campers come from all over the Middle West, the largest number from the Twin Cities and Chicago.[39] For the crowds camping in Whitewater State Park, the Wildlife Management Area provides most of the recreational space and—on long holiday weekends—even additional sites for tenting in the side valleys. The Whitewater Valley has also long been known as a study area for naturalists; in fact, one environmental workshop published a booklet in 1973 using the same pictures of Beaver used by conservation teachers in the 1950s.

The village of Beaver, still on Minnesota road maps, has disappeared under swamps and brush (Fig. 8-9). But former streets can still be recognized through lines of lower second growth. Other survey lines are also recognizable through vegetation (such as juniper trees) along an earlier fence line between two pastures. A former field border along another section line has grown into tall brush (Fig. 8-10). On wooded slopes, fields abandoned in the twenties can be recognized through the lighter green shading of second growth. A straight line of dead trees stands in the middle of Dorer Pool, named after an ardent proponent of the project; they once lined a field or road. From Hoosier Ridge overlooking the Mississippi and the wide opening

Figure 8-10. Section line in Whitewater Wildlife Management Area. Shrub growth along former fence to left; cropped field for feeding wildlife to right.

Figure 8-11. The owner of a 35-acre tract in the Whitewater Valley indicates with his shovel the top of a three-foot high fence post buried by flood deposits (1949). *(Clarence O. Bergeson)*

of the valley, survey directions are recognizable as long borders of trees. A farm of forty acres (where in 1949 an old man showed me the top of a fence which he himself had erected buried in the sand) is no longer recognizable, although a keen observer might wonder about a dying apple tree and a short stretch of broken wire fence among shrubs, reeds, and tree limbs brought by from another flood (Fig. 8-11).

The change in the Whitewater landscape was brought about by many forces—local interest groups, conservation leaders, legislation, and state and federal funds. In view of the time spent by nine federal, ten state, and three county agencies, the actual cost of the purchasing and development program cannot even be estimated. Nor can it be said that the refuge constitutes a case for reversibility of action, for in the valley's "return to nature," scientific expertise and engineering technology have played an important and costly role in the establishment of the largest public recreation area in the region. On the other hand, the Whitewater Valley presents a fine example of a historical process from Indian occupation through European settlement to man-made wilderness. There the public experiences a type of nature that was not glorified by artists such as Albert Bierstadt and Thomas Moran—men whose landscapes of Yellowstone, Yosemite, and the Grand Canyon had heightened the public's expectations and influenced Congress to create national parks. [40]

SMALL PARKS IN THE HILL COUNTRY

Many more small parks and state forests also serve the some twenty million people who live within two-to three-hours drive from the Upper Mississippi. In Minnesota the John A. Latsch, Beaver Creek Valley, and James Carley state parks, none larger than 350 acres, are "scenic" areas of wooded hills and valleys. In the southeastern part of the state is the Minnesota Memorial Hardwood Forest, a long-term project launched in 1962. Land is acquired mainly through tax forfeitures donated by the seven counties involved. Private contributions were solicited initially by the Izaak Walton League, and the first project was a 296-acre campground on the Zumbro River about six miles from the Mississippi. In 1971 the Bureau of Outdoor Recreation provided a matching grant of $93,000 for the purchase of several tracts totaling 2089 acres scattered over the area. In Wisconsin, Merrick State Park covers 133 acres of lowland at Fountain City Bay on the Mississippi, and Wildcat Mountain State Park in Vernon County extends along the Kickapoo Valley, which is being further developed for recreation by a controversial dam in what is largely lakeless country.

In Iowa the Winneshiek County Conservation Board manages Baker Park, a donation of 12 acres on upland and timbered bluff adjacent to the Upper Iowa River; Mayer Lake Park, 126 acres of hardwood timber southwest of Calmar; Kendallville Park, 15 acres of timbered limestone bluffs on the Upper Iowa River; Merlin Moe Memorial Park, another bluff with hardwood timber near Decorah; and Silver Springs Park, once the site of a privately owned creamery. Fort Atkinson State Park was acquired in 1921; its historical reconstruction began in 1958. In Allamakee County the Yellow River State Forest has unusual plant life, trout streams, a state-owned sawmill, and pioneer farm buildings. It consists of scattered areas totaling 5610 acres. The Clayton County Conservation Board manages, under an agreement with the State Conservation Commission, Bixby State Park—69 acres of rugged land—the 135-acre forest preserve of Bloody Run; a 103-acre tract near the headwaters of Buck Creek with hardwood timber and a trout stream; four acres at the Chicken Ridge Scenic Outlook; ten acres on the Turkey River; and on the Volga River, a 22-acre-stand of natural white pine as well as a 60-acre conservation demonstration tree-planting. The Effigy Mounds National Monument and Pikes Peak State Park—over 500 acres covering the highest bluffs along the Mississippi—are also in Clayton

County. Recreational areas in the Iowa Hill Country are not really wild; they are scattered tracts embedded in the rural landscape.

Compared to the great number of public sites, private recreational areas developed for profit are rare in Hill Country. Noteworthy, however, is a retirement and vacation-home project of about 4000 acres east of Galena near the Apple River Canyon. Its clients come from large cities in the Upper Middle West. A less-successful project, so far, is a large skiing and hunting lodge near Alma. Fishing, boating, and summer cottages along the Mississippi have never gone out of fashion and are gaining in popularity. One of the many private cruisers on the Upper Mississippi made news in 1973 by traveling 430 miles from its slip at Hudson, on the Wisconsin side of the St. Croix, to Guttenberg, Iowa, and back; it had to go through nine locks each way. But there is only one tour boat at present that compares with the tour boats of the nineteenth century—the *Delta Queen*, rescued through a special congressional act from demolition. It plies the Ohio and the Mississippi.

DREDGING OF THE MISSISSIPPI—AN ENVIRONMENTAL THREAT

For the past twenty-five years or so, the Hill Country's scenic attraction along certain stretches of the Mississippi has been despoiled by the sand and mud dredged up for maintenance of the navigational channel and deposited along the shores; the dredged waste also impairs the wildlife habitat. Recently a federal judge in Wisconsin ruled that the Army Corps of Engineers must file an environmental impact statement with the federal government to obtain approval for further dumping along the shores. Wisconsin demonstrated its awareness of the value of Hill Country scenery when the state acquired the first scenic easements for the Great River Road in 1952. A 1961 law authorized the purchase of perpetual easements over land abutting selected roads to prevent owners from obstructing scenic views. In 19 the Great River Environmental Action Team (GREAT) was organized, including such groups as the Sierra Club and the Izaak Walton League, federal and state agencies (such as the Fish and Wildlife Service and the Army Corps of Engineers), and planning commissions from Wisconsin, Minnesota, and Iowa. In 1977 GREAT expects to have a management plan ready for the River's environment between the Twin Cities and Guttenberg, Iowa.

The Upper Mississippi Hill Country is easily accessible and its role as a tourists' landscape is on the increase. Society allots "site and sight" values to hills, streams, valleys, and picturesque farms, and recognizing this, the Department of Agriculture recommended in the 1960s that agricultural regions under good management practices be included in the nation's recreational areas for "shun-piking," a new word for Sunday drives.[41] Pleasure driving and hiking, however, usually do not appeal to urbanites when roads are straight. Aesthetic judgments influence the public's acceptance or rejection of landscapes for recreational use.

The last chapter, which will summarize the development of the survey as a system that is increasingly criticized, also invites a discussion of the contemporary scene with its ubiquitous rectilinearity.

9 THE BALANCE SHEET

Rectangularity and Land Use Capability

In 1867 the public domain comprised 78 per cent (1.8 billion acres) of the total land area of the United States, including Alaska. By 1971 the survey had covered over 1.3 billion acres. Most of the unsurveyed land lies in Alaska and the eleven western states. The transfer of so much land to private ownership—"the greatest real estate deal in history"[1]—was greatly facilitated by the survey system, which made possible the unambiguous description of land tracts and guaranteed security of ownership. The system not only made it simple to transfer land, which aided in the success of claim associations, and incidentally, that of speculators, it also contributed toward the attitude that land is a commodity, not a common good under the stewardship of its owners.

The U.S. rectangular survey was the basis of field layout and settlement patterns throughout most of the public domain. Pre-survey claims were extensive only in Louisiana and Missouri.[2] In the Hill Country there were isolated private claims around Prairie du Chien and Dubuque, but most deeds of title begin the description in terms of the survey. Also, metes-and-bounds descriptions were rather widely used for odd-shaped small tracts in subsequent private transactions, to the regret of most registers of deeds.

The design of the survey was not a new invention. Its simplicity is typical of colonizers' plans since Roman times, and strong similarities between colonial settlement patterns of western and non-western literate societies suggest that planners resort to rectangularity all over the world. Grid patterns might well be anthropocentric, possibly a result of the human upright position. As long as humans perceive themselves as the center—often the center of a circle which can be quartered by lines along cardinal directions—the right angle at the crosspoint is an archetype by which they plan assignment of the land. The question of the origin of the

American rectangular survey can probably best be answered by noting that man, but "no man in particular" was the originator.[3]

Right-angled planning is eminently suitable for level, uninterrupted land. But it is foiled in hilly areas. In the United States, regional and local differences challenged settlers to adjust ecologically to the survey's design, and the ways in which they made this adjustment endow the survey with the potential of a regionalism of its own, which as yet is inadequately investigated.

In the Upper Mississippi Hill Country, settled mainly after 1832, the "forty" was an effective modular unit and a formative influence. Had smaller parcels been available, attempts to adjust the layout of pioneer farms to the hills and valleys of the region might have been more sophisticated. But the cost of surveying and mapping tracts smaller than forty acres would have been prohibitive; it also would have been a hindrance to the speed with which the General Land Office had to conduct the survey in order to ready the land for sale. Prairie farmers could have been aided by the direct sale of small woodlots in addition to the farm tracts.

The wood culture in its westward movement met the problem of local scarcity of timber in mixed prairie and forest regions through the subdivision of wooded tracts and their resale. Again, the simple and easily understood description of tracts aided in the transfer of woodlots. The practice of acquiring separate woodlots was continued as far west as watercourses with wooded bands occurred. But in the dry West a different approach was needed; among the few who recognized the need was John Wesley Powell, who urged an adjustment of the survey to geographic conditions—not only through enlarging the size of tracts available to individual settlers under the Homestead Act, but also through changing the survey-derived settlement pattern. Despite the wood scarcity in the prairies and the Great Plains, however, the government made no move to reserve woodlots for settlers, and no new design was created.

But the government was generous in other ways. In the Middle West a large share of federal land was granted to Illinois (6.2 million acres), Iowa (8.1 million acres), Wisconsin (10.2 million acres), and Minnesota (16.4 million acres). At the turn of the century virtually no public land remained open to entry in Illinois and Iowa, and only 314,000 acres remained in Wisconsin. In Minnesota there were more than 4.5 million acres, but none of them in the Hill Country. Some public land has been re-acquired by the government: between Wabasha and Rock Island the Upper Mississippi River Wildlife and Fish Refuge covers 194,031 acres along 284 miles of the river, mostly in intermittent 40-acre tracts that are now slough or under water. Because of many inundated stretches in the floodplain, the survey as an influence on the landscape is not clearly visible along the Great River Road. From most other roads in our region, however, one can see land in crops, wood borders, section roads, and post-survey towns—and all reflect the survey lines of the nineteenth century.

At the time of the survey, maintaining a high degree of accuracy was not so important as the need to provide surveyed land to settlers (and to speculators) on an orderly, workable basis of allotment. Urgency of performance was the order of the day.[4] Surprisingly enough, a high percentage of accuracy *was* maintained; in fact, in the upper Middle West, less than 5 per cent of the surveys carried out before the contract system ended in 1910 were proved fraudulent—a remarkable achievement, which, had the monuments been preserved, would have made the survey usable today.[5]

For clarification of the boundaries of federal lands and most of all in connection with highway construction, the task of resurveying and comparing markers and records with notes of original surveys continues. The latter were available from the Bureau of Land Management (the only federal agency authorized to establish legal boundaries) and, in states where federal lands are still for sale, they still may be bought only at the local land office, a rule that dates back to 1800.

The degree of accuracy attained on the ground cannot compare with the deceptive, right-angled exactness of township maps, tractbooks, county atlases, and modern platbooks, whose geometry reflects the perception of the planners of 1785 or an idealized portrait of tracts. For 200 years no material modification of the non-varying grid has been made. The law of 1796 and subsequent land acts and amendments were always geared to implementing the same design, although certain departures were later permitted in California and Nevada. A surveyor's work was a generally satisfying experience on level land. But working in deeply dissected land with the instruments available around 1850 was difficult for conscientious surveyors.

The survey was generally praised as a system by which the confusion and legal disputes over land titles associated with indiscriminate surveys was prevented.[6] But a historian has recently observed that "the system was not everywhere well-adapted to the land and that it was not everywhere honestly and accurately applied. But as a way of meeting contemporary problems it represented a victory of order over anarchy."[7] Criticism in the nineteenth century was not directed against the survey, but against two indirect results of it, section roads and grid-pattern towns. In 1917 a Canadian official said of the U.S. survey, from which Canada had derived its own system: "Both in its inception and development it appears to have been designed to promote speculation—both private and public—rather than the economic use of land. . . . It permitted no discretion or intelligence to be exercised by the surveyor beyond what was required to accurately define and locate the boundaries according to a rigid and inelastic system."[8]

The need for a generally serviceable classification became gradually apparent. The mandate that surveyors note timber, mineral occurrences, and other "natural objects" was euphemistically called a "classification" in 1884 by Thomas Donaldson, author of the *History of the Public Domain*, the first collection of land laws. Far more sophisticated classifications and discrimination between types of land were needed in the twentieth century. The quality of land was of apparent concern when, at the Agricultural Conference called by President Harding in 1922, it was declared that any land policy not based upon land classification was useless. In 1931 the preamble to the report by the National Conference on Land Utilization stated that federal and state policies mainly "encouraged the rapid transfer of public lands to private ownership with little regard given to the uses to which the land was best adapted."[9] After World War II, development and enacting of zoning laws became a continual task for planning agencies and politicians.

Land classification must be specific and on a regional basis. In the 1930s, public planning still remained suspect. But after World War II the need for (as well as the difficulties of) establishing zoning rights began to be recognized.[10] The development of rural tracts for suburban extensions brought planners, architects, and the public face-to-face with survey lines as a spatially organizing force. In zoning land for agricultural, industrial, commercial, residential, and recreational purposes, planners encountered a strange fact: the surveyors' rigid lines were used to delineate administrative areas.

The survey lines became the object of direct criticism: "One measure taken at the beginning of the land disposal era has left its mark on all the land included in the original public domain. . . . It imposed rigid boundaries which often did not fit topographic and other natural features—a square survey for a rounded countryside, it has been described."[11]

Highways, airports, factories, new homes, and reservoirs were absorbing annually a million acres of mostly agricultural land, and the problem of fitting tracts that had been acquired and developed piecemeal into a coherent pattern became nationwide.[12] The acquisition of areas large enough to accommodate ecologically sound designs for development is a problem under any cadastral system.* However, the survey's square subdivisions are the most arbitrarily shaped of all tracts. The form least easily adjusted to environmental features is a square, and developers should, and often mean to, consider this fact. Still, because they must buy the land in multiples of forties, larger tracts must be acquired than would be necessary had the original tracts been adjusted to the terrain in the first place. An advantage may be the serviceability of the grid for mapping data. For example, the process of land selection can be investigated conveniently by mapping forties.[13] (An illustration is the land-use planning map of Minnesota, for which data on forties were fed into a computer.) On the other hand, the ease

*Prices tend to soar during the process of acquisition.

of mapping sections, townships, and counties may have spurred some investigators to use quantitative data excessively. Furthermore, overly frequent mapping of such units may lead some to believe that units represent a statistically sound random grid system; in fact, they do not. Such tracts are entities with histories of their own.

One problem in land classification is that a serviceable system must integrate many factors in a specific area, a procedure that can become a complex system and an end in itself.[14] In this respect, it is a good idea to heed geographer Carl Sauer when he suggests reducing classification by "paying less attention to the most changeable factors," and by "keeping the number of quality classes to a minimum."[15]

Land-use regulations, it was thought, would loosen the hold of the survey pattern on real estate development and lessen the powerful influence that the existing rural cadastral pattern had on urban planning.[16] The 5-acre block, a basic module in gridiron subdivision and derived from subdividing 40 or 160 acres, was recognized as standardized, monotonous, and inappropriate for hilly terrain. An architect in Barrington, Illinois, observed that subdivision based on soil information could "minimize a variety of problems which application of a rigid arbitrary gridiron system of design ignores or accentuates." At the time of these debates and observations much of the rural-urban fringe was already frozen into the survey pattern by streets, utility installations, and lots.[17] As a countermeasure, town planners used soil maps, which follow the lay of the land, rather than the gridiron pattern. Ian McHarg, for example, accepted soil data as the main determinant for designing the layout of new settlements and called his new method and book *Design with Nature*.[18]

THE MISFORTUNES OF SUBURBIA

Our responses to environment have been researched for extreme conditions largely because such research has generally been underwritten by the armed forces, civil defense agencies, and space agencies.[19] In the 1960s attention finally turned to a more ordinary environment, suburbia, where most Americans lived by 1970. There, the design of houses, size of individual lots, and street alignment were standardized due in large part to the loan policies of the Federal Housing Administration. From Peter Blake's visual onslaught in *God's Own Junkyard* to Richard Neutra's thought-provoking call for action in *Survival Through Design*, a vast literature criticized monotonous rectangular blocks, straight streets, and right-angled corners. "Unfortunately, with but rare exceptions, American city planning has been essentially a two-dimensional pursuit," was John W. Reps's comment on standard designs in his introduction to *The Making of Urban America*.[20]

Euclidean geometry was specifically and disparagingly mentioned by many observers. Many people, perhaps subconsciously, became disdainful of rectangular blocks. Curved streets were preferred. The cul-de-sac was promoted as inducing neighborliness. Overlooked, of course, were the advantages of the grid pattern; among them are easy orientation by numbering or alphabetical naming of streets, and the convenient arrangement of one-way traffic. In most European cities drivers complain that they cannot foresee where winding, one-way streets will lead them.

The section-road system has been recognized as one cause of wasteful suburban growth[21] (Fig. 9-1). Section roads have played a part in spreading homes into the countryside not only in metropolitan areas but around small and medium-sized towns in the Upper Mississippi Country as well. It is often impossible to tell whether a farmstead is the home of a farmer, a part-time farmer, a retired farmer, or a commuter. At the same time, on small hill and valley farms where farming has become uneconomical, the wilderness is taking over again.[22] The distinction between farmstead and suburbia and between farmland and unattended wild growth are increasingly blurred and the countryside looks more untidy.

The ascertainment of property lines, however, continues unabated. Without them it is not possible to uphold the tradition of inviolable property rights—even if we violate them as we build our freeways, using the concept of the "right of public domain" as an excuse in condemning private land along highways.

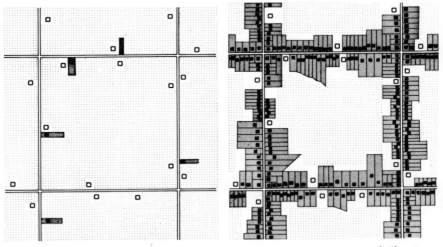

Figure 9-1. Urbanization around section roads. (*Lansing Tri-County Regional Planning Commission*)

The first markers were erected by federal surveyors. Today the government faces the task of resurveying about 50 million acres to redefine boundaries of national parks and other land subject to federal administration. But states and counties also need to resurvey tracts. Soon after their organization, counties often elected surveyors, many of whom were not qualified. In the 1970s subdivisions for urban development, the sale of small tracts on farms for rural non-farm residences, the enforcement of zoning regulations, and most of all, road construction and improvement necessitate much resurveying by state and county surveyors. In Wisconsin the State Plane Coordinate System, developed in the 1960s, was used by the state's Southeastern Regional Planning Commission, which found that "one of the valuable by-products of the system is the restoration and revitalization of the U.S. Public Land Survey System." "Relocated and remonumented U.S. Public Land Survey corners," the commission went on to say, "can be used in an efficient and scientific manner in topographic and cadastral surveying and mapping efforts, and in engineering and land surveys, and can prepare the way for eventual development and application of a modern cadaster suitable to machine data processing methods."[23]

Today the cost of establishing one monument or marker is between $200 and $300, an expense that many counties cannot or do not wish to incur. So the amount of resurveying and the number of markers vary from county to county. Some counties maintain their own equipment and a bureaucracy for surveying; others hire private surveyors on a fee basis. Generalizations are impossible. Of the nine counties in southeastern Minnesota's Hill Country, five had registered surveyors, one had an unregistered surveyor, and three had neither in 1973.[24] Many county surveyors work part-time for counties and part-time for private parties. And in one Minnesota county, surveying has been conducted as a family business since 1926, and is now in the third generation. Methods differ; no standardized monuments are in use.[25] One man might install four "witness" corners of concrete around the crosspoint, while another may use an iron post (Fig. 9-2).

Most original markers have been lost in road construction. Surveyors agree that the best leads for locating the lost cornerstones come from farmers, who always know the lines of their own property. Comparing fence lines with surveyors' original notes is also very helpful.

Original measurements are often found to be incorrect by modern standards: discrepancies of as much as eighty feet are cited by surveyors in the Hill Country. With modern instruments distances now can be measured within an inch or two per mile. States generally observe federal rules regarding the restoration of lost and obliterated corners. But the "record evidence," consisting of field notes and plats duly approved by the authorities, is unchangeable after the title is passed by the United States

Figure 9-2. Modern marker at exterior township line in Trempealeau County, Wisconsin. Resurveying is being promoted in many counties.

according to the government manual for surveyors. The manual goes on to say that the "physical evidence of the original township, section, quarter section, and other monuments must stand as the true corners of the subdivisions they were intended to represent, and will be given controlling preference over the recorded directions and lengths of lines."[26] This means that property lines on the ground are to be respected as originally established.

Today, suburbanites watch their property lines as closely as pioneer farmers did when they cleared as far as the line. They really need no fences: lawns are mowed, leaves raked, dandelions weeded along well-defined lines that exist in their vision. Neighbors will argue over two or three inches of ground; in New York state, disputes involving less than a foot are to be settled out of court according to a recent statute. Observing the line is not regional, but national, and not restricted to rectangular lots. Irregular lots, equally evocative of property-line consciousness, reflect status and often are more expensive than standard regular lots, especially when they front on curved streets. Curvilinearity was considered "natural" after Capability Brown, the English landscape architect, led the movement against formal gardens and made landscaped parks fashionable toward the end of the eighteenth century in the British Isles. English landscape gardening attained increasing popularity in America during the nineteenth century, and rejection of rectangularity was associated with the back-to-nature movement, which imparted great momentum to the protective attitude of wilderness lovers during the twentieth century. Ideas of nature and wilderness became linked to the desire for deliverance from the discipline imposed by straight lines. There are aesthetic dimensions to the ubiquity of and sensitivity to squareness. They warrant reflection here.

Ubiquity and Sensibility

In 1972 Canada honored, by issuing a special stamp, the 22nd International Geographical Congress. The square stamp had as a background a grid of 100 squares on which straight roads, horizontal and vertical, were superimposed. Along the north-south road, rows of rectangles represented buildings. At the opening of the ceremonies of the Congress in Montréal in August, 1972, the Chairman of the Organizing Committee explained that the stamp was not meant to be uniquely Canadian, but that it represented "settlement everywhere in the world as a theme." This is true for colonial settlement, but certainly not for many indigenous African cultures, where shelter, fields, and roads are not rectilinear. It is doubtful that the grid system would have been used for the symbolic presentation of settlement on a global scale at the International Geographical Congress in New Delhi in 1968.

Man's empathy with cultural landscapes is affected by the mode of distribution of houses, utility buildings, roads, and field layout. Most of what we learn of reality we learn through sight, but the percepts and concepts that may play a part in a specific spatial arrangement are immediately apparent to the initiated. Formative elements such as squares, crossroads, and the sites of temples have symbolic spatial meaning for those who experience them within the context of their culture, but rarely for those who analyze the criteria and human experiences of space as outsiders, such as geographers, psychologists, and planners.

Even space itself does not exist, but is created in our minds. Most of us understand how a painter creates space by dropping the horizon close to the lower frame of the picture, and most of us know that balls and cubes, circles and squares imply form and space simultaneously. But we do not fully understand why we conceive of abstract geometrical space so easily.[27] Yet, while it is certain that we can remember the forms of squares, circles, and right-angled triangles, rarely can we recall exactly the forms of curvilinear oblongs or of the pieces in a picture puzzle.

All civilizations appear to create their own space. Architect Constantinos Doxiadis declares that "past societies in their broad terrestrial areas had the wisdom to organize their own space satisfactorily.[28] The American colonists did so, but it can be seen that their "terrestrial skill" included more than ascertaining property boundaries. Political organization and a consistent order by which to subdivide the land were equally necessary. In fact, it is primary in all sedentary societies to organize the land for individual ownership or communal management. But how satisfactory is the rectangular survey as a formal order for America's cultural landscape? Must rectilinearity symbolize merely expedience through a plan, which is all too easy to design, yet contributes an aesthetically oppressive element to the American environment? Perhaps the non-varying grid can be interpreted as the positive statement of a rational order. And perhaps we can accept the grid as part of our culture's roots in the rationalism of the eighteenth century.

In many cultures, cardinal directions still have symbolic meaning. Japanese architect Kenzo Tange laid out the master plan of the 1970 World Exposition at Osaka in quarters and along a strictly north-south and east-west axis. A symbolic area in the middle was for a hall dedicated to the exposition's theme, "Progress and Harmony for Mankind." Possibly there is an innate tendency to favor straightness and even the human quality of the square.

We saw how the roundness of the contour was popularized as being of nature and organic. It seems to imply that rectangularity is peculiarly man's order. Yet consider two versions of eighteenth-century etchings (Fig. 9-3). Both show the shipwrecked Aristippus with his companions stepping on the shores of Rhodes and pointing toward geometric figures drawn in the

Figure 9-3. Two versions of an eighteenth-century etching depicting the
shipwreck of Aristippus as related by
Vitruvius. The philosopher's words,
"Be of good hope, I see the traces of
men," are illustrated by rectilinear
forms in the frontispiece to a 1703 edition of Euclid's *Opera* (above), and (below), by curvilinear forms in the
Clarendon edition of Archimedes'
works (1792). (*The New York Public
Library*)

sand—the traces of men. Yet in one version the figures are straight lines, rectangles, squares, and triangles; in the other they are a circle, curves, and an ellipse. American geographer Clarence Glacken, in *Traces on the Rhodian Shore* includes the "straight-line" version only. But his history of man's attitude and action toward land in western civilization deals with all-important ideas of man as child and part of organic nature and of men as rulers of the earth.

Humans are round and humans are square. Children begin to draw people by drawing circles but are taught to straighten torsoes into angular outlines. They must learn the difference. Van Gogh wrote that life is probably "round." Black Elk, an Ogalala Sioux, found roundness ubiquitous in his world of sky, earth, birds' nests, teepees, in his shoulders, face, and limbs—in contrast to white men's angular altars and rectangular fields; driving posts into the earth to fix property lines was abhorred by the Indians. The poet Rilke wrote a poem about life as a tree which "develops its being into roundness."[29] An Argentinian poet protested against the rectilinearity of a colonial city, Buenos Aires:[30]

> Houses in rows, houses in rows,
> houses in rows,
> Square, square, square,
> Houses in rows,
> People now have square souls,
> Ideas in line,
> And an angle in their spine
> Yesterday I even shed a tear
> My God, square.

(Alfonsina Storni, 1892-1938)*

There is much ambivalence in our responses to forms, which are visually never separated from color and light. Emotionally, their repetition may result in boredom. Norman Newton, in his work on the development of landscape architecture through four centuries, studies the hackneyed assertion that nature abhors a straight line, as well as the fatigue generated by romanticism's embrace of the curved line. Romanticism, Newton said, protested not so much against formal gardens with their "obvious symmetry and man-made character" as against the "unfortunate ways in which these forms had become used." In the eighteenth century, Capability Brown was just as much an engineer when he completely rebuilt the parks of the

---

*Alfonsina Storni, 'Cuadrados y Angulos,' in John E. Englekird, Irving A. Leonard, John T. Reid, and John A. Crow, *An Anthology of Spanish American Literature*, Vol. 2, 2nd ed., © 1968, p. 513. Reprinted by permission of Prentice-Hall, Inc., Englewood Cliffs, N.J.

English manors, changing them from the old geometry to the "natural style," as were earlier landscape architects who created the formal gardens of Villa d'Este and Versailles. An emphasis on sight-line and clear-cut planiform space does not preclude tranquility in such settings. Our search for peace in nature need not be restricted to amorphous wilderness. Still, unspoiled nature became associated with roundness, and the ambling path contrasted with the human world of the straight road. Landscape architects Frederick Law Olmsted and Calvert Vaux recommended curvilinear plans for Riverside, Illinois, in 1869. On the other hand, Horace Cleveland, who campaigned vigorously against the grid pattern for planning towns, criticized the "monotony of variety" (curves), as scarcely less fatiguing than the monotony of the straight road, and proposed grand avenues for some parks.[31]

In the twentieth century the Bauhaus school was not restricted to only one stylistic component, either. The *Neue Sachlichkeit* (new objectivity), which rejected meaningless and tasteless decorations, did not limit itself to rectangularity and unimaginative efficiency. Walter Gropius and Ludwig Mies van der Rohe did not strive for bareness, which the slogan "less is more" implied for followers who were only imitators.

Frank Lloyd Wright, who deeply influenced America's desire for harmonizing shelter and environment, planned his utopian model settlement along grid-pattern lines. In 1924 he conceived Broadacre City, a dispersed interior settlement neither urban nor rural. In the legend that accompanies Broadacre in *The Living City* the architect declared: "Broadacre City makes no change in the existing system of land surveys."[32] The basis of his scheme was the rectangular survey of the United States, and he disciplined his model into the subdivisions of a congressional township. At the same time, two of his most famous buildings are a house built over a waterfall and around trees, and the curvilinear Guggenheim Museum in New York.

Let us look then, for convergences such as Emerson thought of when he wrote: "The feat of imagination is in showing the convertability of everything into every other thing ... . All the facts in nature are nouns of the intellect, and make the grammar of the eternal landscape."[33] One such convergence was revealed in a photograph displayed in a recent exhibition titled "Art and Nature:"[34] when a hexatriacontane crystal is enlarged 28,000 times under an electron microscope, a form emerges that might have been painted by a master of the school of geometric two-and-three dimensional contructivism. Thus aided by advanced technology, the human eye can recognize nature's square elements. Viewing is accompanied by associations; their messages make demands on our minds as forceful as analytical reasoning. Rudolph Arnheim in *Visual Thinking* emphasizes the importance of the "observers attention in searching to find its objective in a perceptual field that has an order of its own." Let us acknowledge Arnheim's challenge and be bold in extracting from the dissimilar the similar mainsprings of man's search for order.

Artist Piet Mondrian has been judged a creator of true reality, not just of another reality. In searching for the supreme conceptual order, he painted natural scenes for nearly twenty years before he began to dedicate himself solely to abstract art. After "Composition in Lines" and "Composition in Color," he painted two checkerboard compositions in light and dark colors. Mondrian called his rectangularity "neoplasticism" and for several years persisted in painting monochromatic rectangles in primary colors with only horizontal and vertical black lines. "I abstract everything until I arrive at the fundamental quality (albeit an external fundamental quality!) of objects." Most of his paintings convey the message that their lines and planes can be extended infinitely beyond the frame of the picture. He based all of his images on the principles of horizontal-vertical rhythm.[35]

The dichotomy between geometric abstract art and nature's roundness was pointed out, not without sarcasm, in a recent painting by Willard Dixon entitled "Mondrian and Cows" (Fig. 9-4).

Figure 9-4. *Mondrian With Cows*, painting by Willard Dixon. (*Courtesy the William Sawyer Gallery, San Francisco*)

Mondrian called his art *beelding*, which is best translated as "formgiving." An American earth artist in 1970 did not give form to his creation himself; he only had an idea of how form might be created on land: the artist, Dennis Oppenheim, telephoned a farmer in the Netherlands and asked him to run a harvester diagonally across a square wheatfield. The request was carried out and the ephemeral creation was entitled "Cancelled Crop."[36] Airline passengers who look down at wheatfields in the Great Plains can see better pictures anytime. In a series "The Farmer as Artist," a Swiss journalist called the aesthetics of strip-cropping, contoured and straight, and of circles created by rotary sprinkling systems, "visually probably more exciting than any other landscape in the United States."[37] Sentiment should not rob us of the ability to appreciate the beauty of the modern technological landscape and its underlying design. We recall the thoughts of another modern artist, Josef Albers, who deliberately restricted himself in the series "Homage to the Square" to one form in order to prove its potential for many moods and significant visual experiences. Albers learned at the Bauhaus that Bacon, Descartes, and the Enlightenment taught that modern ills can be remedied only by more, not less, modern behavior.[38]

Too much rectilinearity, tied to efficiency, in our daily environment has been an American misfortune. Functionalism has become inflated through mass production and cheapened by economic, not aesthetic, standards. It is convenient to produce standardized forms, and easiest to work from blueprints made up of circles and straight lines. Ruler and compass are components of a determining system. "The flatness, straightness, and squareness which more than any other characteristic distinguish man's constructions from the works of God, derive from economy."[39]

In today's environment, products furnished by the tyranny of the straight-edge ruler are omnipresent, from cement sidewalks to tiled floors and slabs on ceilings. Prefabricated blank partitions have replaced the textures of stone and brick walls. Interior decoration has acerbated a rectilinear determinism of which we are hardly aware, from the arrangement of furniture to the magazines stacked "in order" on tables. The specific implication of the American expression "to straighten up (or out)" is not reflected by the words for putting untidy rooms in order in other western languages.* The straight corridors in apartment buildings seem oppressive; the order which they reflect often proves to be deceiving and superficial. Igor Stravinsky said that the view from his last apartment in Manhattan consisted of "Filing cabinet architecture." Ada Louise Huxtable, noted interpreter of

---

*Americans are surrounded in their rooms, their buildings, and their streets by a rectangularity that is rarely interrupted by curvilinear forms. In Europe the heritage from earlier periods, baroque, rococo, and Biedermeyer, left buildings, furniture, and other artifacts that brought relief from omnipresent straight lines and right angles.

America's architectural environment, wrote of "aggressive angularity." In the streets many began to sense the lack of purpose behind the disciplined march of a parade and the common cause uniting the loose formation of street demonstrators. Educators have long promoted the open classroom and the abolition of regimented seating. The creator of a tent-shaped children's playhouse, mass produced and of cement, said it was "a happy curve." Rigid office cubicles have been discovered to be unrelated to communication between workers, and curvilinear "office landscaping," which is designed to conform to movements and behavior, has been declared to achieve "what is truthful and varied."[40]

Most people and business enterprises cannot afford to commission buildings designed for specific sites by master architects. They express preferences by other buying habits. So they rediscover *art nouveau*, buy folk art and crafts, and renovate nineteenth-century houses. Prices reflect the changed taste. Rectangular swimming pools cost less than those of irregular and oval shapes, equally mass produced; the custom-designed pools are "naturalistic."

A real estate firm in the East advertises: "We are building houses on gently curving private lanes and quiet, private courtyards, instead of monotonous grid-pattern blocks." On the West Coast a developer announces: "Because we are abandoning the conventional street grid we can plan an environment for living close to nature."

It is also fashionable to have informal gardens and to seed wild flowers. For modern gardens, according to Elizabeth Kassler, "the certainties of the Renaissance" now are too remote, we must not create order from without by forcing "recalcitrant greenery into Euclid's ideal shapes."[41] In the same context, Kassler, the author of *Modern Gardens and the Landscape*, cites the contour-plowed field of our countryside as "an experience ... intensely extracted from natural land form." She illustrates this experience with a photograph—an oblique view of a contour-stripped field in Texas. But there is also a section road in the background of the photograph which we must, presumably, exclude from our experience. Contour stripping as the symbol of farming with nature reached the point of absurdity in the cover design for *Contours of Change, Yearbook of Agriculture 1970*, where the curves of contoured fields and of freeways are superimposed in garish colors. Still, while we praise and plead for natural landforms and natural order we continue to bulldoze chaos, straight or curved, into "nature."

Abroad, American tourists love "peasant landscapes." But the latter often are no longer fully authenticated by history because of recent complex measures to consolidate small fields unsuited to machinery. When we visit historical farms in the United States or, since the 1960s, vacation on "recreational farms," we are motivated partially by the desire for a change from the urban scene and partially by nostalgia. Variation is the key to the appeal of a landscape as a recreational experience. As a counterpoint to city and suburb, the wilderness ranks first, the survey's rural landscape has no appeal at all.

Consider the landscape of the Red River Valley. Roads are straight in either cardinal direction, flanked by straight ditches, utility poles, and, at times, the track of a railroad. Their lines meet the centerline of the highway in one-point perspective in the distance. Access roads branch off at right angles to farmsteads, most of which face the highway and have shelterbelts planted at right angles (Fig. 9-5). The same lines are followed by rows of round storage bins. There is no need for contour stripping on this almost level plain where the natural hazards are wind erosion, floods, and insufficient drainage. All forms seem to be hardened into plane geometry. The name of one small grid-pattern settlement is Euclid. Enthusiasm over nature's roundness can be stirred only by the spectacle of clouds under the dome of the sky. Today the irony consists not only in the importance of this landscape for the production of food, but also in the near-perfect realization of a design planned 200 years ago. This landscape has the modernity needed to meet our most pressing problems of survival and is a dream of planning come true. But for most people, such values are difficult to reconcile with aesthetic appeal.

Figure 9-5. Shelterbelts in the Red River Valley. (*USDA-Soil Conservation Service*)

When a region has been made popular through literature and song, its aesthetic appeal can be deliberately promoted to meet the public's expectations. An example is the cultivation of heather in Scotland to make reality conform to images that go back to Sir Walter Scott's *Ivanhoe* and the early nineteenth century. Vineyards along some stretches of the Rhine are maintained with government subsidies, in spite of surplus production of wine because people "expect" grapes to grow along the Rhine. Along the Upper Mississippi people expect "scenery." A government study entitled "The Resource Inventory of the Upper Mississippi River Comprehensive Basin Study," has even measured scenery, ranking attraction by points—so many given for acreage of water surface, for average river flow between April and October, for lake-river junctions, for stream junctions, and for water trails suitable for canoes. Variety of relief; that is, change of height from 40 to 60 feet, 60 to 120 feet, and so on, increases the point rating. "Bonus points" are gained by the configuration of water and hills, by clusters of "topo" (number of hills), and "topo" figuration, such as a valley terminus with views in one, two, or three directions, and by "exceptional ridge or valley projections."[42] The scenery of the Upper Mississippi Valley is thus analyzed by categories discernable in the romantic descriptions of travelers in George Catlin's day. But the picturesque Indians are left to history or welfare.

The appeal of the environment in the Upper Mississippi Country is

Figure 9-6. Main Street, Chatfield, Minnesota. Date on cornice of painted brick structure is 1894. (*Rick Ford*)

enhanced by the honest human endeavors to create a productive cultural landscape. In the valleys the first farmsteads were sited through practical and perhaps aesthetic choice. On the upland, farmsteads were located at varying distances from the section roads, accentuated by silos and barns and unified by clusters of trees. Abandoned farms, symbolized by solitary windmills and subsistence farms with leaning barns in the valley, invoke a mood of melancholy in some travelers. Most of the land appears efficiently worked, neither neglected nor beautified. If frontier philosophy directed that man should abandon his nest after fouling it, that philosophy shows itself here and there in junkyards or neglected houses.[43] A Victorian mansion used for storage on Highway 27 near Leon, Wisconsin is an example. The Hill Country presents neither a stark production landscape, as in the Red River Valley, nor a traditional landscape such as people look for in New England. It has no promise of acquiring the urbanity and gentility of some famous European landscapes, such as Tuscany, even if a considerable number of nineteenth-century farmhouses are maintained as usable symbols of the past.

Main Street is still uncertain of itself. The hypocrisy of false fronts is being replaced by another pretense. One- and two-story buildings on main streets have been modernized with window-less bare slabs, adding more rectangularity. The pleasant custom of dating structures—on cornerstones or on a decorative cornice of an upper story—has been abandoned. Some brick buildings· have been renovated by painting, often in garish colors. Those which simply have been cleaned and show their original stone are far more attractive; also, the varying colors and textures of bricks used in different towns reflect the origin from local brick-kilns (Fig. 9-6). Shabbiness is often only a block away from courthouse square or the main thoroughfare; the backs of buildings on main streets usually are neglected. Most river towns look attractive from the bluffs surrounding them but have disappointing waterfronts in spite of attempts at beautification, such as riverside parks. Plastic geraniums in baskets on lamp posts look ludicrous when covered with snow and jar the mind when viewed against the background of a dam as, for example, at Guttenberg, Iowa. We must also resign ourselves to ribbon development ("the strip") which has spoiled many approaches to most medium-sized cities and towns—a national dilemma.

Enthusiasm for the Upper Mississippi Hill Country's aesthetic appeal is local, not regional or national. In Minnesota out-of-state tourists look for the "Land of Lakes." Iowa is not known as a vacation state (although its citizens appreciate their share of "Little Switzerland)". At the edge of Wisconsin's Hill Country, the major tourist attraction is the Wisconsin Dells. Tourists rarely visit Taliesin East, Frank Lloyd Wright's house in Spring Green Valley.

For those who appreciate the significance of human influence on the evolution of a landscape the appeal of the Hill Country may be enhanced by an understanding of the history of the U.S. land survey. There it did not attain the prestige of an unconditional, positive statement by enlightened rationalism as it does on the Middle West's fertile plains. Rather, it offers the opportunity to view the tension between the efforts of surveyors to put a conceptual order upon the land and the country's natural configuration of hills and valleys. For those who enjoy the countryside there are many miles of good roads; for many others, air travel has brought the survey landscape into what Buckminster Fuller calls "informative viewability."

10 POSTSCRIPT

From the air, survey lines show up differently from season to season. In winter, fields often are monochromatic white and the roads grey and darker. Rivers' edges are uncertain. The channel of the Mississippi appears blue; the river is usually open downstream from Lake Pepin. Blowing snow softens the borders between fields and woods and along right-angled fences. Shrubs and trees, black filigree on white, surround the heads of gulches and spread onto what the mind, rather than the eye, must recognize as upland. Bluffs and promontories of valley walls are intermittently covered with snow. On southwestern exposures, where the snow melts fastest, the ground is almost bare. The mud flow of the Chippewa River at its junction with the Mississippi is usually recognizable. By comparing the grid patterns of towns on the floodplains—particularly along the Mississippi—with section roads, one sees that the patterns follow survey lines. Rows of trees at the northwest corners of clusters of farm buildings, straight roads, and fences are aligned with survey directions. Woodlots, planted or left over from originally larger stands, are rectangular. In the valleys the outlines of clearings are related to the gradients of the slopes: rectangles where slopes are moderate, and stretching ribbon-like along the bottom of the steeper hillsides. Strip-cropped fields swing like contour lines on a map; on steep surfaces their widths and directions are more varied and intricate and less solidly white. Some narrow, dark contours look like scribbles on note paper. Being always contained in property lines, they still belong to the survey's order, while the crumpled threads of creeks do not.

Ridge roads are diagonals over fields or through woods and seem to reflect movement; the section road pattern is static in comparison. Between the Twin Cities and Madison, Interstate Highway 94 sweeps along the northern border of the hilly country. But the transition between dissected country and rolling upland is less interesting from the air than on the ground. The ups and downs of section roads are not steep enough to be brought out by shadows when seen from high altitudes. But sudden short curves reveal the spots where they divert from the surveyor's lines. Near the edges of the upland, fields extend towel-shaped into woods that seem thicker toward the inside of valleys. Trees, like strips of black lace, line most creeks and streams, which on maps are merely lines.

With spring's slow arrival clean fields without stubble retain the snow longer than fields where remains from last year's crops were left on the ground. The amount of insolation increases with every bit of surface; due to the warmth received from the sun, old leaves and mulch induce faster melting. Through the process of thawing, the brown lines of hills between white furrows repeat the north-south or east-west direction of the over-all linear pattern. The quality of the soil may vary from one field to the next; this affects the disappearance of the snow cover, making it less uniform. On fields where the snow is completely melted, moisture and evaporation create batik-like or marbled patterns on the rectangular carpets of brown soil. These patterns are more apparent during the ascent or descent of an aircraft.

Budding foliage begins to hide the creeks and the access roads to farmsteads in the valleys. During the morning and late afternoon, the rising and setting sun brings the Hill Country into plastic relief through the interplay of colors—blue, purple, and light green. The eye and mind see lines between contoured fields where curving patterns do not mesh. Concentric rings made by a tractor around a hill reveal it as a separate rise of land. From the contours one can surmise the direction of inclines, but interspersed rectangular fields often make it difficult to determine the steepness and direction of rises on the land below. As for the cardinal directions of straight lines, there is no doubt.

In summer, dark shelterbelts of pine in long rows parallel to section roads contrast with lush green fields. Farm ponds and the metal-covered roofs of barns and silos imbedded in the foliage glitter in the sun. It seems easier to identify towns, rivers, and lakes. Between Milwaukee and Madison one sees drumlins (elongated hillocks composed of till) followed by long, narrow lots adjusted to their southwest-northeast axes. In this area, some woodlots are right-angled triangles formed by diagonal field borders and section road corners. F.J. Marschner explains this curiosity in *Land Use and Its Patterns in the United States*, an invaluable help for studying particular American landscapes from the air.

When a pilot announces that a plane will cross the Mississippi, most passengers are willing to give the Great River a short look. After all, if the United States has a geographic symbol, it is the Mississippi, and Huckleberry Finn rafted the river into world literature. East of the River, in Illinois and Indiana, the impact of the survey is clear: rectangular fields, section roads, grid-pattern towns, and suburban subdivisions of 40-, 80-, and

160-acre tracts stand out. To the west the spectacle gains momentum. In central Iowa for example, farmsteads, four to a square mile, sit at equal distances from section roads. In Main Street towns the main street frequently coincides with a section line. The direction of the flight is immediately apparent from the angle at which the plane's path crosses field lines and section roads. By watching the north-south roads one can identify correction lines; the scanning eye will soon detect a series of jogs, repeated in east-west directions in western Minnesota and the Dakotas. Square quarter sections, rather than forties are subdivided into rectangular fields.

Continuing west, forties are cultivated as one single field and larger farmsteads—three, then two to a square mile—become more common. The furrows of plowed fields provide an exhibit far more varied than the earth artist's idea of a plowed X. Some farmers run strips parallel to section roads. Others plow in a series of lines over rectangles or squares toward the center; then they cut diagonally toward a section-road corner. Diagonal strips, laid out at a ninety-degree angle toward the prevailing wind direction, leave equilateral triangles at the northwest and southeast corners of a section. Contour strips are wider, and make major highways that resolutely follow cardinal directions, look narrower by comparison. Section roads stop abruptly before a rise of land or at a river that is not bridged and resume at some distance on the other side.

Protective measures against wind and water erosion and rotary sprinklers make the landscape in regions of dry farming a bewildering patchwork of lines, stripes, curves, and circles. No more interference from woodlots, farmsteads, and access roads. The roads are thin lines, no longer crossing regularly at one-mile intervals. Field patterns seem unrelated to each other, and wherever the land is too rough or not irrigable, a strip ends abruptly or a circle is incomplete. Many rotary sprinkling systems create circles set into 40- and 160-acre fields. Sprinklers can be set to irrigate half-circles, or circles with a sector cut out, or a series of concentric circles. Green or yellow or brown circles overlap; when four overlap, they appear rather like octagons with diamond-shaped pieces of uncultivated land in the center. (In this way more land can be kept in production than would be possible if the circles merely touched one another at the field line.) Some circles overlap the line between two sections but cover only part of one of them, the remaining part being too rough to cultivate. In the desert, green fields are islands of a few irrigated square miles subdivided along the lines of the non-varying grid. Long straight sprayers that shift on an axis neatly cover any size rectangle. So the survey landscape in the West displays squares, triangles, circles, and curves. The two eighteenth-century interpretations of the traces of man in the sand (Fig. 9-3) represent the lines of the most formalized American landscape of the present, a document of the ideas of the Founding Fathers and twentieth-century technology.

The survey is a marvel of design and planning. But it is not widely understood. On a recent flight to the West Coast as the plane tilted in its descent into Denver, a woman next to me looked up and suddenly saw the land appear through her window. She asked, "What do you suppose those squares are?" "Fields," I replied. "Oh, yes. Like in Dakota." "You recognize them, don't you?" "Yes, but we are from Wisconsin." "They don't look the same there, do they?" "Oh, no. *We* have trees!"

At night, the survey shows up through double rows of lights that cross once or twice in small Main Street towns. Main Street is usually marked by a longer row of lights. Courthouse-square towns are lighted on four streets. The farmyards are lighted by lamps attached to barns or houses at convenient spots and thus are not necessarily equidistant from the section road. Still, they reveal their relation to a road, invisible in the night, and are not distributed at random. The influence of the survey lines on our environment is visible in innumerable ways and runs deep in the living habits of Americans.

NOTES

CHAPTER ONE

1. B. De Voto, *The Course of Empire* (Boston, 1952), pp. 401-2.
2. C. W. Alvord and L. Bidgood, *The First Explorations of the Trans-Allegheny Region by the Virginians*, 1500-1674 (Cleveland, 1912), p. 200.
3. V. W. Crane, "The Tennessee River as the Road to Carolina: The Beginnings of Exploration and Trade," *The Mississippi Valley Historical Review* vol. 3, no. 1 (June 1916), 3-18, 9.
4. H. Broshar, "The First Push Westward of the Albany Traders," *The Mississippi Valley Historical Review* vol. 7, no. 3 (1920-21), 228-41.
5. D. W. Meinig, *Southwest: Three Peoples in Geographical Change*, 1600-1970 (New York, 1971), p. 9.
6. G. Catlin, *Letters and Notes on the Manners, Customs, and Condition of the North American Indians*, vol. 1 (1841; reprint ed., Minneapolis, 1965), pp. 62-65.
7. D. W. Meinig, "Three American Northwests: Some Perspectives in Historical Geography," *Annals* of the Association of American Geographers vol. 47, no. 2 (June 1957), 170-71. Manuscript text kindly loaned by the author.
8. H. W. Odum and H. E. Moore, *American Regionalism, A Cultural-Historical Approach to National Integration* (New York, 1938), pp. 462, 484.
9. T. C. Blegen, "The Fashionable Tour on the Upper Mississippi," *Minnesota History* vol. 20 (1939), 377-96.
10. "The Great Excursion to the Falls of St. Anthony," *Putnam's Monthly Magazine of American Literature, Science and Art* vol. 4 (September 1854), 320-25.
11. H. Lewis, *The Valley of the Mississippi Illustrated*. Translated by A. H. Poatgieter, edited with introduction by B. L. Heilbron (St. Paul, 1967), pp. 5-7. See also P. T. Rathbone, *Mississippi Panorama* (St. Louis, 1950).
12. L. M. Johnson, "Seth Eastman's Water Colors," *Minnesota History* (Fall 1971), 258-67.
13. W. Sypher, *Rococo to Cubism in Art & Literature: Transformations in Style, in Art, and Literature from the 18th to the 20th Century* (New York, 1960), pp. 82-89.
14. Lewis, *The Valley of the Mississippi Illustrated*, Plates 15,30,32.

15. Catlin, *Letters*, vol. 2, p. 129.

16. L. Martin, *The Physical Geography of Wisconsin* (Madison, 1965), p. 41.

17. "By Rail and River to Minnesota in 1854: The Great Excursion to the Falls of St. Anthony, by Catherine M. Sedgwick." *Minnesota History* vol. 25, no. 2 (June 1944), 103-16.

18. W. G. Fearnside, ed., *Tombleson's View of the Rhine* (London, 1852), p. 2.

19. *Minneapolis Tribune* (September 26, 1965), 12-13.

20. F. Marryat, *A Diary in America with Remarks on Its Institutions*, ed. S. Jackman (New York, 1962), p. 180. See also R. C. Bredeson, "Landscape Description in Nineteenth-century American Travel Literature," *American Quarterly* vol. 20 (1968), 86-94.

21. Vincent Scully, *The God and the Earth and the Temple* (New Haven, Conn., 1969), p. 171.

22. L. Leopold, "Landscape Esthetics: How to quantify the scenics of a river valley," *Natural History* vol. 78, no. 8 (October 1969), 40. See also D. L. Linton, "The Assessment of Scenery as a Natural Resource," *Scottish Geographical Magazine* vol. 84 (December 1968), 219-38.

23. B. Zakrzewska, "Valleys of the Driftless Area," *Annals* of the Association of American Geographers vol. 61, no. 3 (September 1971), 441-59.

24. W. J. Peterson, *Steamboating on the Upper Mississippi* (Iowa City, 1968), p. 346.

25. K. Lewis, "Field Theory and Experiment in Social Psychology," in D. Cartwright, ed., *Field Theory in Social Sciences, Selected Theoretical Papers* (New York, 1951), p. 151. G. B. Leonard, *Education and Ecstasy* (New York, 1968), Chapter 3. A. N. Whitehead, *Adventures of Ideas* (New York, 1956), p. 198. R.W. Kates, "The Perception of Storm Hazard on the Shores of Megalopolis," in D. Lowenthal, ed., *Environmental Perception and Behavior*, University of Chicago Department of Geography Research Paper No. 109 (Chicago, 1967), p. 65.

26. F. Münch, *Gesammelte Schriften* (St. Louis, 1902), pp. 352, 354, and passim.

27. A. J. Schem, ed., *Deutsch-amerikanisches Conversations-Lexicon* (New York, 1869-1874).

28. R. C. Overton, *Burlington West: A Colonization History of the Burlington Railroad*, (Cambridge, Mass., 1941), pp. 159, 160.

29. M. Birkbeck, *Notes on a Journey in America* (London, 1818)(Ann Arbor, Mich.: University Microfilms, 1966), pp. 86, 105, 111.

30. G. Flowers, *History of the English Settlement in Edwards County, Illinois* (Chicago, 1882), p. 121.

31. D. R. McManis, *The Initial Evaluation and Utilization of the Illinois Prairies, 1815-1840*, The University of Chicago Department of Geography Research Paper No. 94 (Chicago, 1964).

32. J. F. Davis, "Images of the Plains: A Commentary," *Historical Geography Newsletter* vol. 3, no. 2 (Fall 1973), 11-13.

33. W. P. Webb, *The Great Plains* (Waltham, Mass., 1931, 1959), p. 422 and *passim*.

34. J. W. Powell, *Report on the Lands of the Arid Region of the United States*, 1879 (Washington, D.C., U.S. Government Printing Office), pp. 23, 28, 29, 37, 38.

35. P. W. Gates, *The Farmer's Age: Agriculture 1815-1860* (New York, 1960), Chapter 4. D. E. Clark, "The Westward Movement in the Upper Mississippi Valley during the Fifties," *Mississippi Valley Historical Association Proceedings* vol. 7 (1913-14), 212-19.

Chapter Two

1. A. C. Ford, "Colonial Precedents of our National Land System as it existed in 1800," *Bulletin of the University of Wisconsin*, no. 352, History Series vol. 2, no. 2 (1908).

2. For a contemporary discussion of the *rang*, see R. Benoit, "Les Cultures Légumières de la Côte de Beauport," *Cahiers de Géographie de Québec* vol. 6, no 37 (April 1972), 31-56.

3. M. Derruau, "A l'origine du 'rang' Canadien," *Cahiers de Géographie de Québec* no. 1 (October 1956), 39-47.

4. R. C. Harris, *The Seigneurial System in Early Canada: A Geographical Study* (Madison, 1966), p. 199 and passim.

5. M. Trudel, *Atlas de la Nouvelle France* (Québec: Les Presses de l'Université Laval, 1968), pp. 163, 167.

6. Harris, *The Seigneurial System in Early Canada*, p. 135.

7. P. Deffontaines, "Le Rang, Type de Peuplement Rural du Canada Franccaise," *Cahiers de Géographie de Québec* no. 5 (1953), 21.

8. L. Trotier, ed. *Studies in Canadian Geography: Québec* (Montréal, 1972), pp. 35-36.

9. J. M. Peck, *The Traveler's Directory for Illinois* (New York, 1839), foldout map. N. M. Belting, "Kaskaskia, the Versailles of the West," *Indiana Magazine of History* vol. 12, no. 1 (March 1945), 14-15. C. E. Peterson, "Notes on Old Cahokia," *Journal of Illinois Historical Society* vol. 42 (1949), no. 1, p. 16, no. 2, p. 200.

10. "Private Land Claims of Prairie du Chien." *American State Papers: Public Lands*, vol. 1 (Washington, D.C., 1834), p. 867, see also map, p. 186. See also F. N. Trowbridge, "Confirming Land Titles in Early Wisconsin," *Wisconsin Magazine of History* vol. 26 (1943), 314-22. G. T. Trewartha, "The Prairie du Chien Terrace: Geography of a Confluence Site," *Annals* of the Association of American Geographers vol. 22 (1932), 119, 158.

11. U.S. Public Land Commission, *Local Laws* vol. E1, part 2, (Washington, D.C.), pp. 256, 276, 277, 284.

12. J. F. Jameson, *Narratives of New Netherland* 1609-1664 (New York, 1909), pp. 89-96.

13. D. W. Meinig, "The Colonial Period" in John H. Thompson, *Geography of New York State* (Syracuse, N.Y., 1966.), pp. 122-26. Jameson, *Narratives*, p. 202.

14. Jameson, *Narratives*, p. 271.

15. H. Konigsberger, *Holland and the United States* (Netherlands Information Service, New York, undated), p. 17.

16. B. B. James, *The Labadist Colony in Maryland*, Johns Hopkins University Studies in Historical and Political Science, Series XVII, no. 6 (Baltimore, 1899), pp. 31-37.

17. G. T. Trewartha, "Types of Rural Settlement in Colonial America," *The Geographical Review* vol. 36 (1946), 571. C. M. Andrews, *The River Towns in Connecticut: A Study of Wethersfield, Hartford, and Windsor*, Johns Hopkins University Studies in Historical and Political Science, Series VII (Baltimore, 1899), pp. 43 ff.

18. D. W. Meinig, "The American Colonial Era, A Geographic Commentary," *Proceedings of the Royal Geographical Society, South Australian Branch* (1957-58), 1-22,6. F. J. Marschner, *Land Use and its Patterns in the United States*, Agricultural Handbook no. 153 (Washington, D.C., U.S. Government Printing Office, 1959). This book illustrates through an informative collection of air photos the diversity of settlement forms and field patterns.

19. Peter Force, *Tracts and Other Papers Relating Principally to the Virgin settlement and*

Progress of North America, vol. 3 (1641; reprint ed., Gloucester, Mass., 1963), p. 8. See also J. B. Jackson, "The Westward-Moving House," *Landscape* vol. 2, no. 3 (Spring 1953) and M. Eggleston, *The Land System of the New England Colonies*, The Johns Hopkins University Studies in Historical and Political Science, Series IV (Baltimore, 1886), p. 22.

20. D. H. Davies, *The Earth and Man* (New York, 1948), examples from Appendix.

21. A. C. Ford, "Colonial Precedents of our National Land System as it existed in 1800," 24,43,44.

22. A. C. Leiby, *The Early Dutch and Swedish Settlers of New Jersey*, The New Jersey Historical Series, vol. 10 (Princeton, N.J., 1964), p. 53. For Dutch precedents in the Netherlands see A. M. Lambert, *The Making of the Dutch Landscape* (London, 1971), passim.

23. J. W. Reps, *The Making of Urban America, A History of City Planning* (Princeton, N.J., 1965), p. 126.

24. The Azilia plan is published in R. H. Brown, *Historical Geography of the United States* (New York, 1948), p. 66, and in Peter Force, *Tracts*, vol. 1, part 1. C. Jones, *The History of Georgia*, vol. 1 (Boston, 1883), opposite p. 72.

25. W. J. Murtagh, *Moravian Architecture and Town Planning* (Chapel Hill, N.C., 1967).

26. For a discussion see N. B. Wainwright, "Plan of Philadelphia," *Pennsylvania Magazine of History and Biography* vol. 80 (April 1956), 164-226.

27. J. T. Lemon, *The Best Poor Man's Country, A Geographical Study of Southeastern Pennsylvania* (Baltimore, 1972), pp. 52-55, 98-102, 108.

28. J. W. Hall, "Sitios in Northwestern Louisiana," *North Louisiana Historical Association Journal* vol. 1, no. 3 (Spring 1970), 1-9.

29. H. J. Nelson, "Townscapes of Mexico: An Example of the Regional Variation of Townscapes," *Economic Geography* vol. 39, no. 1 (January 1963), 74-83.

30. J. Bradford, *Ancient Landscapes* (London, 1957), particularly Chap. IV, "Roman Centuriation: A Planned Landscape."

31. G. Kish, "Centuriation: The Roman Rectangular Survey," *Surveying and Mapping* vol. 22, no. 2 (June 1962), 233-544.

32. W. Mueller, *Kreis und Kreuz* (Berlin, 1938), p. 16.

33. ———*Die Heilige Stadt, Roma Quadrata, himmlisches Jerusalem und die Mythe vom Weltnabel* (Stuttgart, 1961), pp. 19-21, and H. Nissen, *Das Templum* (Berlin, 1869), passim.

34. Bradford, *Ancient Landscapes*, photographs between pp. 174-75.

35. ibid, p. 146.

36. Examples are D. Stanislawski, "The Origin and Spread of the Grid-Pattern Town," *Geographical Review* vol. 36 (1946), 105-20; B. B. Dutt, *Town Planning in Ancient India* (Calcutta, 1925); and Kwoh-Ting Wan, *History of the Land System in China* (Nanking, 1933, in Chinese).

37. J. Yonekura, "The Development of the Grid-Pattern Land Allotment System in East Asia," *Proceedings* of the International Geographical Union Regional Conference, Japan, 1957 (Tokyo, 1959), p. 545; ———*The Historical Geography of Settlements in East Asia* (Tokyo, 1960), English summary; and *Hokkaido Guidebook* (Tokyo, 1957).

38. R. Guenon, *Symbolism of the Cross*, (London, 1958), p. 10. For background reading see Mircea Eliade, *Cosmos and History* (New York, 1959), pp. 16-17; ———*The Sacred and the Profane* (New York, 1959); Yi-Fu Tuan, *Man and Nature*, Commission on College Geography, Resource Paper no. 10 (Washington, D.C., 1971); J. E. Cirlot, *A Dictionary of Symbols* (New York, 1962).

39. J. Klein, *A Commentary on Plato's Meno* (Chapel Hill, N. C., 1965, pp. 100-101.

40. D. J. Struik, *A Concise History of Mathematics* (New York), 1946, pp. 58-68.

41. W. D. Pattison, *Beginnings of the American Rectangular Land Survey System*, 1784-1800, University of Chicago Department of Geography Research Paper No. 50 (Chicago, 1957), p. 64.

42. J. Needham, *Science and Civilization in China*, vol. 1 (Cambridge, England), 1954, p. 227.

43. J. H. Rowe, "Diffusionism and Archeology," *American Antiquity* vol. 31, no. 3 (January 1966), 337.

44. E. C. Semple, *Influences of Geographic Environment on the basis of Ratzel's System of Anthropo-Geography* (New York, 1911), p. 44.

45. H. B. Johnson, "French Canada and the Ohio Country," *The Canadian Geographer* no. 12, (1958), 110.————"Science and Historical Truth on French Maps of the 17th and 18th Centuries," *Proceedings* of the Minnesota Academy of Science vol. 25 (1957) and vol. 26 (1958), 327-37.

46. H. S. Commager, ed., *Documents of American History*, 3d ed. (New York, 1946), pp. 2, 3, 11, 17, 48.

47. D. W. Thompson, *Men and Meridians: The History of Surveying and Mapping in Canada*, vol. 1 (Ottawa, 1966), pp. 98, 100, 220-22.

48. *The Charter of Maryland*, June 20, 1632, Sec. 3 in F.N. Thorpe, ed., *Federal and State Constitutions*, vol. 3 (Washington, D.C.: U.S. Government Printing Office, 1909), pp. 1677-78.

CHAPTER THREE

1. P. Laslett, *John Locke: Two Treatises of Government* (Cambridge, 1963), p. 308.

2. D. R. McManis, *Colonial New England: A Historical Geography* (New York, 1975), pp. 57-60.

3. J. H. Adams, "The Land Surveyor and His Influence on the Scottish Rural Landscape," *Scottish Geographical Magazine* vol. 84, no. 3 (December 1968), 248-55, 249.

4. The *Report* is reprinted in the *Introduction to Contemporary Civilization in the West*, vol. 2, 3d ed. (New York, 1962), pp. 235-40.

5. F. de Coulange, *The Origin of Property in Land*. Translated by Margaret Ashley. (London, 1891). A short bibliography about village community and property conditions appears in Lowry Nelson, *The Mormon Village* (Salt Lake City, Utah, 1952), pp. 28-29.

6. Arthur Bestor, *Backwoods Utopias*, 2d ed. (Philadelphia, 1970), p. 31.

7. W. J. Murtagh, *Moravian Architecture and Town Planning*. (Chapel Hill, N.C.), p. 19.

8. W. C. Ford, et al, eds., *Journals of the Continental Congress* 1774-1789, vol. 30 (Washington, D.C., 1930), pp. 230-31.

9. P. L. Ford, ed., *The Writings of Thomas Jefferson*, vol. 3, 1781-1784 (New York, 1894), pp. 407-11.

10. The map is reproduced in color in *The American Heritage Pictorial Atlas of United States History* (New York, 1966), p. 120. A thorough discussion of the map of the proposed states

is in J. P. Boyd, ed., *The Papers of Thomas Jefferson*, vol. 6 (Princeton, N.J., 1952), pp. 588-98.

11. W. Pattison, *Beginnings of the American Rectangular Land Survey System*, 1784-1800 University of Chicago Department of Geography Research Paper No. 50 (Chicago, 1957), pp. 15-29, 37ff. Payson Jackson Treat, *The National Land System* 1785-1820 (New York, 1910), pp. 15ff.

12. W. Clark, ed., *The State Records of North Carolina*, vol. 17, 1781-1785 (Goldsboro, N.C., 1899), p. 82.

13. Ford, *The Writings of Thomas Jefferson*, pp. 475-83.

14. Text of the Ordinance in Ford, et al, eds., *Journals of the Continental Congress 1774-1789*, vol. 28, pp. 375-81.

15. P. Webster, *An Essay on the Extent and Value of Our Western Unlocated Lands and Their Proper Method of Disposing of Them*, 1781. Reprinted in *Political Essays on the Nature and Operation of Money, Public Finances and other Subjects* (New York, 1969), pp. 492-93.

16. Ford, et al, *Journal of the Continental Congress 1774-1789*, pp. 230-31.

17. *Hokkaido Guidebook* (Tokyo, 1957). Field observations in Nara basin and in Hokkaido, 1969. For general distribution of grid pattern in Asia, examples are D. Stanislawski, "The Origin and Spread of the Grid-Pattern Town," *Geographical Review* vol. 36 (1946), 105-20. B. B. Dutt, *Town Planning in Ancient India*, (Calcutta, 1925).

18. C. R. King, ed., *The Life and Correspondence of Rufus King*, vol. I, 1755-1794 (New York, 1894), pp. 43-44.

19. Pattison, *Beginnings of the American Rectangular Land Survey System*, Chapters 6, 7, 8.

20. N. J. Thrower, *Original Survey and Land Subdivision; A Comparative Study of the Form and Effect of Contrasting Cadastral Surveys* (Chicago, 1967).

CHAPTER FOUR

1. M. J. Rohrbough, *The Land Office Business: The Settlement and Administration of American Public Lands*, 1789-1837 (New York, 1968), p. 4.

2. L. O. Stewart, *Public Land Surveys* (Ames, Iowa, 1935), p. 23.

3. *American State Papers*: Legislative and Executive Documents of the Congress of the United States, vol. 6, p. 123.

4. Ibid., pp. 182-84.

5. Ibid., p. 185.

6. Stewart, *Public Land Surveys*, p. 29.

7. *Manual of Instructions for the Survey of Public Lands of the United States* 1947. U.S. Department of the Interior, Bureau of Land Management. (Washington, D.C.: U.S. Government Printing Office, 1947), p. 10.

8. W. V. Johnson and R. Barlowe, *Land Problems and Land Policies* (New York, 1954), p. 39.

9. Pre-emption Act of 1841 in U. S. Statutes at Large, vol. 5, p. 453ff; partially reprinted in H. S. Commager, *Documents of American History*, vol. 1, 3d ed. (New York, 1946), pp. 291-92.

10. A. G. Bogue, "The Iowa Claim Club: Symbol or Substance," *The Mississippi Valley Historical Review* vol. 45 (1958), 231-53.

11. R. E. Lokken, *Iowa Public Land Disposal* (State Historical Society of Iowa, 1942), p. 69.

12. T. Donaldson, *The Public Domain* (Washington, D.C. 1884), pp. 347-48.

13. H. N. Smith, *Virgin Land: The American West as a Symbol and Myth* (New York, 1950), p. 190.

14. J. F. Hart, "The Middle West," *Annals* of the Association of American Geographers vol. 62 (June 1972), pp. 258-82.

15. P. W. Gates, *Agriculture and the Civil War* (New York, 1965), pp. 272, 276.

16. Hart, "The Middle West," p. 264.

17. Norman J. Thrower, *Original Survey and Land Subdivision*; A Comparative Study of the Form and Effect of Contrasting Cadastral Surveys (Chicago, 1967).

18. D. R. McManis, *The Initial Evaluation and Utilization of the Illinois Prairies*, 1815-1840. University of Chicago Department of Geography Research Paper no. 94 (Chicago, 1963), p. 52.

19. J. Schafer, *The Wisconsin Lead Mining Region*. Wisconsin Domesday Book, General Studies, vol. 3 (Madison, 1932), p. 151.

20. A. G. Bogue, *From Prairie to Corn Belt: Farming on the Illinois and Iowa Prairies in the Nineteenth Century* (Chicago, 1963), p. 52.

21. H. B. Johnson, "Rational and Ecological Aspects of the Quarter Section, An Example from Minnesota," *The Geographical Review* vol. 47, no. 3 (1957, 330-48.

22. J. Schafer, *The Winnebago-Horicon Basin, A Type Study in Western History*, Wisconsin Domesday Book, General Studies, vol. 4 (Madison, 1937), Chapters 11, 12.

23. R. C. Overton, *Burlington West: A Colonization History of the Burlington Railroad* (Cambridge, Mass., 1941), pp. 139, 143.

24. H. F. Peterson, "Early Minnesota Railroads and the Quest for Settlers," *Minnesota History* vol. 13 (March 1932), 25-44, 35.

25. W. F. H. Horton, *Land Buyer's, Settler's and Explorer's Guide* (Minneapolis, 1902), p. 38.

26. M. B. Bogue, *Patterns from the Sod: Land use and Tenure in the Grand Prairie 1850-1900*. Collections, Illinois State Historical Library, vol. 34, Land Series, vol. 1 (Springfield, Ill., 1959), pp. 25, 34, 50, 131.

27. M. P. Conzen, *Frontier Farming in an Urban Shadow* (Madison, 1971), pp. 12, 13, 66.

28. Pamphlet explaining Minnesota land-use map, (St. Paul, Minn.: Minnesota State Planning Agency, March 1972).

29. Stewart, *Public Land Surveys*, p. 46.

30. J. F. Hart, "Field Patterns in Indiana," *Geographical Review* vol. 58, no. 3 (July 1968), 450-71.

31. O. F. Whitney, *History of Utah* (Salt Lake City, Utah, 1892), p. 339. D. L. Morgan, "The Changing Face of Salt Lake City," *Utah Historical Quarterly* vol. 27, no. 3 (July 1959), pp. 9-14. A. Jensen, *Encyclopedic History of the Church of Jesus Christ of Latter-Day Saints* (Salt Lake City, 1941), p. 740. L. Nelson, *The Mormon Village: A Pattern and Technique of Land Settlement* (Salt Lake City, 1952). D. W. Meinig, "The Mormon Culture Region: Strategies and Patterns in the Geography of the American West, 1847-1965," *Annals* of the Association of American Geographers vol. 55 (June 1965), 191-220.

32. J. M. Peck, *The Traveler's Directory for Illinois* (New York, 1839), pp. 138-39. Reproductions of samples of a plat map, entries in a Land Office Record Book and an original surveyor's map in Johnson, "Rational and Ecological Aspects of the Quarter Section," *Geographical Review* vol. 47, no. 3 (1957), 342-43.

33. Stewart, *Public Land Surveys*, p. 45.

34. Ibid., p. 159.

35. J. S. Dodds, *Original Instructions Governing Public Land Surveys of Iowa* (Ames, Iowa, 1943), p. 22.

36. Ibid., pp. 121-22.

37. D. L. Agnew, "The Government Land Surveyor as a Pioneer," *Journal of American History* vol. 28 (1941), 369-82. Malcolm J. Rohrbough, *The Land Office Business*, 74-75.

38. A. H. Strahler, "Forests of the Fairfax Line," *Annals* of the Association of American Geographers vol. 62, no. 4 (December 1972), 664-84.

39. R. H. Brown, *Historical Geography of the United States* (New York, 1948), p. 328.

40. J. J. Marschner's map "Original Vegetation in Minnesota" (1930), retraced and published by North Central Forest Experiment Station, St. Paul, Minn., 1974. R. W. Finley, "The Original Forest Cover of Wisconsin." PH.D. diss., University of Wisconsin, 1951. For other less extensive composites, see W. Pattison, "Uses of the U. S. Public Land Survey Plats and Notes as Descriptive Sources," *The Professional Geographer* vol. 8, no. 1 (January 1956), 10-14.

41. N. J. Thrower, "Cadastral Survey and County Atlases of the United States," *The Cartographic Journal* (June 1972), pp. 43-51.

Chapter Five

1. The Ordnance Museum of the U. S. Military Academy has eighteen watercolors by Peter Rindisbacher, who was particularly interested in Indian transportation. Several of them show Chippewa traveling in possibly the earliest faithful representation of dog trains. See G. Lee Nute, "Rindisbacher Minnesota Water Colors," *Minnesota History* vol. 20 (March 1939), 54-57. A biography of the artist is in J. F. McDermott, "Peter Rindisbacher: Frontier Reporter," *Art Quarterly* vol. 12 (Spring 1949), 129-45; and J. C. Ewers, *Artists of the Old West* (Garden City, N.Y. 1965), pp. 53-65.

2. W. W. Folwell, *A History of Minnesota*, vol. I (St. Paul, Minn., 1921, reprinted 1956), p. 93.

3. Historical Committee of St. Charles, *A History of St. Charles* (St. Charles, Minn., 1954), p. 11. F. Curtiss-Wedge, *The History of Winona County, Minnesota* (Chicago, 1883), p. 536.

4. A. J. Larsen, "Roads and the Settlement of Minnesota," *Minnesota History*, vol. 21, no. 3 (September 1940), 225-44, 234.

5. H. E. Cole, "The Old Military Road," *Wisconsin Magazine of History* vol. 9 (1925-26), 47-62. *Map of the Settled Part of Wisconsin Territory* (Philadelphia, 1838).

6. I. A. Lapham, *Wisconsin: Its Geography and Topography*, 2d ed. (Milwaukee, 1846), p. 182.

7. "Abner Morse's Diary of Emigrant Travel, 1855-1856," *Wisconsin Magazine of History* vol. 22 (1938-39), 329-43.

8.   Letter of Traveler in Galena area in *Weekly Reveille*, St. Louis, August 11, 1845.

9.   D. R. Fatzinger, *Historical Geography of Lead and Zinc Mining in Southwest Wisconsin, 1820-1920. A Century of Change*. Ph.D. dissertation, Michigan State University, 1971, p. 13.

10. G. T. Trewartha, "A Second Epoch of Destructive Occupance in the Driftless Hill Land," *Annals* of the Association of American Geographers vol. 30 (1940), 109-42.

11. W. J. Petersen, "The El Dorado of Iowa," *The Palimpsest* (November 1964), 401-8.

12. T. Donaldson, *The Public Domain* (Washington, D.C., 1884), pp. 306-7.

13. Early plats of Dubuque in Petersen, "The El Dorado of Iowa," p. 436 and in A. T. Andreas, *Illustrated Historical Atlas of the State of Iowa* (Chicago, 1875), p. 111.

14. *Galena Guide*. American Guide Series, Federal Writers' Project (The City of Galena, 1937), p. 26.

15. G. Fiedler, *Mineral Point, A History* (Mineral Point, Wisc., 1962), Chap. 5.

16. Trewartha, "A Second Epoch," p. 140.

17. Schafer, *The Wisconsin Lead Mining Region* (Madison, Wisc., 1932), pp. 112-23.

18. Lapham, pp. 34-35. For recognition of lead miners' pre-emption rights, see Wisconsin Legislative Assembly, *Journal of the Council*, 1837-38, pp. 32-33, quoted in Roscoe L. Lokken, *Iowa: Public Land Disposal* (Iowa City, 1942), pp. 283-85.

19. Fiedler, *Mineral Point, A History*, pp. 88-89.

20. J. F. McDermott, "An Upper Mississippi Excursion of 1845," *Minnesota History* vol. 22, no. 1 (March 1941), 13-34, 24.

21. M. J. Rohrbough, *The Land Office Business: The Settlement and Administration of American Public Lands*, 1789-1837 (New York, 1968), p. 236.

22. D. D. Owen, *Report of a Geological Reconnaissance of the Chippewa Land District of Wisconsin; and incidentally, of a Portion of the Kickapoo Country, and a Part of Iowa and of the Minnesota Territory*, Senate Executive Document 57, 30th Cong., 1st sess., Washington, D.C., 1848.

23. For a classic description of the Driftless Area, see T. G. Chamberlin and R. D. Salisbury, "The Driftless Area of the Upper Mississippi," *Sixth Annual Report of the United States Geological Survey, (Washington, D.C., 1884-1885)*, 205-308. A recent study is G. T. Trewartha and Guy-Harold Smith, "Surface Configuration in the Driftless Cuestaform Hill Land," *Annals* of the Association of American Geographers vol. 31, no. 1 (March 1941), 25-45.

24. G. Forrester, *Historical and Biographical Album of the Chippewa Valley, Wisconsin* (Chicago, 1891-92), p. 76. W. W. Bartlett, *History, Tradition and Adventure in the Chippewa Valley* (Chippewa Falls, Wisc., 1929), passim.

25. T. Donaldson, *The Public Domain*, p. 357.

26. R. F. Fries, *Empire in Pine, The Story of Lumbering in Wisconsin* (Madison, 1951), p. 8.

27. Folwell, *A History of Minnesota*, vol. I, p. 237.

28. A. E. Smith, *From Exploration to Statehood, The History of Wisconsin*, vol. I (Madison, 1973).

29. Fries, *Empire in Pine*, p. 15.

30. Owen, *Report of Geographical Reconnaissance of the Chippewa Land District*, p. 67.

31. Smith, The History of Wisconsin, vol. I, pp. 90, 165-66. *Wisconsin, A Guide to the Badger State*, American Guide Series (New York, 1941), pp. 441-43. P. L. Scanlan, *Prairie du Chien: French, British, American* (Menasha, Wisc., 1937), pp. 191, 196, 199.

32. A. H. Sanford and J. J. Hirshheimer, *A History of La Crosse, Wisconsin* (La Crosse, 1951), pp. 42-47. *History of La Crosse County, Wisconsin* (Chicago, 1881), p. 345.

33. *City of Winona and Southern Minnesota* (Winona, Minn., 1858). A. T. Andreas, *Illustrated Historical Atlas of the State of Minnesota* (Chicago, 1874), pp. 106-7. F. Curtiss-Wedge, *The History of Winona County*, pp. 140-48.
140-48.

34. Folwell, *A History of Minnesota*, p. 322.

35. "Proposed Plan of Village," *The Western Farm and Village Advocate* (January 1, 1852), title page.

36. "Editorial Correspondence No. 3, Up the Mississippi, Minnesota Territory," *The Western Farm and Village Advocate* (April 10, 1852).

37. Curtiss-Wedge, *History of Winona County*, footnote #3, p. 207.

38. F. Curtiss-Wedge, *The History of Houston County, Minnesota* (Winona, Minn., 1919), pp. 146-48.

39. Ibid., pp. 167-69.

40. *Standard Atlas of Fillmore County, Minnesota* (Chicago, 1896).

41. M. Snyder, *The Chosen Valley, The Story of a Pioneer Town* (New York, 1948), pp. 15, 22, 40, 59. *Our First Hundred Years* (Chatfield, Minn., 1953).

Chapter Six

1. *History of Wabash County* (Chicago, 1884), p. 759.

2. State Highway Commissioner's maps, Madison, Wisc., 1966, 1972.

3. M. Curti, *The Making of an American Community, A Case Study of Democracy in a Frontier County* (Stanford, Calif., 1959), pp. 25-29.

4. Ibid., pp. 6, 26-27, 373.

5. S. B. Jones, "Interstate Boundaries in Oregon," *The Commonwealth Review* vol. 16 (1934), 105-26.

6. L. Martin, *The Physical Geography of Wisconsin* (Madison, Wisc., 1965), pp. 486-87. A. E. Smith, *The History of Wisconsin*, vol. I: *From Exploration to Statehood* (Madison, Wisc., 1973), pp. 652-53.

7. Martin, *The Physical Geography of Wisconsin*, pp. 447-51.

8. L. Pelzer, *Augustus Ceasar Dodge: A Study in American Politics* (Iowa City, 1909), pp. 116-18.

9. R. L. Lokken, *Iowa Public Land Disposal* (Iowa City, 1942), Chapter 1.

10. Ibid., Chapter 8. Field observations, May 1971. A pictorial report of this line in O. Knauth, "A Fascinating Report of Boundary Surveyors," *Des Moines Sunday Register*, Picture Section, July 12 and 19, 1970.

11. J. Schafer, *Four Wisconsin Counties, Prairie and Forest* (Madison, Wisc., 1927), p. 55.

12. Lokken, *Iowa Public Land Disposal*, p. 86.

13. Pelzer, *Augustus Caesar Dodge, A Study in American Politics*, pp. 56-57.

14. Smith, *The History of Wisconsin*, vol. 1, pp. 190, 331, 340. G. Fiedler, *Mineral Point, A History* (Mineral Point, Wisc., 1962), p. 74.

15. Lokken, *Iowa Public Land Disposal*, pp. 109, 113.

16. *History of La Crosse County* (Chicago, 1881), pp. 403, 670.

17. A. H. Sanford and H. J. Hirshheimer, *A History of La Crosse, Wisconsin*, 1841-1900 (La Crosse, Wisc., 1951), pp. 79-80.

18. *A Sketch of the Public Surveys in Wisconsin*, November 30, 1848, House Executive Documents, 30th Cong., 2d sess., no. 12, Serial 539. E. D. Neill and Y. F. Williams, *History of Washington County and the St. Croix Valley* (Minneapolis, 1881), p. 195.

19. J. T. Dunn, *The St. Croix: Midwest Border River* (New York, 1965), pp. 51-53.

20. T. D. Hall, "Hudson and Its Tributary Region," *Collections of the State Historical Society of Wisconsin* (Madison, Wisc., 1857), 466-77, 564.

21. R. S. Maxwell, *The Public Land Records of the Federal Government, 1800-1950, and their Statistical Significance*, Preliminary Draft, National Archives, May 1968, Appendix 11, p. 15. Lokken, *Iowa Public Land Disposal*, pp. 131ff.

22. G. Forrester, ed., *Historical and Biographical Album of the Chippewa Valley, Wisconsin* (Chicago, 1891-92), p. 299.

23. Lokken, *Iowa Public Land Disposal*, pp. 122-24.

24. "Report of the Commissioner of the General Land Office," *The Annual Report of the Secretary of the Interior for the year* 1860, (Washington, D.C., 1860), pp. 3, 4, 50, 52.

25. B. H. Hibbard, *A History of Public Land Policies* (New York, 1939), p. 300.

26. H. B. Johnson, "Rational and Ecological Aspects of the Quarter Section," *The Geographical Review* vol. 47 (1947), 330-48.

27. Entries from Winona Land Office Record Book compared with Minnesota Plainview quadrangle and Minnesota-Wisconsin Cochrane Quadrangle (U. S. Geological Survey, scale 1:62,500), aerial photographs and field observations.

28. R. W. Harrison, "Public Land Records of the Federal Government," *Mississippi Historical Review* vol. 41 (1954), 277.

29. From abstracts of titles in Winona County Abstract Office, November 28, 1882, and in office of Register of Deeds, Wabasha County, September 25, 1895.

30. The diary of Irvin Washington Rollins in *Plainview*, 1856-1956 (Plainview, Minn., 1956), p. 23.

31. *One Hundred Years of History* (West Liberty, Iowa, 1938), p. 277.

32. *United States Land Office Report*, 1865 (Washington, D.C., U.S. Government Printing Office), p. 26.

33. L. Hewes, "Some Features of Early Woodland and Prairie Settlement in a Central Iowa County," *Annals* of the Association of American Geographers vol. 30 (1940), 40-47, 51.

34. H. B. Johnson, "King Wheat in Southeastern Minnesota: A Case Study of Pioneer Agriculture," *Annals* of the Association of American Geographers vol. 47 (1957), 350-62.

35. G. Catlin, *Letters and Notes on the Manners, Customs, and Conditions of the North American Indians*, vol. 2, 1841 (Minneapolis, 1965), p. 158.

36. L. Vacher, *Le Homestead aux Etats-Unis* (Paris, 1895), p. 39. P. Haggett, *Geography: A Modern Synthesis* (New York, 1972), p. 276. H. Boesch, *U.S.A. Die Erschliessung eines Kontinents* (Bern, Switzerland, 1956), p. 38.

37. D. A. Williams, "Urbanization of Productive Farmland," *Soil Conservation* vol. 22 (October 1956), 64.

38. *U.S. Statutes at Large*, 1835-1845, vol. 5 (Washington, D.C., U.S. Government Printing Office), pp. 454, 456.

39. Hibbard, *A History of Public Land Policies*, pp. 233-44.

40. R. M. Robbins, *Our Landed Heritage: The Public Domain 1776-1936* (New York, 1950), p. 148.

41. H. G. Pearson, *An American Railroad Builder: John M. Forbes* (Boston, 1911), pp. 67-68.

42. Quoted from certified copy of records, No. 5 Deed, February 26, 1872, State Office, St. Paul, Minnesota.

43. O. Paullin, *Atlas of the Historical Geography of the United States* (New York, 1932), Plate 55c. R. H. Brown, *Historical Geography of the United States* (New York, 1948), p. 408. R. S. Henry, "The Railroad Land Grant Legend in American History Texts," *Mississippi Valley Historical Review* 32 (1945), 171-94, reprinted in V. Carstensen, ed., *The Public Lands* (Madison, Wisc., 1963).

44. T. D. Hall, "Hudson and Neighborhood," *Wisconsin Historical Collections*, vol. 3, 1845-57 (Madison, Wisc., 1904), p. 470.

45. R. W. Stephenson, *Land Ownership Maps: A Checklist of Nineteenth Century United States County Maps in the Library of Congress* (Washington, D.C., 1967), xiii-xxii. Maps are published for the following counties: Iowa—Allamakee ·(1872), Dubuque (1900), Jackson (1867); Minnesota—Houston (1871); Wisconsin—Eau Claire (1878), Grant (1857, 1868), Green (1861), Iowa (1870), Juneau (1876), La Crosse (1874, 1874, 1890), Monroe (1877), Sauk (1859), Trempealeau (1877).

46. Examples are from: E. D. Neill, *History of Fillmore County* (Minneapolis, 1882), pp. 501, 511, 540. *History of Crawford and Richland Counties, Wisconsin* (Springfield, Ill., 1884), pp. 566, 745, 1005. *History of Vernon County, Wisconsin* (Springfield, Ill., 1884), pp. 409, 485. E. D. Neill, *History of Houston County* (Minneapolis, 1882), p. 352.

47. F. Curtiss-Wedge, *The History of Winona County, Minnesota*, vol. 2 (Chicago, 1913), p.· 414. *History of Houston County, Minnesota* (Winona, Minn., 1919), pp. 414, 577. L. Barland, *Sawdust City, A History of Eau Claire, Wisconsin, from Earliest Times to 1910* (Stevens Point, Wisc., 1960), pp. 10, 12, 13

48. J. F. Hart, "The Middle West," *Annals* of the Association of American Geographers vol. 62 (June 1972), 263.

CHAPTER SEVEN

1. R. H. Whitbeck, "Economic Aspects of the Glaciation of Wisconsin," *Annals* of the Association of American Geographers vol. 3 (1913), 64-87.

2. M. L. Primack, "Land Clearing under Nineteenth Century Techniques: Some Preliminary Calculations," *Journal of Economic History*, vol. 22 (1962), 484-97. H. Thompson and E. D. Strait, *Cost and Methods of Clearing Land in the Lake States*, U.S. Department of Agriculture Bulletin, vol. 91 (Washington, D.C., 1914). A. J. McGuire, *Land Clearing*, University of Minnesota Agricultural Experiment Station, Bulletin 134 (St. Paul, Minn., 1913).

3. D. E. Schob, "Sodbusting on the Upper Midwestern Frontier, 1820-1860," *Agricultural History* vol. 7 (1973).

4. L. White, Jr., *Medieval Technology and Social Change* (New York, 1962), p. 55.

5. C. L. Flint, "A Hundred Years of Progress," in *Report of the Commissioner of Agriculture for the Year* 1872 (Washington, D.C., 1872), pp. 274-304. An instructive booklet with drawings of pioneer farming techniques is E. T. Letterman, *Farming in Early Minnesota* (St. Paul, Minn., 1966). More illustrations are in *Power to Produce*, Yearbook of Agriculture, 1960 (U.S. Government Printing Office, Washington, D.C., 1960), pp. 20-24. Illustrations and explanation of farm machinery in L. Rogin, *The Introduction of Farm Machinery*, Publications in Economics, vol. 9 (Berkeley, Calif., 1931), passim.

6. *Power to Produce*, p. 13.

7. M. E. Jarchow, *The Earth Brought Forth, A History of Minnesota Agriculture to* 1885 (St. Paul, Minn., 1949), p. 135.

8. *Plainview, Plateau of Plenty*, (Plainview, Minn., 1956), pp. 26, 29.

9. W. D. Rasmussen, "The Impact of Technological Change on American Agriculture, 1862-1962," *Journal of Economic History* vol. 22 (1962), 578-91.

10. E. H. Graham, *Natural Principles of Land Use* (New York, 1944), p. 103.

11. E. Sloane, *Our Vanishing Landscape* (New York, 1955), pp. 28-30.

12. Jarchow, *The Earth Brought Forth*, pp. 7, 264.

13. *Report of the Commissioner of Agriculture for the Year* 1869, (Washington, D.C., 1871), p. 332. "Statistics of Fences in the United States" in *Report of the Commissioner of Agriculture*, 1871 (Washington, D.C., 1872), pp. 497-512, 510.

14. E. C. Burnett, "The Passing of the old Rail Fence," *Agricultural History* vol. 22 (January 1948), 31-32. H. J. Carman, "English Views of Middle Western Agriculture, 1850-1870," *Agricultural History* vol. 8 (January 1934), 3-19, 19.

15. H. Quick, *One Man's Life* (Indianapolis, 1925), p. 191.

16. A. G. Bogue, *From Prairie to Corn Belt* (Chicago, 1963), p. 76.

17. *Plainview, Plateau of Plenty*, p. 25.

18. Bogue, *From Prairie to Corn Belt*, pp. 78-79.

19. W. H. Mitchell, *Geographical and Statistical History of the County of Olmsted* (Rochester, Minn., 1870), passim.

20. Jarchow, *The Earth Brought Forth*, p. 106.

21. *History of Winona and Wabasha Counties* (Chicago, 1884), p. 1257.

22. Henry D. and Frances T. McCallum, *The Wire That Fenced The West* (Norman, Okla., 1865), p. 40.

23. E. C. Mather and J. F. Hart, "Fences and Farms," *The Geographical Review* vol. 44 (1954), 201-23.

24. N. J. Thrower, *Original Survey and Land Subdivision* (Chicago, 1966), pp. 83-85. W. E. Kiefer, "An Agricultural Settlement Complex in Indiana," *Annals* of the Association of American Geographers vol. 62 (1972), 490.

25. J. F. Hart, "Field Patterns in Indiana," *The Geographical Review* vol. 58 (1968), 451-71.

26. Thrower, *Original Survey and Land Subdivision*, pp. 103, 107.

27. G. S. May, "The Old Roads," *The Palimpsest* vol. 36 (1955), 1-6. *A History of Wisconsin Highway Development 1835-1945* (Madison, Wisc., 1947), pp. 60-61.

28. D. W. Thompson, *Men and Meridians: The History of Surveying and Mapping in Canada*, vol. 2 (Ottawa, 1972), pp. 28-35, 54. *Manual of Instructions for the Survey of Dominion Lands* (Ottawa, 1918), p. 44.

29. W. M. Gillespie, *Manual of Principles and Practice of Roadmaking; Comprising the Location, Construction and Improvement of Roads and Railroads* (New York, 1854), p. 3.

30. P. D. Jordan, *The National Road* (Indianapolis, 1948), p. 80.

31. Gillespie, *Manual*, pp. 26, 29-30, 45.

32. W. O. Hotchkiss, *Rural Highways of Wisconsin* (Madison, Wisc., 1906), pp. 89-90.

33. *History of Winona County* (Chicago, 1883), p. 440.

34. M. Curti, *The Making of an American Community* (Stanford, Calif., 1959), pp. 49-50.

35. F. Curtiss-Wedge, *The History of Houston County, Minnesota* (Winona, Minn., 1919), pp. 78-80.

36. *A History of Wisconsin Highway Development 1835-1945*, p. 16.

37. J. W. Jenks, "Road Legislation for the American State," *Publications of the American Economic Association* vol. 4 (1889), 49-52, tables, appendix ii.

38. *Iowa Laws of Fifth General Assembly*, Chap. 45, p. 3. Letter from Iowa State Highway Commission, May 17, 1973.

39. Thrower, *Original Survey and Land Subdivision*, pp. 98-99.

40. W. E. Fuller, *R F D: The Changing Face of Rural America* (Bloomington, Ind., 1966), p. 159.

41. Ibid., pp. 99-101.

42. W. E. Fuller, "Good Roads and Rural Free Delivery of Mail," *The Mississippi Valley Historical Review* vol. 42 (1955), 67-83.

43. Fuller, *R F D*, pp. 193-95, 271-75.

44. J. F. Brindley and J. S. Dodds, *Good Roads and Community Life in Iowa*, Bulletin 39, Engineering Experiment Station (Ames, Iowa, 1917), p. 25.

45. E. G. Smith, "Road Functions in a Changing Rural Environment," (Ph.D. diss., University of Minnesota, 1966), pp. 5-6, 8, 46, 49, 51, 57, 62, 74, 89-90. E. G. Smith, Jr., "Fragmented Farms in the United States," *Annals* of the Association of American Geographers vol. 65 (March 1975), 58-70.

46. S. S. King, "Rural Crime, Too, Often Pays," *The New York Times*, June 6, 1970.

47. G. T. Trewartha, "Some Characteristics of American Farmsteads," *Annals* of the Association of American Geographers vol. 38 (1948), 169-225.

48. W. A. Burt, *Key to the Solar Compass* (New York, 1894), p. 35.

49. H. W. S. Cleveland, *A Few Hints on Landscape Gardening in the West* (Chicago, 1871), p. 3.

50. H. W. S. Cleveland, Roy Lubove, ed., *Landscape Architecture as Applied to the Wants of the West* (Pittsburgh, 1965), p. x.

51. H. A. Caparn, "Parallelogram Park: Suburban Life by the Square Mile," *Craftsman*, vol. 10 (1906), 767-74.

52. E. M. Fisher, *Principles of Real Estate Practice* (New York, 1926), p. 212.

53. L. O. Stewart, *Public Land Surveys, History, Instructions, Methods* (Ames, Iowa, 1935), p. 1.

54. W. W. Ristow, "Simon de Witt, Pioneer American Cartographer," in K. H. Meine, ed., *Kartengeschichte und Kartenbearbeitung*, Festschrift for Dr. Wilhelm Bonacker (Bad Godesberg, Germany), pp. 103-14.

55. R. C. Wade, *The Urban Frontier, The Rise of Western Cities, 1790-1830* (Cambridge, Mass., 1959), p. 314. E. T. Price, "The Central Courthouse Square in the American County Seat," *The Geographical Review* vol. 58 (1968), 29-60.

56. R. Pillsbury, "Urban Street Patterns and Topography: A Pennsylvania Case Study," *The Professional Geographer* vol. 22 (1970), 21-25.

57. *Statutes of the United States of America*, vol. 5, 1844, p. 657, and vol. 9, 1877, pp. 392-93. *Revised Statutes of the United States*, 2d. ed., 1873-74 (Washington, D.C., 1878).

58. *Manual of Instructions for the Survey of the Public Lands of the United States*, Bureau of Management (Washington, D.C., 1947), p. 352.

59. T. Donaldson, *The Public Domain* (Washington, D.C., 1884). List of townsites with date of entry as listed by the General Land Office until June 30, 1880, pp. 300-305.

60. I. de Wolfe, *Italian Landscape* (New York, 1966) p. 257. H. C. Brookfield, *Progress in Geography*, vol. 2 (London, 1970), p. 53.

61. G. T. Trewartha, "The Unincoporated Hamlet, One Element of the American Settlement Fabric," *Annals* of the Association of American Geographers vol. 33 (1943), 32-81. *Plat Book of Vernon County, Wisconsin*, (1896), p. 48.

62. R. E. Dickinson, "Rural Settelements in the German Lands," *Annals* of Association of American Geographers vol. 39 (1949), 239-63.

63. P. Schrag, "Is Main Street Still There?" *Saturday Review* (January 1970), 2025.

64. C. Gauss, "Sinclair Lewis vs. His Education," *The Saturday Evening Post* (December 1931).

65. F. Marryat, *A Diary in America*, edited by Sidney Jackman (New York, 1962), p. 91.

66. *Platbook of Winneshiek County, Iowa*, (Minneapolis 1886), p. 34. E. C. Baily, *Past and Present of Winneshiek County, Iowa*, vol. 1 (Chicago, 1913), p. 205.

67. E. T. Price, "The Central Courthouse Square in the American County Seat," 29-60.

68. "The Almost Perfect Town," in E. H. Zube, ed., *Landscapes, Selected Writings of J. B. Jackson* (Boston, 1970), pp. 116-31.

CHAPTER EIGHT

1. H. Quick, *One Man's Life* (Indianapolis, Ind., 1925), p. 71.

2. R. H. Whitbeck, "Economic Aspects of the Glaciation of Wisconsin," *Annals* of the Association of American Geographers vol. 3 (1913), 62-87.

3. H. C. Prince, "Wet Prairie and Marsh: An Essay on Draining in the Middle West," unpublished manuscript, Dept. of Geography, University of Wisconsin. Kindly furnished by the author.

4. T. W. Small, "Morphological Properties of Driftless Area Soils Relative to Slope Aspect and Position," *The Professional Geographer* vol. 24, no. 4 (1972), 321-26.

5. U.S. Department of Agriculture, Bureau of Chemistry and Soils, Series 1923. An example is *Soil Survey of Olmsted County, Minnesota*, no. 30 (U.S. Government Printing Office, Washington, D.C., 1928).

6. U.S. Department of Agriculture, *Soil Erosion: A National Menace* (U.S. Government Printing Office, Washington, D.C. 1928).

7. W. Brink, *Big Hugh, The Father of Conservation* (New York, 1953). An example of criticism is C. M. Hardin, *The Politics of Agriculture, Soil Conservation, and the Struggle for Power in Rural America* (Glencoe, Ill., 1952).

8. B. H. Hibbard, *A History of the Public Land Policies* (New York, 1939), p. 488.

9. F. de Dainville, "From the Depths to the Heights," *Surveying and Mapping* vol. 30, no. 3 (1970), 389-403. A. H. Robinson, "The Genealogy of the Isopleth," *Surveying and Mapping* vol. 32, no. 3 (1972), 331-38.

10. C. A. Browne, "Thomas Jefferson and the Scientific Trends of His Time," *Chronica Botanica* vol. 8, no. 3 (1944), 409.

11. A. R. Hall, *Early Erosion Control Practices in Virginia*, U.S. Department of Agriculture Misc. Pub. 256, 1937 (U.S. Government Printing Office, Washington, D.C., 1938), pp. 2, 7, 13, 14, 15, 16, 46.

12. N. T. Sorsby, *Horizontal Plowing and Hill Ditching* (Mobile, Ala., 1860). Sorsby's plan is reproduced in *Early American Soil Conservationists*. U.S. Department of Agriculture Misc. Pub. 449 (U.S. Government Printing Office, Washington, D.C., 1941), p. 40.

13. G. D. Garvey, "Centennial of Stripcropping," *Soil Conservation* vol. 27 (June 1962), 25556. I. J. Hygard and L. E. Bullard, "Effect of Erosion on Long-Time Stripcropping in Bush Valley, Minnesota," *Soil Conservation* vol. 4 (April 1939), 239-41, 249.

14. J. Coffman, "Farmer Practices to Plow the 'Old Sod' in Tournament," *Minneapolis Tribune*, September 18, 1973.

15. R. Blythe, *Akenfield, Portrait of an English Village* (New York, 1969), p. 68.

16. *A Century of Farming in Iowa 1846-1946* (Ames, Iowa, 1946), plate II.

17. G. Lloyd, "Singing Plowboy Plows Crooked to Win," *Soil Conservation* vol. 7, no. 7 (1942), 169-71.

18. C. A. Dambock, "Fence Row Facts, *Soil Conservation* vol. 7, no. 10 (1942), 238.

19. *Land Use Regulations in Soil Conservation Districts*, U.S. Department of Agriculture, Soil Conservation Service (U.S. Government Printing Office, Washington D.C., 1947), p. 29. M. A. Thorfinnson, "County Attorneys in Vital Role," *Soil Conservation* vol. 2, no. 8 (1947), 178-79.

20. M. Harris, "Private Interests in Private Lands: Intra- and Inter-Private," in H. W. Ottoson, ed., *Land Use Policy and Problems in the U.S.* (Lincoln, Neb., 1963), pp. 307-35.

21. U.S. Congress, *Conservation and Watershed Programs*, Hearing Before the Committee on Agriculture, 83d Cong., 1st Sess., April, May, 1953 (U.S. Government Printing Office, Washington, D.C., 1953). U.S. Congress, *Public Law* 566, 83d Cong., 2d Sess., H.R. 6788, 4 August, 1954. U.S. Congress, *Watershed Conservation and Flood Prevention: A Discussion of the Watershed Protection and Flood Prevention Act*, 1954, Committee on Agriculture (Washington, D.C., 1954).

22. K. Alverson, "Buffalo County Hits the Watershed Trail," *Soil Conservation* vol. 25, no. 10 (1960), 229-31.

23. M. J. Peterson, "The Laws of the Watershed," *The Conservation Volunteer*, Minnesota Department of Conservation (January, February 1958), 1-8. The League of Women Voters of the United States, *On the Waterfront: An Introduction to the administrative, legislative, and economic problems involved in Water Resource Development* (Washington, D.C., 1957).

24. R. Reed, "Soil Erosion Control is a Victim of Shifting Priorities," *The New York Times*, March 13, 1973.

25. F. Fournier, "Rational Use and Conservation of Soil," *Geoforum* vol. 10 (1972), 35-48.

26. T. Moore, *The Great Error of American Agriculture Exposed* (Baltimore, 1801), pp. 6-7.

27. E. H. Faulkner, *Plowman's Folly* (Norman, Okla., 1943).

28. L. D. Meyer, W. H. Wischmeier, and G. R. Foster, "Mulch Rates Required for Erosion Control on Steep Slopes." *Proceedings* of the Soil Society of America vol. 34, no. 6 (1970), 928-31. *Mulch Tillage in Modern Farming*, Leaflet 554, U. S. Department of Agriculture (Washington, D.C., U. S. Government Printing Office, 1971). C. A. Van Doren, "The Effectiveness of Erosion and Sediment Control Practices, an Overview," address, Minnesota Chapter, Soil Conservation Society of America, 1971.

29. H. Lehmann, "The Role of Law and Tradition in the Use of Agricultural Resources," Department of Geography, University of Chicago, 1952.

30. N. T. Newton, *Design on the Land. The Development of Landscape Architecture* (Cambridge, Mass. 1971), Chapter 37. "The State Park Movement: 1864-1933," p. 564. J. E. Trotter, *State Park System in Illinois*, The University of Chicago Department of Geography Research Paper No. 74 (Chicago, 1962, pp. 66-67, 90, 98, 99; LeRoy G. Pratt, *Discovering Historic Iowa*, Iowa Department of Public Instruction (Des Moines, 1972), p. 40; *Among the Wisconsin State Parks and Forests*, Wisconsin Conservation Department, no. 400-57 (Madison, undated), *passim. The Conservation Volunteer* vol. 16 (May-June 1953), Special Issue, "Minnesota's State Parks."

31. *Minnesota's Paradise* (St. Charles, Minn., 1917), foreword.

32. *History of Winona County* (Chicago, 1883), p. 102. Record Deed, No. 1691, State Auditor's Office, Saint Paul, Minn.

33. Tract data based on abstracts of deed (between May 26 and December 29, 1932) in State Auditor's Office, St. Paul, Minn.

34. *Detailed Examination Report on the Whitewater River Watershed, Minnesota*, U.S. Department of Agriculture, Soil Conservation Service, 1941, revised 1942. Appendix III, pp. 1, 17.

35. T. Beck, J. N. Darling, A. Leopold, *Report of the President's Committee on Wildlife Restoration*, U.S. Department of Agriculture (Washington, D.C., 1934). *A Report on National Planning and Public Works in Relation to Natural Resources*) U. S. Government Printing Office, Washington, D.C., 1934), p. 14.

36. *Laws Relating to Forestry, Game Conservation, Flood Control, and Related Subjects*, compiled by G. G. Udell (U.S. Government Printing Office, Washington, D.C., 1958). Public Law No. 415, September 1937 (Pittman-Robertson Wildlife Restoration Act), pp. 97-100.

37. Letter from Minnesota's Director of Game and Fish to the Secretary of the Interior, January 12, 1948.

38. Based on the study of 74 abstracts of records of deed (1950-1960), State Auditor's Office, St. Paul, Minn.

39. J. McKane, "A Walk Thru the Whitewater," *The Conservation Volunteer* vol. 31, no. 182 (November-December 1968), 31, 37. H. B. Johnson, "Geographic Research in Outdoor Recreation: A Case Study of Recreational Usage of the Whitewater Valley" in Station Paper 89, *Outdoor Recreation in the Upper Great Lakes Area*, The Lake States Forest Experiment Station, St. Paul, Minn. (August 1961), pp. 69-78.

40. M. S. Haverstock, "Can Nature Imitate Art?" *Art in America* vol. 54 no. 3 (January-February 1966) 73-80.

41. "Federal Report Doubles as a Guide for Travelers," *The New York Times*, February 25, 1968, Section 10.

CHAPTER NINE

1. A. A. Schmid, *Converting Land from Rural to Urban Uses* (Baltimore, Md., 1968), p. vi.

2. *American State Papers, Public Lands*, vol. 8, pp. 20-246.

3. W. A. Truesdell, "The Rectangular System of Surveying," *Association of Engineering Societies* vol. 61 (November 1908), 207-30.

4. D. W. Thompson, *Men and Meridians*, vol. 2, 1867-1917 (Ottawa, reprinted 1972), p. 38.

5. H. H. Dunham, *Government Handout, A Study in the Administration of the Public Lands: 1875-1891* (New York, 1941), pp. 242-60. J. E. Fant, *Public Land Survey in Minnesota*, Department of Civil Engineering, University of Minnesota (Minneapolis, 1970), p. 5.

6. G. F. Tyrell, "Background and Development of Cadastral Surveys," *Surveying and Mapping* vol. 17 (1957), 33-41.

7. T. Le Duc, "History and Appraisal of U. S. Land Policy to 1862," in H. W. Ottoson, ed., *Land Use Policy and Problems in the United States* (Lincoln, Neb., 1964), p. 6.

8. T. Adams, *Rural Planning and Development* (Ottawa, 1917), pp. 45-46.

9. *Proceedings of the National Conference on Land Utilization, Chicago, 1931* (Washington, D.C., U.S. Government Printing Office, 1932).

10. W. O. Winter, *The Urban Policy* (New York, 1969), pp. 436-40.

11. M. Clawson and B. Held, *The Federal Lands* (Baltimore, Md., 1956), pp. 23-24.

12. D. J. Bogue, *Metropolitan Growth and the Conversion of Land to Non-Agricultural Uses* (Chicago, 1956), pp. 4-5.

13. K. K. Keffer, Jr., "Original Land Entry in Eastern Iowa," MA thesis, University of Iowa, 1954.

14. D. Hudson, "The Contributions of Geography in Land Classification," *Bulletin 421, Land Classification*, Missouri Agricultural Experiment Station, Columbia, Mo. (1940), pp. 174-83.

15. C. O. Sauer, "The Problems of Land Classification," *Annals* of the Association of American Geographers vol. 2 (March 1921), 3-16.

16. M. Conzen, "Fringe Location Land Uses: Relict Patterns in Madison, Wisconsin," paper delivered at the Association of American Geographers, West Lakes Division meeting, October 1968, p. 3.

17. J. R. Quay, "Use of Soil Surveys in Subdivision Design," in *Soil Surveys and Land Use Planning*, edited by L. Y. Bartelli (Soil Science Society of America and American Society of Agronomy, Madison, Wisc., 1966). Chapter 8, pp. 76-77. G. S. Wehrwein, "The Rural-Urban Fringe," *Economic Geography* vol. 18 (July 1949), 217-28.

18. Ian McHarg, *Design With Nature* (Garden City, N.Y., 1969).

19. W. R. Ewald, Jr., ed., *Environment for Man, the Next Fifty Years* (Bloomington, Ind., 1967), pp. 28-29.

20. P. Blake, *God's Own Junkyard: The Planned Deterioration of America's Landscape* (New York, 1964). R. Neutra, *Survival Through Design* (New York, 1954). J. W. Reps, *The Making of Urban America, A History of City Planning* (Princeton, N.J., 1965), p. 15.

21. C. Tunnard and B. Pushkarev, *Man-Made America: Chaos or Control? An Inquiry into Selected Problems of Design in the Urbanized Landscape* (New Haven, Conn., 1963), p. 81.

22. C. O. Sauer, "Status and Change in the Rural Middle West—A Retrospect," *Mitteilungen der Oestereichischen Geographischen Gesellschaft* vol. 105 (1965), 357-65.

23. K. W. Bauer, "Revitalization of the U. S. Public Survey System in Southeastern Wisconsin," *Surveying and Mapping* vol. 24 (June 1969), 231-42.

24. *Minnesota Land Surveyors–Disclosures* vol. 2 (Minneapolis, 1973), pp. 3, 5, 6.

25. J. E. Fant and W. A. Maher, *Platting and County Survey Records in Minnesota*, Department of Civil Engineering, University of Minnesota (Minneapolis, 1970), p. 11.

26. *Manual of Instructions for the Survey of the Public Lands of the United States*, 1947, Bureau of Land Management (Washington, D.C., U.S. Government Printing Office, 1947), p. 10. *Restoration of Lost or Obliterated Corners, and Subdivisions of Sections ... A Guide for Surveyors*, Bureau of Land Management (Washington, D.C., 1963), p. 2.

27. J. J. Gibson, *The Perception of the Visual World* (Boston, 1950), p. 183.

28. L. G. Moholy-Nagy, *Vision in Motion* (Chicago, 1947), p. 244. C. A. Doxiadis, *Ekistics: An Introduction to the Science of Human Settlements* (New York, 1968), pp. 25, 71.

29. G. Bachelard, *The Poetics of Space* (New York, 1964), Chapter 10, "The Phenomenology of Roundness," pp. 232, 240.

30. A. Torres-Roseco, *The Epic of Latin-American Literature* (Berkeley, Calif., 1959), pp. 120, 123.

31. N. T. Newton, *Design on the Land, The Development of Landscape Architecture* (Cambridge, Mass., 1973), pp. 210, 212, 217, 311, 376, 428, 466.

32. Frank Lloyd Wright, *The Living City* (New York, 1958).

33. Ralph Waldo Emerson, *The Basic Writings of America's Sage*, edited by Edward C. Lindeman (New York, 1947), p. 114.

34. G. Schmidt and R. Schenk, eds., *Kunst und Naturform–Art and Nature–Art et Nature* (Basel, Switzerland, 1960), passim., note illustrations of crystals on p. 66.

35. *Piet Mondrian, 1872-1944*, Centennial Exhibition (The Solomon R. Guggenheim Museum, New York, 1971), pp. 25, 35, 61, 75, 80, 86. Composition "Checkerboard, Dark Colors," 1919, reproduced in black and white, p. 64. Color reproduction of the painting in I. Tomassoni, *Piet Mondrian* (Florence, 1969).

36. Color reproduction in R. Bongartz, "It's Called Earth Art—And Boulderdash," *The New York Times Magazine*, February 1, 1970, pp. 16-30.

37. G. Gerster, "Der Bauer als Kuenstler," *Neue Zürcher Zeitung*, Sect. Wochenende, July 22, 29, and August 5, 1973.

38. *Joseph Albers at the Metropolitan Museum of Art*, an exhibition of his paintings and prints (New York, 1971), p. 10.

39. D. Pye, *The Nature of Design* (New York, 1967), p. 52.

40. J. F. Pile, "The Nature of Office Landscaping," *AIA Journal* (The American Institute of Architects) vol. 52, no. 1 (July 1969), 40-48, 47.

41. E. B. Kassler, *Modern Gardens and the Landscape*, (New York, 1964), pp. 5, 6, 14.

42. *Upper Mississippi River Comprehensive Basin Study*, vol. 2, appendix B, 1970; "Aesthetic and Cultural Values."

43. E. K. Faltermeyer, *Redoing America* (New York, 1968), p. 47.

INDEX

Gillmore Valley Watershed project (1935), 197, 200
Glacken, Clarence, 230
Glidden, Joseph, 163
Graduation Act (1854), 64, 134
Grayson, William, 43–44
Great Northwest (Oregon Territory), 8
GREAT (Great River Environmental Action Team), 217
Great River Road, 14, 86, 127, 217, 220
Grid pattern: archetype, 30–31, 219, 224, 227; colonial towns, 26–27; nineteenth-century, 178, 221; pre-survey plats, 111–13; in Wisconsin, 180–81; accepted by immigrants, 184–86
Gunter's chain, 42, 55, 158
Guthrie, Woody, 4
Guttenberg, 185, 217, 237

Half Breed Tract, *see* Wabasha Reservation
Hart, John Fraser, 150
Hastings, Minn., 12, 105–6, 111
Hazel Green, Wisc., 87, 97
"Heartland," 7
High Forest, Minn., 116
Hokah, Minn., 112, 181
Homestead Act (1862), 64, 66, 220
Hudson, Wisc., 132, 134, 145–46, 217
Hundredth Meridian, 4, 18
Huxtable, Ada Louise, 233–34

Iowa City, 131
Ice Age National Scientific Reserve, 205
Immigration routes to Upper Middle West, 15
Improvements (of claims): clearing and stump removal, 152; shelters, 151; sod-breaking, 153; Whitewater Valley, 155–57
Indiscriminate location, 25, 43, 53, 221
Indians: Black Hawk War, 64, 84, 87, 122; cessions, 50, 72, 100, 122–23; in Ordinance of 1785, 45; resentment of property lines,

230; romanticized, 10; under Spanish, 6; trails, 83–84; Wabasha Reservation (Half-Breed Tract), 108
Izaak Walton League, 203, 207, 216, 217

Jefferson, Thomas, 30, 39, 196; writes Ordinance of 1784, 40–44, 46
Jefferson's "Hundreds," 30, 42–43, 47
Jori land division system (Japan), 46–47

Kaskaskia, Ill., 24, 59
Kassler, Elizabeth, 234
Kickapoo River, 98, 149, 181, 216, 202

Labadist colony, 24
La Crosse, Wisc., 86, 100, 106, 111, 131, 132, 186; Agricultural Experiment Station, 198
La Crosse River, 97, 100, 105, 119
Lake City, Minn., 106, 112, 186
Lake Pepin, 97, 122
Land Act of 1796, 53
Land classification, 195, 221–23
Land offices, 57, 61, 114, 127–34
Land sales at Winona, Minn., 136–40
Land-use capability, *see* land classification
Lead mining: Dubuque, 87; Galena, 88–90, surveying in mining area, 92–95; sale of mining land, 95; population density in mining region, 151
Leopold, Aldo, 193
Lewis, Henry, 9, 10, 12
Lewis, Sinclair, 182–84
Lincoln, Abraham, 4, 127
Lindstrom, Minn., 185
"Linemindedness," 149, 227
Locke, John, 37, 144
Long lots: Canada, 22–24; Prairie du Chien, 105–6
Lumbering: 97–100; wood supply in Hill Country, 162
Luxemburg, Iowa, 185

McCormick reaper, 153
McGregor Watershed project, 200